PROPERTY AND ITS FORMS IN CLASSICAL GERMAN PHILOSOPHY

The theme of property is directly relevant to some of the most divisive social and political issues today, such as wealth inequality and the question of whether governments should limit it by introducing measures that restrict the right to property. Yet what is property? And when seeking to answer this question, do we tend to identify the concept with just one dominant historical form of property? In this book, David James reconstructs the theories of property developed by four key figures in classical German philosophy – Kant, Fichte, Hegel and Marx. He argues that although their theories of property are different, the concept of social recognition plays a crucial role in all of them, and assesses these philosophers' arguments for the specific forms of property they claim should exist in a society that is genuinely committed to the idea of freedom.

DAVID JAMES is Reader in Philosophy at the University of Warwick. His previous publications include *Rousseau and German Idealism: Freedom, Dependence and Necessity* (Cambridge, 2013), and *Practical Necessity, Freedom, and History: From Hobbes to Marx* (2021).

PROPERTY AND ITS FORMS IN CLASSICAL GERMAN PHILOSOPHY

DAVID JAMES
University of Warwick

Shaftesbury Road, Cambridge CB2 8EA, United Kingdom

One Liberty Plaza, 20th Floor, New York, NY 10006, USA

477 Williamstown Road, Port Melbourne, VIC 3207, Australia

314–321, 3rd Floor, Plot 3, Splendor Forum, Jasola District Centre, New Delhi – 110025, India

103 Penang Road, #05–06/07, Visioncrest Commercial, Singapore 238467

Cambridge University Press is part of Cambridge University Press & Assessment, a department of the University of Cambridge.

We share the University's mission to contribute to society through the pursuit of education, learning and research at the highest international levels of excellence.

www.cambridge.org
Information on this title: www.cambridge.org/9781009288101

DOI: 10.1017/9781009288118

© David James 2023

This publication is in copyright. Subject to statutory exception and to the provisions of relevant collective licensing agreements, no reproduction of any part may take place without the written permission of Cambridge University Press & Assessment.

First published 2023
First paperback edition 2024

A catalogue record for this publication is available from the British Library

ISBN 978-1-009-28814-9 Hardback
ISBN 978-1-009-28810-1 Paperback

Cambridge University Press & Assessment has no responsibility for the persistence or accuracy of URLs for external or third-party internet websites referred to in this publication and does not guarantee that any content on such websites is, or will remain, accurate or appropriate.

Contents

Acknowledgements		*page* vii
List of Abbreviations		viii
	Introduction	1
	I.1 The Mystery of the Right to Property	1
	I.2 The Concept of Property and Forms of Property	11
1	Property, Freedom and Enlightenment: Kant's *Rechtslehre*	14
	1.1 Freedom, Equality and Property	14
	1.2 Property and Domination	20
	1.3 Kant's Justification of the Right to (Private) Property	27
	1.4 Property and Enlightenment	40
2	Fichte on Property and Labour	48
	2.1 Fichte's Early Theory of Property	48
	2.2 The Relation between the Concept of Right and the Concept of Property	56
	2.3 Property and Labour	65
	2.4 Absolute Property	75
3	Property and Ethical Life: Hegel's System of Right	89
	3.1 Property and the Science of Right	89
	3.2 Property and Abstract Right	92
	3.3 The Embodiment Interpretation of Hegel's Argument for Private Property	95
	3.4 The Recognition Interpretation of Hegel's Argument for Private Property	103
	3.5 The Integration of Private Property into Ethical Life	110
	3.6 Inalienable Property	121
	3.7 Ethical Property	125

4 Equality, Exchange Value and Individuality:
   Marx's Critique of Private Property   139
   4.1 Property and Equality   139
   4.2 The Origin of the Idea of Equality   147
   4.3 Exchange Value and the Idea of Equality   151
   4.4 Freedom and the Abolition of Private Property   164
   4.5 Communist Property and the Free Development of the
        Social Individual   174

   Concluding Remark   189

Bibliography   198
Index   201

Acknowledgements

I am very grateful for the award of an Alexander von Humboldt Research Fellowship for Experienced Researchers during which most of the first draft of this book was written. I would like to thank Rahel Jaeggi for agreeing to host me at the Humboldt-Universität zu Berlin and for her hospitality during the fellowship. I am also grateful to Bernardo Ferro and two anonymous readers for Cambridge University Press for their comments on later drafts of the book. I have benefited from presenting early versions of sections of the book in talks at the University of Vechta; the University of Edinburgh Philosophy Society; the Katholische Privat-Universität Linz; the Faculty of Political Science of the University of Zagreb Summer School in Modern Political Theory held in Grožnjan, Croatia; the 'An Ethical Modernity? Hegel's Concept of Ethical Life Today – Its Limits and Potential' conference organized by the International Network Hegel's Relevance held in Prague and the University of Zagreb. I would like to thank the organizers of these events for inviting me and the audiences for their comments and questions. Chapter 1 is an extended and substantially revised version of my article 'Property and Independence in Kant's *Rechtslehre*', *British Journal for the History of Philosophy* 24(2) (2016), and sections of Chapter 4 contain revised material from the article 'Marx's Genealogy of the Idea of Equality', *European Journal of Philosophy* 27(4) (2020).

Abbreviations

Writings by Kant

AA	*Kant's gesammelte Schriften*, ed. Königliche Preußische (later Deutsche) Akademie der Wissenschaften (Berlin: Reimer/de Gruyter, 1900–). Cited by volume and page number.
CPR	*Critique of Pure Reason*, ed. Paul Guyer and Allen W. Wood (Cambridge: Cambridge University Press, 1998).
E	'An Answer to the Question: What Is Enlightenment?', in *Practical Philosophy*, trans. and ed. Mary J. Gregor (Cambridge: Cambridge University Press, 1996).
GMM	*Groundwork of the Metaphysics of Morals*, in *Practical Philosophy*, trans. and ed. Mary J. Gregor (Cambridge: Cambridge University Press, 1996).
KrV	*Kritik der reinen Vernunft*, ed. Jens Timmermann (Hamburg: Felix Meiner, 1998).
MM	*The Metaphysics of Morals*, in *Practical Philosophy*, trans. and ed. Mary J. Gregor (Cambridge: Cambridge University Press, 1996).
TP	'On the Common Saying: That May Be Correct in Theory, but It Is of No Use in Practice', in *Practical Philosophy*, trans. and ed. Mary J. Gregor (Cambridge: Cambridge University Press, 1996).

Writings by Fichte

CCS	*The Closed Commercial State*, trans. Anthony Curtis Adler (Albany: State University of New York Press, 2012).

FNR	*Foundations of Natural Right*, ed. Frederick Neuhouser, trans. Michael Baur (Cambridge: Cambridge University Press, 2000).
GA	*J. G. Fichte – Gesamtausgabe der Bayerischen Akademie der Wissenschaften*, eds. Reinhard Lauth, Erich Fuchs and Hans Gliwitzky (Stuttgart and Bad Canstatt: Frommann-Holzboog, 1962–2012). Cited by series, volume and page number.
RPP	'Review of Immanuel Kant, *Perpetual Peace: A Philosophical Sketch*', trans. Daniel Breazeale, *The Philosophical Forum* 32(4) (2001): 311–21.
SE	*The System of Ethics*, trans. and eds. Daniel Breazeale and Günter Zöller (Cambridge: Cambridge University Press, 2005).

Writings by Hegel

PhG	*Phänomenologie des Geistes*, eds. Hans-Friedrich Wessels and Heinrich Clairmont (Hamburg: Felix Meiner, 1988).
PR	*Grundlinien der Philosophie des Rechts oder Naturrecht und Staatswissenschaft im Grundrisse*, in *Werke*, ed. E. Moldenhauer and K. M. Michel (Suhrkamp: Frankfurt am Main, 1969–1971), Vol. 7. English translation: *Elements of the Philosophy of Right*, ed. A. W. Wood, trans. H. B. Nisbet (Cambridge: Cambridge University Press, 1991). Cited according to paragraph (§) numbers. R indicates a remark which Hegel himself added to the paragraph, while A indicates an addition derived from student lecture notes. The only exception is the preface, which is cited by the page number of the German edition followed by that of the English translation.
PR 1819/20	*Philosophie des Rechts. Die Vorlesung von 1819/20 in einer Nachschrift*, ed. Dieter Henrich (Frankfurt am Main: Suhrkamp, 1983).
PR 1821/22	*Die Philosophie des Rechts. Vorlesung von 1821/22*, ed. Hansgeorg Hoppe (Frankfurt am Main: Suhrkamp, 2005). Cited by paragraph (§) number.
PS	*Phenomenology of Spirit*, trans. A. V. Miller (Oxford: Oxford University Press, 1977).

SL	*Science of Logic*, trans. A. V. Miller (New York: Humanities Books, 1999).
WL 1	*Wissenschaft der Logik I*, in *Werke*, ed. E. Moldenhauer and K. M. Michel (Suhrkamp: Frankfurt am Main, 1969–1971), Vol. 5.

Writings by Marx

Cap. 1	*Capital: Volume I*, trans. Ben Fowkes (London: Penguin, 1990).
Cap. 3	*Capital: Volume III*, trans. David Fernbach (London: Penguin, 1991).
CGP	*Critique of the Gotha Programme*, in *Later Political Writings*, ed. and trans. Terrell Carver (Cambridge: Cambridge University Press, 1996).
EB	*The Eighteenth Brumaire of Louis Bonaparte*, in *Later Political Writings*, ed. and trans. Terrell Carver (Cambridge: Cambridge University Press, 1996).
EJM	*Excerpts from James Mill's* Elements of Political Economy, in *Early Writings*, trans. Rodney Livingstone and Gregor Benton (London: Penguin, 1992).
EPM	*Economic and Philosophical Manuscripts*, in *Early Writings*, trans. Rodney Livingstone and Gregor Benton (London: Penguin, 1992).
G	*Grundrisse*, trans. Martin Nicolaus (London: Penguin, 1993).
GI	*The German Ideology*, ed. C. J. Arthur, 2nd edn (London: Lawrence and Wishart, 1974).
JQ	'On the Jewish Question', in *Early Writings*, trans. Rodney Livingstone and Gregor Benton (London: Penguin, 1992).
MCP	*Manifesto of the Communist Party*, in *Later Political Writings*, ed. and trans. Terrell Carver (Cambridge: Cambridge University Press, 1996).
MEGA	*Marx-Engels-Gesamtausgabe*, ed. Institut für Marxismus-Leninismus beim Zentralkomitee der Kommunistischen Partei der Sowjetunion and Institut für Marxismus-Leninismus beim Zentralkomitee der Sozialistischen Einheitspartei Deutschlands/Internationale Marx-Engels-Stiftung Amsterdam (Berlin: Dietz Verlag/De

	Gruyter, 1975–). Cited by section, volume and page number.
MEW	*Marx-Engels-Werke*, ed. Institut für Marxismus-Leninismus beim Zentralkomitee der Sozialistischen Einheitspartei Deutschlands (Berlin: Dietz Verlag, 1956–1990). Cited by volume and page number.
MP	*Misère de la philosophie: réponse à la Philosophie de la misère de M. Proudhon* (Paris: A. Frank, 1847).
MZC	'Marx Zasulich Correspondence: Letters and Drafts', in *Late Marx and the Russian Road: Marx and the Peripheries of Capitalism*, ed. Teodor Shanin (London: Verso, 2018).
PCPE	'"Preface" to *A Contribution to the Critique of Political Economy*', in *Later Political Writings*, ed. and trans. Terrell Carver (Cambridge: Cambridge University Press, 1996).
PP	*The Poverty of Philosophy: Answer to the* Philosophy of Poverty *by M. Proudhon*, in Karl Marx and Friedrich Engels, *Collected Works*, Vol. 6 (London: Lawrence and Wishart, 1976).

Introduction

I.1 The Mystery of the Right to Property

In two notes found in his desk after his death, the German-speaking Czech Jewish writer Franz Kafka instructed his friend Max Brod to burn his remaining notebooks, manuscripts and letters. Brod did not obey Kafka's instructions. Instead, Kafka's papers came to form part of Brod's own literary estate, which he subsequently bequeathed to his secretary and confidante Esther Hoffe. After Esther Hoffe's death, a long legal process began when the National Library of Israel laid claim to Kafka's papers, citing both their status as cultural assets of national significance and evidence that Brod had intended that they be donated to a public archive. Another party to this legal dispute was the German Literature Archive in Marbach, which was negotiating with one of Esther Hoffe's daughters to purchase those of Kafka's papers that had not already been sold. Like the National Library of Israel, the German Literature Archive cited the papers' status as cultural assets of national significance. This time, however, Kafka's place in the history of German literature was emphasized rather than his Jewishness. Unlike the National Library of Israel, the German Literature Archive did not contest the legal right of Esther Hoffe's daughter to sell Kafka's papers, and so there was no attempt to appropriate these papers from someone who claimed to be their legal owner with the right to dispose of them freely. Eventually, Israel's Supreme Court ruled in favour of the National Library of Israel, which was not required to provide any compensation for the papers of which it became the legal owner.[1]

This case illustrates various issues relating to the right to property. To begin with, there is the question of what originally gave Max Brod the legal right to Kafka's papers that his right to dispose of them freely presupposed, when they were neither given to him as a gift by their original owner, who in fact instructed Brod to destroy them, nor formed the object

---

[1] The details of this case are presented in Balint, *Kafka's Last Trial*.

of any legally binding contract through which they were transferred to him. This legal right appears to derive from the fact that Brod was the first person to gain effective control over the papers after Kafka's death, unless one assumes that Brod's interpretation of Kafka's true intentions was not only correct but also generated a legal right to the papers. Yet why should being the first person to take possession of a thing establish a right to dispose of it freely and the right to deny others access to this thing even though they can make a reasonable moral claim to it, such as the type of claim that scholars wishing to consult Kafka's papers might make? Even if one were to provide a plausible account of how Brod gained a right to these papers, this account would have to be supplemented by an account of how this right was transferred to Esther Hoffe, given that no obvious reason for thinking that Kafka intended this outcome suggests itself. Indeed, Esther Hoffe's right to these papers appears so mysterious that it is reasonable to claim that this right, even if we assume that it has some basis, is so tenuous that it could be easily overridden by other considerations and values. The considerations might include the need to provide certain people with guaranteed regular public access to the papers, as opposed to making access to them dependent on the arbitrary will of their legal owner. The values might include the cultural value that derives from the national significance of the papers, which can be explained in terms of a common language, culture and history.

In this book, I intend to examine the theories of property developed in a philosophical tradition that extends from Immanuel Kant, through Johann Gottlieb Fichte and G. W. F. Hegel, to Karl Marx.[2] Although my main aim is to reconstruct these philosophers' arguments concerning property and to evaluate these arguments, I hope thereby to show that these theories of property make a significant contribution to the dissolution of the mysteries surrounding property rights, even if they fail to provide definitive answers to the questions identified above. In contrast, the mysterious nature of property rights persists when the question of how goods that include monetary wealth and access to resources such as healthcare should

---

[2] The claim that Kant, Fichte and Hegel belong to the same philosophical tradition is uncontroversial, given Kant's influence on the other philosophers and Hegel's direct engagement with key elements of Fichte's philosophy. Although the claim that Marx belongs to the same philosophical tradition may appear less obvious, there are some common concerns and themes, especially freedom, that allow us to situate Marx within this tradition. See Wood, *The Free Development of Each*, 1f. My account of how Marx adopts a similar concept of property to the one adopted by Kant, Fichte and Hegel and relates it to the common theme of freedom provides an indirect defence of the claim that we should situate him within the relevant philosophical tradition.

be distributed is posed in such a way as to presuppose the legitimacy of one specific form of property to the exclusion of other possible forms of it. For example, redistribution may be justified in terms of some higher good or value, such as equality or justice, at the same time as it is assumed that a person in all other respects enjoys the right to any property of which he or she is the legal owner. As well as the right to exclude others from the use or other benefits of a thing, this right includes the right to do whatever one pleases with one's property, provided that the use of it does not threaten to harm other persons or to violate their property rights and does not otherwise constitute a danger to society.

In order to make clearer why a more critical approach to the concept of property and any specific forms of it is needed, I shall now turn to one example of how this concept in the specific form of private property plays a *structuring* role in debates about distributive justice. Property rights structure human relations by establishing entitlements to parts of the world and objects within it and by generating an obligation on the part of others to respect these entitlements. Property rights can therefore be classed among the general norms that order and regulate human interaction within a society. These norms typically take the form of laws that are enforced by the state. The way in which property rights play this structuring role has social implications, in that the possession and protection of these rights will result in individuals and social groups coming to possess different degrees of economic and social power in relation to one another that may enable one social agent to dominate another social agent. Moreover, different forms of property may structure society in substantially different ways. The example in question concerns a well-known objection to distributive justice that appeals to the value of freedom.

According to Robert Nozick, any pattern of distribution that arises from an existing just pattern of distribution will itself be just. Thus property rights, or 'holdings' as he calls them, would be just if the following conditions were satisfied: a moral right to a thing, to which no one originally enjoyed such a right, has been established by one person and another person, who subsequently acquires this right, does so by means of a voluntary act through which the thing is exchanged for another thing or is transferred to him or her by its original owner in the form of a gift.[3] These two conditions can be described as the just appropriation condition and the just transfer condition, respectively. The argument is simple

---

[3] Nozick, *Anarchy, State, and Utopia*, 150ff.

and does not rule out the legitimacy of redistributive acts, for a pattern of distribution may, in fact, fail to satisfy one or both of the relevant conditions, in which case there may be grounds for distributing a thing to another person. This person would presumably be either the first person to have appropriated it or someone to whom the right to the thing had been transferred in the appropriate way but who was then unjustly deprived of this thing by means of force or fraud. Yet the simplicity of this argument conceals certain difficulties and presuppositions relevant to the theme of the right to property. Let us begin with the just appropriation condition.

This condition invites the question as to *how* an exclusive moral right to a thing which everyone originally had the right to use or to benefit from in another way can be established. The obvious answer would consist in an appeal to an act of appropriation of the right moral kind. A classic example of this approach is John Locke's argument that individuals were able to establish rights to things in the state of nature by 'mixing' their labour with them, despite how the world originally belonged to everyone. This argument rests on the claim that each individual is the owner or 'master' of his or her own person and anything immediately connected with it, including his or her capacity to bring about changes in that which is external to him or her through purposive action.[4] In the following passage, it is assumed that the connection thus established between one's own person and a thing is sufficient to generate an exclusive right to this thing:

> [E]very Man has a *Property* in his own *Person*. This no Body has any Right to but himself. The *Labour* of his Body, and the *Work* of his Hands, we may say, are properly his. Whatsoever then he removes out of the State that Nature hath provided, and left it in, he hath mixed his *Labour* with, and joyned to it something that is his own, and thereby makes it his *Property*. It being by him removed from the common state Nature placed it in, it hath by this *labour* something annexed to it, that excludes the common right of other Men.[5]

---

[4] Locke includes among this original property animals and servants, so that changes brought about by them may also establish property rights for their owner: 'the Grass my Horse has bit; the Turfs my Servant has cut' (*Two Treatises of Government*, Second Treatise, Ch. V, § 28). Yet even if the truth of the claim that a person's body and associated powers are his or her original property by virtue of the unique, immediate relation in which he or she stands with them is granted, the same reasoning cannot be extended to other human beings or to non-human animals without any further justification. To fill this gap in the argument, Locke would have to show either that there is, in fact, a direct, immediate relation of the relevant kind or that independently of any such relation a person's labour can establish a right to other human beings and non-human animals, in which case there would not be an *original* right to them.

[5] Locke, *Two Treatises of Government*, Second Treatise, Ch. V, § 27.

A right to a thing is here established by means of a causal relation between a person's original 'property' and a thing that all human beings were originally entitled to use or to benefit from in another way. This transformation of a 'common' right into a 'private' right is not limited to instances of the direct appropriation of nature, such as the consumption or the act of taking physical possession of a thing, both of which necessarily exclude the simultaneous possession or use of the thing by another person. Rather, Locke extends it to land, even though the possession and use of parts of the same piece of land are not self-evidently incompatible with common ownership of it, provided there are collectively agreed-upon rules governing the allocation, possession and use of parts of the relevant piece of land.

Locke introduces a further requirement when he argues that the act of appropriation must also be of a value-enhancing kind.[6] In this way, the right to property is partly justified in terms of the use of natural resources 'to the best advantage of Life, and convenience',[7] and how it is '[*l*]*abour* ... that *puts the difference of value* on every thing'.[8] Presumably, if the effects were less beneficial and even harmful ones, then the appropriate moral relation between an individual and an external object would not obtain, even if a person had 'mixed' something to which he or she is assumed to possess an original right with a thing to which he or she did not originally possess a right. This additional consideration, however, invites such questions as the following ones. Who is to decide whether the property rights thus established are sufficiently value-enhancing ones, and if they are, whether the relevant benefits could not have been achieved in ways that avoid the harmful effects of property rights? Does society as a whole or only a privileged group within society have the authority to decide such matters? If the latter is the case, is this privileged group made up of people who already possess extensive property rights? If so, could one not then object that those people who benefit most from a state of affairs cannot be expected to be impartial judges of its legitimacy, given their personal interest in the perpetuation of this state of affairs? Moreover, would those people

---

[6] In addition, Locke introduces a moral constraint on the right to property in the form of the condition that 'there is enough, and as good left in common for others' (*Two Treatises of Government*, Second Treatise, Ch. V, § 27). Yet he argues that the improved productivity facilitated by the appropriation of nature and the right to property would satisfy this condition by making more things available to consume and to use than was originally the case. See *Two Treatises of Government*, Second Treatise, Ch. V, § 37, §§ 41–2. Locke also appears to view the opportunities that colonies offer to the dispossessed as another way of satisfying the condition in question. See *Two Treatises of Government*, Second Treatise, Ch. V, § 36
[7] Locke, *Two Treatises of Government*, Second Treatise, Ch. V, § 26.
[8] Locke, *Two Treatises of Government*, Second Treatise, Ch. V, § 40.

who already benefit from existing property rights not employ the social power that these rights give them to define what is or is not of social utility whenever sufficient consensus concerning this matter is lacking?

We can here already see how there might be a fundamental problem with reducing the right to property to a relation between a person and a thing, namely, that this model cannot accommodate the moment of recognition implied by the claim that a full justification of the right to property must take into consideration social factors.[9] There is the claim that the 'mixing' of a person's immediate, original property in the form of his or her body and labour with an external object is sufficient to 'join' together two things that did not previously belong together in such a way that a moral right to a thing is established. This relation between a person and a thing does not imply a necessary relation to other persons, for a right of the relevant kind could be established by someone living in complete isolation, even though such a right may then be considered unnecessary, given the absence of any threat to a person's possession and use of things. This right would nevertheless generate an obligation on the part of any imaginary others who might one day be present. Thus the right to property and the obligations that follow from it do not depend on the consent of others or any other signs of their recognition of property rights that are claimed to satisfy the just appropriation condition. Yet there is equally a sense in which the right to property cannot be understood independently of social relations, for this right appears to require sufficient social recognition of its benefits and the claim that these benefits cannot be achieved in potentially less harmful ways. One may therefore argue that a truly adequate account of the right to property must incorporate the moment of social recognition in a more convincing way. We shall see that Kant, Fichte, Hegel and Marx attempt to provide such an account by adopting a model of property that explicitly incorporates a moment of recognition.

---

[9] Locke himself implies that the right to property consists in more than a relation between a person and a thing when he connects property rights with an agreement concerning the introduction of money. See *Two Treatises of Government*, Second Treatise, Ch. V, § 36. The introduction of money removes any moral constraints on the accumulation of property rights, for although Locke limits the right of appropriation by making it conditional on whether that which is appropriated can be used 'before it spoils' (*Two Treatises of Government*, Second Treatise, Ch. V, § 31), money can be accumulated without decaying and exchanged for objects of consumption and use. See *Two Treatises of Government*, Second Treatise, Ch. V, § 47. One may nevertheless wonder if anyone other than those who already own a significant amount of property could reasonably consent to an arrangement that enables some people to increase their property to such an extent that there is nothing, or at least very little, left for others to appropriate. In Chapter 2, we shall see that Fichte provides a counter-argument to the claim that a rational agent would consent to such an arrangement.

1.1   The Mystery of the Right to Property

With respect to the just transfer condition, Nozick commits himself to the claim that private property is the only form of property that satisfies this condition when he, in effect, defines this condition in terms of a feature of private property that distinguishes it from other forms of property. This is the right to dispose freely of a thing to which one has established a right. When I speak of 'private' property, I intend *modern* private property. There are features of the right to property that are compatible with different forms of property. For example, although the exclusive right to the possession and use of a thing is a defining feature of private property, this right is compatible with goods and resources being collectively owned and allocated to individuals according to rules to which all the relevant agents have agreed. Moreover, although clearly defined restrictions on the use or neglect of things characterize common or collective forms of ownership, private property is typically understood not to involve an absolute right on the part of the legal owner to do whatever he or she pleases with his or her property. Rather, there is the general prohibition not to cause physical harm to others or to damage *their* property through the use or neglect one's property, as well as restrictions on the right to dispose freely of this property that can be justified in the name of the general well-being of society, such as restrictions aimed at preventing environmental damage. Nevertheless, there is a presumption in favour of minimizing such restrictions on the right to dispose freely of one's property. For example, the fact that one person may find another person's neglect of his or her property or the irrational use of it morally offensive is not sufficient to justify legal constraints on the right to dispose freely of one's property. Any justifiable constraints on the exercise of this right will concern its potential consequences, which are judged in terms of considerations, goals and values that do not relate to the concept of property itself. Ultimately, however, the *absolute* right to dispose freely of property is viewed as an *optimal* condition whose full realization is nevertheless acknowledged to be highly unlikely, and even impossible, within society.

The right to dispose freely of property is a presupposition of certain specific rights associated with private property, including the right to bequeath one's property to whomsoever one pleases and the right to participate in a market economy, the functioning of which depends on the free exchange of items of property. Nozick presupposes this defining feature of private property when he speaks of 'voluntary' acts of exchange or gift-giving, for the permissibility of such acts presupposes a person's entitlement to do whatever he or she pleases with the property of which he or she is the legal owner, provided that he or she does not thereby harm other persons or damage their property. The exercise of the right to dispose freely of property may be irrational, but this is not an issue. As Pierre-Joseph Proudhon puts it: 'The proprietor has the power to let his crops rot underfoot, sow his field with salt, milk his cows on the sand, turn his vineyard into a desert, and use his vegetable garden as a park.'[10] Yet does the appropriation of a previously ownerless thing entail the additional right to dispose of it freely?

Nozick assumes that the right to dispose freely of property follows from the right to freedom, which is thereby presupposed. He also presupposes the existence and justifiability of an economic and social condition in which this right can be exercised, namely, a monetized system of exchange in which things are viewed as exchangeable with one another irrespective of their specific nature and qualities. The legitimate exercise of the right in question presupposes both that the just appropriation condition was once satisfied in relation to items of property to which specific persons now enjoy a legal right and that the just transfer condition has been consistently satisfied within the relevant type of economic and social system. Nozick's argument is here susceptible to an empirically based objection. This is the objection that even if the just appropriation and the just transfer conditions are assumed to be valid ones, the claim that the way in which property has come to be distributed in the course of history satisfies them, or could ever do so, is either naïve or a purely ideological move. We might here speak of the myth of private property's pure, uncontaminated origins. Marx seeks to undermine this myth with his account of 'primitive accumulation'. This is the process whereby people were forcibly deprived of access to land and resources that were previously owned in common, thereby creating the division between people who control the means of production and people who own only their labour power that is a historical presupposition of the capitalist mode of production (MEGA II/8: 667–70; Cap. 1: 873–76).[11]

We have now seen that Nozick presupposes the justifiability of private property. We have also seen that Locke's attempt to explain how property

---

[10] Proudhon, *What Is Property?*, 35.
[11] In response to this objection, one might claim that a situation in which both the just appropriation condition and the just transfer condition are satisfied is treated as a purely hypothetical one that demonstrates the validity of these conditions irrespective of the lack of sufficient historical evidence of the consistent application of them. The idea of a hypothetical situation of this kind may well be attractive to property owners who already enjoy the social power that the institution of private property gives them because it implies that they have a moral right to their property, but this condition can then be viewed as an abstract, ideal picture that is too divorced from history and actual social relations to be of any genuine value.

I.I The Mystery of the Right to Property

rights are established implies a model of property that fails to do justice to the moment of social recognition to which he himself alludes. Is a theory of property available that justifies private property in preference to other forms of property in such a way as to incorporate the moment of social recognition more effectively? One candidate is a consequentialist justification of private property, which argues that the right to property is established by convention, so that if the conditions that justify it no longer obtain, this right itself will lack sufficient justification. The fundamental difference between a justification of private property that appeals to an act of original appropriation and a justification of it in terms of human convention is articulated by David Hume in the following passage:

> What other reason, indeed, could writers ever give, why this must be *mine* and that *yours*; since uninstructed nature, surely, never made any such distinction? The objects, which receive those appellations, are, of themselves, foreign to us; they are totally disjoined and separated from us; and nothing but the general interests of society can form the connexion.[12]

Hume does not appeal to the type of connection between the object of a property right and the bearer of such a right that we encounter in Locke's account of how a property right can be established by the act of mixing one's labour with a thing. Although Locke also appeals to the social benefits of the right thus established, Hume goes further than this by reducing the justification of private property to a matter of social utility. Thus the right to property is understood in terms of human and social ends, rather than in terms of a mysterious process whereby a right that did not previously exist is established through a specific way of interacting with material objects. Yet the question of what explains the greater social utility of *private* property, which is a specific form of property, then arises. This question needs to be addressed if the possibility of the equal or superior utility of other forms of property is not to be dogmatically excluded.

Hume himself concedes that social and political arrangements that favour equality, which he understands in terms of perfect quantitative equality, can produce certain benefits, whereas arrangements that are incompatible with this equality 'rob the poor of more satisfaction than we add to the rich, and that slight gratification of a frivolous vanity, in one individual, frequently costs more than bread to many families, and even provinces'.[13] This statement testifies to Hume's recognition of how wealth

---

[12] *An Enquiry Concerning the Principles of Morals*, Section 3, Part 2, § 30.
[13] *An Enquiry Concerning the Principles of Morals*, Section 3, Part 2, § 25.

inequality and the property rights on which it is founded favour the desires and interests of some individuals and social groups at the expense of the desires and interests of other individuals and social groups. Nevertheless, Hume asserts that the overall utility of the inequalities generated by private property is greater than their disutility. In his attempt to justify this claim, Hume is, however, reduced to appealing to unnamed historical sources, common sense, practicability and certain beneficial effects on human motivation and psychology together with their social consequences.[14] He is thereby led to introduce a set of claims concerning the greater desirability of certain things relative to other ones and the necessary means of achieving the desired goods that themselves require justification.[15]

We shall see that there is, in contrast, an internal connection between the concept of property and that which justifies specific forms of property in the theories of property discussed in this book. The institution of property and the rights connected with it are held to structure social relations in such a way that freedom becomes genuinely possible. By seeking to explain the concept of property and justify specific forms of property in terms of the idea of freedom, these theories of property avoid both the need to demonstrate how certain ends, such as equality, security and the generation of wealth, possess more value relative to other ones and the need to show that specific legal, social and political arrangements that promote these ends ought to be established and maintained in preference to other possible arrangements. Instead, freedom is accorded an overriding value and the necessity of property is explained in terms of how it is a condition of freedom rather than a way of maximizing it. Moreover, none of these theories of property seeks to justify the right to property by appealing to an act of original appropriation, thereby reducing this right to a relation between a person and a thing. Instead, a relation between persons is viewed as a constitutive feature of property rights. To understand not only

---

[14] See *An Enquiry Concerning the Principles of Morals*, Section 3, Part 2, §§ 26–28.
[15] I have used both Locke's and Hume's arguments for private property with the intention of making explicit the presuppositions of some standard arguments for this form of property. This is not to claim that Kant's, Fichte's, Hegel's and Marx's accounts of the concept of property and the forms of it are directly influenced by these specific attempts to justify private property. There are hybrid or mixed theories of property that appeal to various considerations that include first occupancy or possession, a convention agreed upon by all the relevant parties and matters of utility such as the promotion of peace and industry. This approach is exemplified by the seventeenth-century natural law tradition, whose main representatives are Hugo Grotius and Samuel Pufendorf. See Pierson, *Just Property: A History in the Latin West, Volume 1: Wealth, Virtue, and the Law*, Chapter 8. Given that my focus will be on the arguments and theories themselves, I do not intend to engage with the question of who might have influenced whom, as valuable as such an inquiry may be.

what is common to these theories of property but also what makes them different from one another, we must distinguish between the *concept* of property and the *forms* of property that instantiate this concept. It is therefore to this distinction that I shall now turn.

I.2 The Concept of Property and Forms of Property

In the theories of property constructed by Kant, Fichte, Hegel and Marx, the concept of property is understood in terms of a triadic structure that incorporates a moment of social recognition, in that property rights are held to consist in a relation between persons that is mediated by things, rather than in a relation between a person and a thing from which an obligation then follows. This triadic structure becomes explicit in Fichte's theory of property, but it is already present in Kant's theory of right, and although Hegel's argument for private property may appear to rest on the idea of an act of original appropriation that reduces the right to property to a relation between a person and a thing, I shall show that a proper understanding of this argument reveals the same triadic structure, which becomes explicit at the stage of contract. This triadic structure is for Marx a basic feature of property that does not require any independent justification. In this respect, the concept of property is essentially the same one.

Kant, Fichte, Hegel and Marx also appeal to the same fundamental idea and value, namely freedom, and apply it to the concept of property. Yet freedom is not reduced to the freedom to do what one desires to do with items of property to which one is assumed to possess a moral or legal right. Moreover, the justification or criticism of property rights in each case fundamentally differs from a conventionalist, consequentialist one because there is here no appeal to *external* considerations whose relative value might be contested. Instead, there is a single value that stands in a *necessary* relation to the concept of property, for although property promotes freedom, it is equally a condition of the actualization of freedom, so that in the absence of property, human beings could not be genuinely or fully free. This approach does not reduce the institution of property and the rights associated with it to conventions that serve to promote a good that is logically independent of them. The institution of property and any rights that define it are instead constitutive moments of freedom. Although the value accorded to freedom may itself require justification, the focus on freedom has the advantage that it relates the concept of property to a fundamental idea and value associated with modernity that is historically bound up with arguments surrounding the right to property.

Although Kant, Fichte, Hegel and Marx work with what is essentially the same *concept* of property, they provide different accounts of the specific *form* in which this concept is best instantiated. Kant and Hegel seek to justify private property, whereas Fichte and Marx seek to justify forms of common or collective property. Yet this distinction between the concept of property and forms of property does not mean that concept and form are separable from one another in so far as property is a social, historical and political phenomenon. Rather, concept and form are inseparable in that property is an institution that is characterized by specific rights or other entitlements and corresponding obligations, and it is the nature and the extent of these rights, entitlements and obligations that distinguish one form of property from another one.

The differing accounts of the form of property invite the question as to whether one of the theories of property examined in this book is more successful than the other ones in arguing for a specific form of property. Answering this question will require analysing and evaluating Kant's, Fichte's, Hegel's and Marx's arguments. I shall show that the way in which Kant appears to favour private property is, in fact, unsupported by his theory of right, that Fichte commits himself to a form of common property that, as his own attempt to 'apply' the concept of property shows, may justify repressive measures that are incompatible with the idea of freedom in terms of which he seeks to justify this form of property and that Hegel's concept of ethical life implies a form of property different from private property, even though the latter occupies a privileged place in his system of right. Like Fichte, Marx argues for a form of common or collective property, which is this time justified in terms of a free but social individuality. Yet explaining how this property can perform the function that Marx assigns to it will be shown to be difficult.

The different arguments and the problems with them may suggest that we should compare these philosophers' theories of property with the aim of deciding which of them is the most coherent or in some other way most convincing one. There is, however, a different conclusion that one might draw from this disagreement concerning the specific form that the same concept of property ought to assume. This is the conclusion that ultimately no single form of property ought to be favoured to the exclusion of other ones. One might then argue that we should therefore favour a pluralist theory of property, by which I mean a theory of property that accepts that different forms of property are justifiable in terms of such considerations as the type of thing involved and the aspect of freedom at stake.[16] This approach would be consistent with the intersubjective nature of property rights that is made explicit in the concept of property employed by Kant, Fichte, Hegel and Marx, in that this intersubjective element suggests that the precise form that the concept of property assumes within a society must be decided by a complex social and political process in which there is meaningful consideration of different proposals concerning how property rights can structure social relations in ways that secure and promote free agency. This would prevent the dogmatic acceptance of the inherent superiority of one specific form of property. It would require consideration of how to secure and promote not only the personal freedom intended by Nozick, which finds expression in the right to dispose freely of one's property, but also the democratic freedom that enables citizens to shape the fundamental normative structures that govern a society and thus influence their own lives. This type of freedom may well require the introduction of significant constraints on the right to dispose freely of one's property, and thus on the personal freedom of which this right is an expression.

If a philosophical theory cannot settle such questions, and arguably ought not to attempt to do so, it can nevertheless make a substantial contribution to the clarification of them. It can also indicate the types of answers that one might provide. In this book, I hope to show that Kant, Fichte, Hegel and Marx make contributions of precisely this kind and that recognizing this does not require showing that one of the theories of property analysed in this book is right or at least more defensible than the other ones. This approach also does not require an attempt to combine the different theories into a harmonious whole, as if disagreements about the nature of property and the rights associated with it did not reflect how this institution and these rights have been and continue to be sources of social and political conflict even when no direct appeal to the concept of property and specific forms of it is made.

---

[16] This theory is therefore not a pluralist one in the sense that it accepts different grounds of the right to property, such as desert, utility and justice. For the idea of this type of pluralist theory of property, see Munzer, *A Theory of Property*, 3ff. This type of theory faces the challenge of either showing how the different grounds create no irresolvable conflicts or specifying other grounds that enable us to determine which of these grounds ought to take precedence whenever the different grounds turn out to be incompatible. Although making freedom the ground of the right to property faces similar challenges in that there are competing conceptions of freedom that support different forms of property, the theories of property that I discuss at least provide a framework within which the nature of such challenges becomes clearer.

CHAPTER I

Property, Freedom and Enlightenment
Kant's Rechtslehre

1.1 Freedom, Equality and Property

The *Rechtslehre* (doctrine of right) that forms the first part of Kant's *Metaphysics of Morals* is founded on the 'universal' principle of right. The application of this principle explains how the freedom of one person can coexist with the freedom of other persons. The principle of right forms the basis of Kant's account of specific rights, including the right to property, in such a way as to invite the following question: what kind of freedom is to be secured? An action is claimed to be right only 'if on its maxim the freedom of choice [*die Freiheit der Willkür*] of each can coexist with everyone's freedom in accordance with a universal law' (AA 6 [MM]: 230). If we assume that 'everyone's freedom' refers to each person's 'freedom of choice', then the aim of Kant's *Rechtslehre* will be to explain the coexistence of the freedom of choice of one person with the freedom of choice of all other persons. Moreover, the assumption that freedom of choice is that which right must both delimit and secure appears to be justified by Kant's definition of right as 'the sum of the conditions under which the choice [*die Willkür*] of one can be united with the choice of another in accordance with a universal law of freedom' (AA 6 [MM]: 230).

Kant's *Rechtslehre* seeks to identify '[t]he sum of those laws for which an external lawgiving is possible' (AA 6 [MM]: 229). The mutual limitation of freedom of choice must therefore be thought to take the form of a set of enforceable laws. A person's freedom of choice is to be limited, however, only if the exercise of it would make it impossible for another person to exercise his or her freedom of choice. The 'universal law of right' is accordingly identified with the following command: 'so act externally that the free use of your choice can coexist with the freedom of everyone in accordance with a universal law' (AA 6 [MM]: 231). The right to property must be explained in terms of the aim of delimiting and securing the permissible freedom of choice of each person. This right itself will then serve to delimit and secure legitimate freedom of choice in the form of a person's right to dispose freely of his or her property, provided that this exercise of freedom of choice is compatible with the freedom of choice of others. Thus a further question arises: what does it mean for the freedom of choice of one person to be compatible with the freedom of choice of all other persons in so far as this freedom relates to the right to property?

In seeking to address this question, I shall be led to argue that some of Kant's statements concerning the principle or law of right point to an alternative interpretation of the freedom for the sake of which the freedom of choice of each person is to be limited, because these statements imply that there is a form of freedom on which meaningful freedom of choice itself depends. This more fundamental notion of freedom has implications with respect to the question of the form that the concept of property ought to assume in a legal and political order that aims to secure the relevant type of freedom for all its members. This is not to say that Kant himself was aware of these implications. Indeed, there are statements that indicate that he did not think that this more fundamental notion of freedom was significant in relation to the right to property.

The idea that right concerns not only freedom of choice but also a more fundamental type of freedom that represents a negative condition of freedom of choice is signalled by Kant's claim that 'the only original right' which individuals possess by virtue of their humanity alone is the following one: '*Freedom* (independence from being constrained by another's choice [*Unabhängigkeit von eines Anderen nöthigender Willkür*]), insofar as it can coexist with the freedom of every other in accordance with a universal law' (AA 6 [MM]: 237). This statement implies that the freedom that right guarantees ultimately concerns how each person's will is not subject to the choices of any other person. It is therefore the *state* of being independent rather than the *act* of choosing that is fundamental. Indeed, the possibility of choosing freely depends on being free in the negative sense that one is not constrained by the choices of others, for only then can a person exercise his or her *own* power of choice. Independence from the wills of other persons and freedom of choice are in this respect logically distinct but practically related types of freedom. Limiting the freedom of choice of others in accordance with a universal law with the aim of securing the freedom of each person will then require ensuring that each person is sufficiently free of the choices of others to be able to make his or her own choices, unless being subject to the choices of another person can be justified in terms of an exercise of free choice on the part of the affected agent.

This supports the claim that independence from the choices of others is the foundation of Kant's *Rechtslehre*.[1] Independence of this kind is fundamental to Kant's *Rechtslehre* not only because it is the freedom that right must ultimately secure so as to make the freedom of choice of one person compatible with the freedom of choice of other persons, but also because it thereby determines what actions can be classed as rightful ones and what laws and institutions follow from the concept of right in that they are the conditions of this concept's application. It is therefore not merely a matter of securing or promoting a certain outcome (that is, independence), in which case right would be reduced to a means to an end that remains external to it. Rather, the end of securing independence is constitutive of the concept of right. This means that Kant's justification of the right to property must be thought to rest on the claim that this right is necessary to secure each person's independence. In order to explain the independence from the choices of other persons that right must secure and how this independence relates to the right to property, I shall now turn to the concept of equality with which Kant associates the freedom that right is to secure. We shall see that Kant's theory of property is not entirely consistent with the idea that independence from the choices of others is the freedom that right must secure once this independence is understood in a more robust way than Kant appears to understand it.

Kant speaks of an 'innate *equality*', which he describes as 'independence from being bound by others to more than one can in turn bind them; hence a human being's quality of being *his own master* (*sui iuris*)' (AA 6 [MM]: 237–38). This claim provides an important clue as to the nature of the independence that right must secure and how this independence can be secured within a legal and political order whose members are accorded an equal status. For it tells us that this independence consists in a condition in which no human being is either more or less obliged to obey other human beings than they are obliged to obey him or her. Thus there is a type of reciprocity that involves recognizing only those obligations that individuals are willing to impose both on themselves and on others. Freedom is here identified with the condition of being one's own master in the sense that one is not subject to the freedom of choice of another person whom one is obliged to obey without being equally entitled to command this other person. Since the sources of obligation are here understood to be rights, it is a matter of being one's own master in the sense of enjoying equal rights

---

[1] For this claim, see Ripstein, *Force and Freedom*, 13ff., and Wood, *The Free Development of Each*, 72ff.

that include the right to make one's own choices, provided the exercise of this right is compatible with the freedom of others to do the same.

By describing the equality that he identifies with the relevant type of independence as 'innate', Kant implies that every human being originally enjoys it. This can be understood to mean that all human beings possess the *capacity* for independence and are thus, potentially at least, their own masters, in the sense of agents who can decide for themselves how they should act and what they should be. The question of the conditions under which an individual can become aware of this capacity and exercise it properly then arises. An individual could not exercise the right in question, even if he or she were conscious of his or her capacity to be his or her own master, in a condition in which he or she is subject to the freedom of choice of another person, because this person would then be able to decide what this individual does and thus what he or she may become. Yet what precisely does it mean for one person to be subject to the will of another person in this way? Does it concern only direct interference in another person's life? Or does it also concern the possibility of interfering in another person's life on an arbitrary basis in such a way as to limit, and even determine, the choices that this person makes, as defenders of the republican idea of freedom argue?[2]

Kant's theory of right as it has been presented so far is too abstract to provide any clear answers to such questions. I shall now show how the characterization of the independence that right is to secure provided above is compatible with a robust understanding of this independence, and thus a correspondingly more demanding account of how right must delimit and secure each person's freedom. This robust understanding of independence can be illustrated with reference to some key features of Jean-Jacques Rousseau's account of the foundations of a rightful legal and political order that secures the freedom of its members. As we shall see, it is not evident that Kant himself is committed to such a robust understanding of independence, thereby inviting the question as to whether he nevertheless ought to endorse it.

Kant's characterization of independence as not 'being bound by others to more than one can in turn bind them' echoes Rousseau's claim that a legitimate social contract demands that those who enter into this contract completely give up any rights that they claim to possess, because only then will the condition be 'equal for all' and no one will, therefore, have 'any

---

[2] See Pettit's *Republicanism* and Skinner's *Liberty before Liberalism* for accounts of this idea of republican freedom and how it differs from the classical liberal idea of freedom.

interest in making it burdensome to the rest'.[3] In other words, a fundamental requirement of a legal and political order founded on a legitimate social contract is that each person remains equal in the sense that he or she subjects himself or herself only to the same laws as others, thereby incurring the same obligations and acquiring the same rights as they do. The outcome will then be a condition in which each person is subject to the same constraints on his or her freedom of choice and subject to them to the same extent, as opposed to a condition in which some individuals or social groups enjoy privileges that derive from a different and superior status. At the same time, the laws, and thus the obligations to which they give rise, secure the freedom of individuals who are now no longer in danger of becoming subject to the arbitrary will of any other person, as they would be if the relations between individuals in society were governed by force and thereby depended on the amount of power that one individual or social group happened to possess relative to others.

It is therefore ultimately freedom in the sense of independence from the arbitrary wills of others that ought to be equally distributed in such a way that the freedom of choice of each person is secured and its rightful extent delimited. If, in contrast, some members of the legal and political order established by the social contract were to become subject to constraints on their freedom of choice to which other members of society were not subject, they would bear additional burdens. Yet this state of affairs would be incompatible with the idea of equality. Moreover, any person who came to bear such additional burdens would be in danger of becoming dependent on the arbitrary will of any person who is not subject to the same constraints, for the second person would be able to constrain the choices of the first person by demanding that he or she fulfil obligations without his or her own freedom of choice being constrained in turn. This conflicts with the demand that the conditions to which individuals subject themselves be 'equal for all'.

Although we shall see that Kant does not directly endorse the robust idea of independence implied by Rousseau's account of the conditions that a legitimate social contract must satisfy, Kant's debt to Rousseau is evident from his understanding of the role that each person's interests play in deciding what rights would define a rightful legal and political order. Kant assumes that no one would willingly wrong himself or herself by submitting himself or herself to conditions that are incompatible with his

---

[3] Rousseau, *Of the Social Contract*, 1.6.6.

or her fundamental interests even if he or she would willingly harm others. Among these interests, we may include the interest in securing one's independence from the arbitrary wills of others, given how this independence enables one to remain or to become one's own master. Even if voluntary submission to conditions that are incompatible with one's true interests may render them legitimate in the case of oneself because it can be traced back to an act of free choice, this would not apply to others who have not consented to these conditions or cannot be thought to do so. For one may not assume that *they* would also willingly harm themselves in this way. According to Kant, the procedure of universalizing the principle that no one would willingly wrong himself or herself by submitting himself or herself to conditions that are incompatible with his or her fundamental interests provides the key to identifying the fundamental laws to which all rational agents could subject themselves and others in conformity with the idea of a united will:

> Now when someone makes arrangements about *another*, it is always possible for him to do the other wrong; but he can never do wrong in what he decides upon with regard to himself (for *volenti non fit iniuria*). Therefore only the concurring and united will of all, insofar as each decides the same thing for all and all for each, and so only the general united will of the people, can be legislative. (AA 6 [MM]: 313–14)

Yet what are the conditions discoverable by means of the universalization of the relevant principle to which all individuals could reasonably consent, given certain fundamental interests that they share, especially the interest in securing their independence in relation to the freedom of choice of other persons? Is it simply a matter of being subject to the same laws and being subject to them to the same extent as others? Or is something more required, such as the removal of other real or potential threats to freedom understood as independence from the arbitrary wills of other persons?

The fact that for Kant himself nothing more than being subject to the same laws and being subject to them to the same extent as others is required is suggested by his acceptance of a specific type of social relation that is structured by property rights. This social relation threatens to make one individual or social group subject to the arbitrary will of another individual or social group *within* a rightful legal and political order. I shall shortly turn to the relevant type of social relation. First, though, I want to emphasize its importance for the question of how property rights that explain a lack of genuine independence in the case of some citizens can be justified when Kant himself not only identifies independence as the single original right that a human being possesses, but also proposes the universalization of the principle that no one would willingly wrong himself or herself as the means of identifying the fundamental laws of right. As we have seen, these laws are ones to which rational agents who are seeking to secure their common interest in freedom could reasonably subject not only themselves but also others. This potential tension between Kant's commitment to the idea of independence and his acceptance of a lack of genuine independence that can be explained in terms of property rights makes his account of the right to property central to the question of the coherence of his *Rechtslehre*.

Although Kant's attempt to justify the right to property will be shown to indicate a presumption in favour of private property, I shall argue that there is no necessary connection between the freedom that right is to secure and the idea of independence that Kant himself accepts. Indeed, other forms of property may be necessary to secure a more robust type of independence that is more compatible with Kant's account of how right must ensure that the freedom of choice of one person is compatible with the freedom of choice of all other persons. I shall go on to relate this argument to Kant's concept of enlightenment, thereby providing an additional reason for claiming that forms of property other than private property are compatible with the aims of his *Rechtslehre* at least in some cases. Kant's *Rechtslehre* features a constellation of concepts that are historically associated with the Enlightenment, namely freedom, equality and property. Yet is private property the only form of property that may legitimately figure in this constellation? I shall argue that common or collective forms of property may, in fact, be viewed as more favourable to the genuinely independent way of thinking that is central to Kant's concept of enlightenment.

1.2 Property and Domination

Kant's acceptance of one-sided forms of dependence whose source is a specific type of social relation structured by property rights is evident from the distinction that he draws between active and passive citizenship.[4] For Kant, the status of citizen is the only relevant qualification with respect to the right to vote. Yet he restricts active citizenship, which includes the right to vote, to individuals who are independent by virtue of their status

---

[4] For an account of the historical background to this distinction as it is drawn by Kant himself, see Maliks, *Kant's Politics in Context*, 80ff. The important thing here is the distinction itself, rather than whether Kant applies it successfully in all the examples that he himself provides.

as owners of a certain type of property. This is the property that enables the owners of it either to engage in a productive activity in such a way that they can live from their own labour without becoming dependent on the arbitrary will of another person or to purchase the goods and services of others in such a way that these others become subject to their freedom of choice.

The role played by property rights in explaining this independence is evident from some of Kant's examples of people who are *not* independent in the relevant sense and who are therefore denied the right to vote. Although the 'woodcutter I hire to work in my yard' may own certain productive means, such as the axe that he uses to chop wood, he does not own other necessary ones, such as the wood to chop, which another person supplies. He is also dependent on the willingness of others to purchase his labour. Tenant farmers do not own the land that they cultivate and thus also lack sufficient productive means, making them dependent on another person's will, namely, the will of the person who owns the land and is willing to lease it to them (AA 6 [MM]: 314–15). These examples imply that the lack of political independence ultimately derives from how a person's ability to live from his or her labour depends on the will of another person. This is made more explicit in the following statement from another of Kant's writings:

> The quality ... of *being one's own master* (*sui iuris*), hence having some *property* (and any art, craft, fine art, or science can be counted as property) that supports him – that is, if he must acquire from others in order to live, he does so only by *alienating* what *is his* and not by giving others permission to make use of his powers. (AA 8 [TP]: 295)

This statement shows how the relevant type of dependence is a product of existing property rights, including the nature of the property to which a person possesses a right, for these rights explain the existence of a specific type of social relation and the asymmetries in social power that accompany it. This illustrates the structuring role that property rights play in society. The relevant type of social relation is exemplified by the relation that exists between the wage labourer and the person who pays for his or her labour power and the relation that exists between the tenant farmer and the landowner because there is, in both cases, a relation of economic dependence that can be explained in terms of the absence of legal ownership of any property other than one's own labour, on the one hand, and legal ownership of productive resources or the means of purchasing another person's labour, on the other. Social agents who enjoy the second type of property right can dominate social agents who enjoy only the first type of property right by subjecting them to their own choices and what follows from them. This is shown by how an employer may agree to purchase a person's labour power or a landowner may agree to lease a person a piece of land only on the condition that the person in question agrees to act in ways that further some political goal that the employer or the landowner favours because of how it accords with his or her private interests or those of a social group to which he or she belongs.

Although this type of dependence is incompatible with the robust idea of independence that I have attributed to Rousseau, Kant claims that this dependence on the will of another person and the political inequality that follows from it are compatible with the freedom and equality that passive citizens enjoy in common with other citizens. This is because lacking the right to vote and other political rights is compatible with the other attributes of citizenship, including equal legal status. Moreover, it must be possible to work oneself up from the position of a passive citizen to that of an active citizen, and thus to acquire the additional rights required to become truly one's own master (AA 6 [MM]: 315). It is not, then, a matter of *never* being subject to the arbitrary will of another person. Rather, what matters is that one can *become* fully independent because there are no legal or political obstacles to achieving this goal. There are nevertheless grounds for claiming that a more robust idea of independence is not only equally compatible with the law of right because this law does not entail Kant's less robust notion of independence but also more defensible than this less robust notion of independence.

To begin with, Kant's distinction between active and passive citizenship concerns a type of status rather than a principle that strictly follows from his definition of right. The members of specific social groups are accorded a status to which either fewer or more rights are attached. This status and the rights that accompany it are explained in terms of an idea of independence based on property rights. Thus one way of explaining the tension between the principles of freedom and equality, on the one hand, and Kant's acceptance of forms of social domination founded on property rights, on the other, is that it reflects a more fundamental tension between a priori principles of right and an a posteriori view of independence. The concept of right, which is a concept of pure practical reason, and the normative implications of this concept are compromised by being associated with an idea of what it means to be a citizen, and thus to enjoy a specific status, that is uncritically derived from traditional views of what qualifies an individual to be a citizen.⁵ Although the possibility of acquiring the relevant status may make Kant's distinction between active and passive citizenship compatible in a formal sense with the type of freedom that right is to secure, one may object that only the type of status that characterizes active citizenship is genuinely compatible with the idea of a rightful legal and political order. This opens the way for the argument that property rights should be distributed with the aim of guaranteeing this status for all citizens, rather than allowing existing property rights to determine who enjoys it.⁶

As we have seen, the specific normative structure of a rightful legal and political order can be identified by universalizing the principle that no one would willingly wrong himself or herself by submitting himself or herself to conditions that are incompatible with his or her fundamental interests. Kant agrees with Rousseau that this procedure cannot be reduced to a matter of what any single individual is willing to accept, for the universalization of this principle entails consideration of what others would be willing to accept. It is hardly self-evident that other people can be reasonably expected to accept the status of a passive citizen at the same time as others enjoy the status of an active citizen. Moreover, the possibility of achieving the status of an active citizen does not look like a sufficient safeguard, because those who are currently active citizens may employ their greater social and political power to prevent this possibility from becoming a reality in the case of others. I shall later identify an ambiguity in Kant's account of the right to property, the removal of which implies that this right cannot be reduced to the relation between a person and a thing. Rather, it must be understood in terms of a relation between persons concerning a thing in such a way that the right to property is founded on mutual recognition. Once the demand for mutual recognition is introduced, it becomes even more questionable whether the members of a specific social group could reasonably accept the existence of a system of property rights that reduces them to passive citizens. Thus the following question arises: why should property rights and the social relations founded on them be allowed to override the original right to independence that a rightful legal and political order ought to secure?

---

⁵ See Riedel, 'Die Aporie von Herrschaft und Vereinbarung in Kants Idee des Sozialvertrags'.
⁶ Regular secure access to goods and resources that enables individuals to become genuinely independent of the arbitrary wills of others would address a concern that may have motivated Kant's distinction between active and passive citizenship. This is the concern that individuals who are economically dependent on others may be indirectly forced to vote, and thus exercise their capacity to choose, in ways that do not reflect their own preferences, in order to protect their livelihoods.

Kant does not restrict possible violations of the external freedom which is the object of right to direct forms of interference, for he identifies the concept of right more broadly 'with the external and indeed practical relation of one person to another, insofar as their actions, as deeds, can have (direct or indirect) influence on each other' (AA 6 [MM]: 230). Among indirect ways of influencing another person, we may include a type of interference that consists in attempting to determine another person's freedom of choice by stating the potential negative consequences of his or her failure to act in conformity with one's own choices, which are here assumed to be those of an economically and socially more powerful agent. A person with greater economic and social power may choose not to interfere with another person's freedom of choice in this way. He or she may, in fact, be benevolently disposed towards this person and consequently act with a paternalistic sense of duty in relation to him or her. Yet this situation would itself be incompatible with a robust idea of independence because the mere possibility of suffering interference on an arbitrary basis can be judged to be sufficient to render a person unfree.[7] If protection from possible as well as actual interference is a necessary condition of genuine independence, then it becomes difficult to see why the removal of obstacles to an economic form of independence as well as a political one should not be a matter of right.

Kant himself appears uncomfortable with certain features of the property relations that underpin his distinction between active and passive citizenship. This distinction presupposes the right to any objects that are bought and sold as part of a contract between their legal owners, one of whom has only his or her labour to sell, while the other possesses the means of purchasing this labour and then limits the seller's freedom of choice by determining what he or she does. Kant accepts the legitimacy of any contractual relation founded on the act of 'granting another the use of my powers for a specified price' (AA 6 [MM]: 285). He also accepts the legitimacy of the 'possession of another's choice, in the sense of my capacity to determine it by my own choice to a certain deed in accordance with laws of freedom' to which this contractual relation entitles one party (AA 6 [MM]: 271). Yet Kant also imposes moral constraints on the permissible use of another person's labour when discussing the contract between a master and a servant. For he states that the 'contract of the head of a household with servants can ... not be such that his *use* of them would

---

[7] The classic example is the slave whose master just happens not to practise interference on an arbitrary basis but could nevertheless do so at will and with impunity if he wished to do so. See Pettit, *Republicanism*, 22f., 31ff. and Skinner, *Liberty before Liberalism*, 39ff.

amount to using them up; and it is not for him alone to judge about this, but also for the servants (who, accordingly, can never be serfs)' (AA 6 [MM]: 283). This example could be extended to any contract between an employer and a person who sells his or her labour to him or her. It implies that even when a person has sold his or her labour to another person for a specified period of time, restrictions on the permissible use of this labour ought to exist. Moreover, these restrictions ought to be decided by the employee as well as by the employer. Kant also appears hostile to the idea that human beings own themselves and therefore have the right to dispose of themselves howsoever they please, when he states that 'someone can be his own master [*sein eigener Herr*] (*sui iuris*) but cannot be the owner [*Eigenthümer*] of himself (*sui dominus*) (cannot dispose of himself as he pleases)' (AA 6 [MM]: 270). This suggests that Kant does not endorse the idea of self-ownership in so far as it entails the right to dispose freely of one's body or labour irrespective of the specific terms of any contract into which one has entered with another person.

Let us now turn to Kant's account of the right to property. The fact that property rights typically relate to material objects makes the right to a thing an obvious example of the external freedom with which the concept of right is concerned. Kant discusses rights of the relevant type under the heading 'Concerning what is externally mine and yours in general'. He appears to want to justify the existence of certain pre-political property rights that would limit how and to what extent a legal and political order may seek to achieve the goal of securing the independence of all its members, in that any violation of these property rights would undermine a person's independence in so far as it expresses itself in the right to dispose freely of items of property to which one has established a right independently of the choices of others. In other words, property rights are held to be constitutive of the independence that right guarantees because these rights are conditions of genuine freedom of choice.[8]

This type of argument depends on the premise that independence requires the right to dispose freely of one's property. Yet this begs the question of assuming that this specific right is a condition of independence. If this right can be shown to be incompatible with the genuine independence of others, then this assumption becomes even more problematic. For not only will any positive argument in favour of the claim that genuine independence requires private property be lacking, but there would also be grounds for viewing this form of property as a threat to such

[8] See Ripstein, *Force and Freedom*, 19, 63f., 66f., 86.

independence. For Kant himself, the right to property is only an acquired right, whereas independence is an original one. This suggests that any claims in favour of a specific form of property will be justified only if the relevant form of property secures the genuine independence of *all* citizens in a way that other forms of property cannot do. Independence here provides the criterion in accordance with which any property rights are to be judged, rather than the idea of independence being defined in terms of property rights of a specific kind. I shall now turn to Kant's attempt to justify the right to property, beginning with a problem faced by the notion of a pre-political version of this right.

Rousseau's account of the transition from a state of natural freedom to a law-governed society founded on a legitimate social contract illustrates a difficulty faced by any attempt to demonstrate the existence of provisional property rights that act as a constraint on how the legal and political order instituted by means of such a contract may seek to secure the independence of its members. The republican ideas of equality and freedom are central to this account. Rousseau asserts that the clauses of the contract 'all come down to just one, namely the total alienation of each associate with all of his rights to the whole community'.[9] This claim can be taken to mean that the legitimacy of any provisional property rights, assuming that it is meaningful to speak of such rights at all, cannot be taken for granted once the transition in question has been accomplished. Rather, all such rights must be examined in the light of the principle of equality and the idea of freedom that are the foundations of the law-governed society that has been established. If these provisional property rights turn out to be incompatible with the principle of equality and the idea of freedom understood as a person's independence of the arbitrary will from any other person, then these rights must be rejected because of their incompatibility with the foundations of right itself.[10]

In the next section, I shall argue that if Kant is seeking to justify a provisional right to property that serves as a moral constraint on what a state may rightfully do with the aim of securing the independence of all its

---

[9] Rousseau, *Of the Social Contract*, 1.6.6.

[10] This goes potentially further than the claim that property rights can be subordinated to the right to be independent of the choices of others in the restricted sense that property may have to be redistributed so as to guarantee the independence of all citizens. See, for example, Wood, *The Free Development of Each*, 85f. This type of claim assumes the legitimacy of private property, in that it concerns itself only with how the right to property understood in terms of private property is to be distributed, instead of considering whether other forms of property may not, in fact, better secure each citizen's independence.

citizens, his more fundamental commitment to the principle of equality and to the republican idea of freedom as independence from the arbitrary wills of others makes such a right appear so insecure that it becomes essentially meaningless. Moreover, there are good reasons for thinking that Kant understands this provisional, pre-political right in terms of private property. This is not to say that private property would be unjustifiable in those cases where it does not unduly limit the independence of others but does serve to secure or enhance the independence of the owners of property. I shall nevertheless argue that there are Kantian reasons for claiming that genuine independence, in so far as it ought to manifest itself in the publicly expressed thoughts of enlightened citizens, will require a different form of property in some significant cases.[11]

1.3 Kant's Justification of the Right to (Private) Property

Kant indicates the possibility of a provisional, pre-political right to property when he identifies private right (*Privatrecht*) with natural right (*Naturrecht*) and claims that private right would exist in a state of nature, thereby contrasting it with public right (*das öffentliche Recht*), which becomes possible only with the establishment of a legal and political order, or, as Kant terms it, the 'civil condition' (AA 6 [MM]: 242). Kant's statements concerning private right imply a form of right founded on principles of pure practical reason that precedes the existence of explicit legal norms and a state that enforces these norms. Kant's account of private right can, in fact, be seen to develop an argument that serves to justify public right, in that although the status of things as the exclusive property of individuals ('mine and yours') can be justified in terms of private right, public right is shown to be necessary to secure the relevant property rights.[12]

Private right is the topic of the first part of the *Rechtslehre*. It is here that we encounter Kant's account of rights of possession. This account develops into what looks like an attempt to justify private property, for in the section on 'property right' (*Sachenrecht*), Kant claims that '[a]n external object which in terms of its substance belongs to someone is his *property*

---

[11] The argument has been made that for Kant a market economy, as well as equal civil liberty, explains how it is possible for a passive citizen to become an active citizen. See Maliks, *Kant's Politics in Context*, 93, 109. Given that a market economy presupposes private property, especially the right to dispose freely of property, my argument that other forms of property may be necessary to secure independence implies that the logic of a market economy can, in fact, pose a threat to the independence of citizens when it is extended to certain spheres of social and political life.

[12] See Herb and Ludwig, *Naturzustand, Eigentum und Staat*, 289ff.

(*dominium*), in which all rights in this thing inhere (as accidents of a substance) and which the owner (*dominus*) can, accordingly, dispose of as he pleases (*ius disponendi de re sua*)' (AA 6 [MM]: 270). The right to dispose of a thing as one pleases (*nach Belieben*), that is, according to freedom of choice, distinguishes private property from other possible forms of property, such as when a person has the right to use a thing only under certain conditions and he or she does not have the right to exchange this thing for another thing or to give it to another person as a gift. Moreover, Kant's use of the phrase 'mine and yours' implies the *exclusive* possession of a thing, as does the statement that '[t]hat is *rightfully mine* (*meum iuris*) with which I am so connected that another's use of it without my consent would wrong me' (AA 6 [MM]: 245). Thus there are some *prima facie* grounds for viewing Kant's account of private right as an attempt to justify private property as opposed to mere rights of possession and use.[13] As an instance of natural right, this form of property and the rights that define it would be provisionally valid even in a state of nature, thereby acting as a moral constraint on how any legal and political order may seek to secure the independence of all its members.

Kant explains the possibility of the rightful possession of external objects in terms of the idea of 'intelligible' or 'rational' possession. This type of possession is independent of space and time in that it does not depend on having direct physical control over an object that is external to oneself. Intelligible possession does not, therefore, involve the possession of this object in *this* location and at *this* time. This means that someone other than the owner could exercise direct physical control over the object in such a way as to alter its location while lacking any right to this object other than the right to use it with the owner's permission. Thus the object remains the property of the original owner until such time as he or she chooses to dispose of it by destroying it, giving it to another person as a gift or exchanging it for another thing by means of a contract. The idea of intelligible possession nevertheless presupposes a connection between the owner of the object and the object itself that gives the former an exclusive right to the latter. Does this mean that there is a non-physical relation between a person and an external object that is sufficient to establish the person's right to this object, and from which the obligation to respect this right on the part of others then follows, making the relation to other persons an indirect one?

---

[13] For the claim that Kant's aim is in fact to provide only a justification of possession and use in the section on private right, see Westphal, 'A Kantian Justification of Possession'.

1.3 Kant's Justification of the Right to (Private) Property

The reduction of intelligible possession to a connection of this kind would be problematic because the most obvious way of understanding this form of possession is in terms of a normative relation that consists in the owner of the object having a right to it that can be violated by the actions of another person who would thereby wrong the owner. Yet how can a normative relation of this kind exist if the right in question is reduced to a relation between a person and an external object or 'thing' that is incapable of recognizing any normative claims because it is not a person? Kant himself draws attention to the absurdity of this way of understanding intelligible possession:

> Could this external rightful relation of my choice be a *direct* relation to a corporeal thing? Someone who thinks that this right is a direct relation to things rather than to persons would have to think (though only obscurely) that since there corresponds to a right on one side a duty on the other, an external thing always remains *under obligation* to the first possessor even though it has left his hands; that, because it is already under obligation to him, it rejects anyone else who pretends to be the possessor of it. So he would think of my right as if it were a *guardian spirit* accompanying the thing, always pointing me out to whoever else wanted to take possession of it and protecting it against any incursions by them. (AA 6 [MM]: 260)

Only another person can recognize a normative claim of the relevant kind and thus enter into an appropriate relation both to the thing and to the person who claims to possess an exclusive right to this thing. Intelligible possession must therefore be construed as a relation between two or more persons with respect to one and the same thing, in which one person possesses a right to the thing that does not depend on the physical possession of it and this same right entails an obligation on the part of others not to take possession of this thing without the first person's permission. The relation between the person and the thing is therefore not a direct one. Rather, it is mediated by a relation between persons.

Thus, when properly understood, the right to a thing presupposes prior recognition of the obligation to respect this right. This obligation cannot, therefore, be established independently of a relation to other persons whose own rights and legitimate expectations must be considered, given the requirement to universalize the principle that no one would willingly wrong himself or herself by submitting himself or herself to conditions that are incompatible with his or her fundamental interests. In Chapter 2, we shall see how Fichte makes this understanding of the right to property explicit by treating right itself primarily as a relation between persons who recognize one another as such. We shall then see how the procedure of universalizing the principle that no one would willingly wrong himself or herself by submitting himself or herself to conditions that are incompatible with his or her fundamental interests can be applied to the right to property in such a way as to show that one person cannot expect another person to recognize a system of property rights that significantly disadvantages himself or herself while benefiting others, as when an inferior social and political status is claimed to follow from how a person lacks property rights of a certain kind.

Unlike one person's direct physical possession of an external object and another person's attempt to dispossess this person of the object by means of force, the normative, recognitive relation between one person and another person with respect to one and the same thing cannot be an object of experience. Rather, this relation is an object of thought, that is to say, a concept. Hence Kant's description of the right to an external object as 'an intellectual possession of an object' (AA 6 [MM]: 249). This description by itself does not explicitly acknowledge how the normative relation in question is fundamentally a relation between persons with respect to one and the same thing. The same is true of the claim that 'such a concept of possession (*possessio noumenon*)' concerns 'an obligation … laid upon all others, which they would not otherwise have, to refrain from using the object' (AA 6 [MM]: 253). For Kant, however, an obligation of this kind cannot be derived from a right to a thing because this would require thinking of the thing itself as somehow having an obligation in relation to its owner from which the obligation to respect this right to a thing on the part of other persons follows. Yet Kant describes the thought of 'a right to a thing as if the thing had an obligation to me, from which my right against every other possessor of it is then derived' as 'an absurd way' of representing the matter (AA 6 [MM]: 261).

The way in which the right in question, and thus the corresponding obligation to respect it, is grounded in a relation of recognition between persons helps to avoid this absurdity and to make the right to property appear less mysterious. Moreover, the concept of intelligible possession can explain how property rights structure the relations of economic dependence described in the previous section. This is because one person can promise another person to provide a service or to fulfil a task as part of an agreement through which he or she receives something in return. Thus, as Kant himself points out, there must be some way in which the obligation to provide the service or to fulfil the task extends beyond the moment in time in which such commitments are made (AA 6 [MM]: 248). The external object is here an action that a person has promised to perform instead

1.3 Kant's Justification of the Right to (Private) Property

of an inert physical object, while the intelligible possession of this action is explained in terms of the choices of two persons: the person who agrees to perform the action at some point in the future and the person who agrees to provide some benefit in return either before or afterwards in such a way as to establish a right to this action.

If explaining the normative relation that exists between one person and another person with respect to one and the same thing requires the idea of intelligible or 'intellectual' possession, then this type of possession 'must be assumed to be possible if something external is to be mine or yours' (AA 6 [MM]: 249). Kant here assumes that there is the rightful possession of external objects and proceeds to identify the necessary conditions of this type of possession. This explains his use of the term 'deduction' in the relevant section of the *Rechtslehre*. Kant's use of this term in the *Critique of Pure Reason* indicates that he means a justification of our employment of a concept that consists in demonstrating this concept's necessity. The necessity concerns how this concept must be introduced in order to explain our general experience of the world (KrV [CPR], A 84–85/B 116–17). In the case of intelligible possession, the world would be one in which people claim to be the rightful owners of things and such claims are recognized by others, who in turn make the same type of claim in relation to other things. Moreover, Kant's use of the phrase 'mine and yours' and the way in which he speaks of the right to dispose of an object as one pleases imply that in this world people enjoy not only the exclusive possession of things but also the right to choose what to do with them, provided the exercise of this right does not violate the rights of others.

For reasons already stated, this implies that Kant has in mind private property. The object of the deduction would then concern a form of property whose justifiability has been, and continues to be, disputed. Kant cannot, therefore, merely presuppose general recognition of this object, and so it is not surprising that his attempt to demonstrate the existence of an exclusive right to a thing appeals to the conditions of the possibility of the *use* of a thing. This approach presupposes a relatively uncontroversial feature of human experience in general, namely, the fact that human beings are, for the most part, able to interact effectively with objects located within the natural and human environments in which they find themselves in such a way as to achieve ends that they have set themselves. Kant argues that the free and effective use of things would not be possible in the absence of the exclusive possession of parts of the world and objects within it. If this argument is meant to justify private property, however, it must assume that the right to dispose freely of one's property is also a condition of the free and effective use of things.[14] Yet is the possibility of using things in accordance with freely chosen ends sufficient to explain not only the right to exclude others from the use or other benefits of a thing but also the right to dispose of this thing as one pleases, with even another person's actions being among those things in relation to which a person may enjoy both rights?

From the following passage, it is evident that for Kant the conditions of free and effective use play a key role in his justification of the right to the exclusive possession of parts of the world and objects within it:

> For an object of my choice is something that I have the *physical* power to use. If it were nevertheless absolutely not within my *rightful* power to make use of it, that is, if the use of it could not coexist with the freedom of everyone in accordance with a universal law (would be wrong), then freedom would be depriving itself of the use of its choice with regard to an object of choice, by putting *usable* objects beyond any possibility of being *used*; in other words, it would annihilate them in a practical respect and make them into *res nullius*, even though in the use of things choice was formally consistent with everyone's outer freedom in accordance with universal laws. (AA 6: 246; MM, 405)[15]

Towards the end of this passage, a rightful condition in which the freedom of choice of one person can coexist with the freedom of choice of others with respect to the use of things is assumed to exist, or at least to be possible. Moreover, Kant asks us to conceive of a situation in which an exclusive right to things that are assumed to be compatible with the freedom of choice of others was prohibited. He claims that this would be an absurd situation precisely because the free use of things thereby becomes impossible. Since it is a matter of the exercise of freedom of choice, the use of external objects can here be taken to mean the use of them in accordance with ends that a person has formed independently of the choices of others. Thus the right to property, understood as the exclusive right to the use of a thing, is identified as a necessary condition of the free use of things. This right to property presupposes the concept of intelligible possession.

---

[14] This type of assumption is suggested by Ripstein's claim that '[f]reedom requires that you be able to have usable things fully at your disposal, to use as you see fit, and so to decide which purposes to pursue with them, subject only to such constraints imposed by the entitlement of others to use whatever usable things *they* have. Any other arrangement would subject your ability to set your own ends to the choice of others, since they would be entitled to veto any particular use you wished to make of things other than your body' (*Force and Freedom*, 19).

[15] MM does not here follow AA. I have therefore on this occasion provided the MM page number as well.

1.3 Kant's Justification of the Right to (Private) Property

Consequently, the validity of this concept is demonstrated by how it turns out to be a necessary condition of the free and effective use of things. Yet does the free and effective use of things always require more than the exclusive possession of them, in that a person must also be entitled to dispose freely of his or her property, provided the exercise of this right is compatible with the freedom of choice of other persons? Does the free and effective use of a thing even require the *unlimited* exclusive right to it?

Kant claims that a maxim whose universalization through becoming a law implies that an external object belongs to no one or, more literally, is without a master (*herrenlos*), is contrary to right (*rechtswidrig*), and that this is demonstrated by the possibility of having 'any external object of my choice as mine' (AA 6 [MM]: 246; MM, 404–5).[16] Yet even if we assume the truth of this claim, must the 'master' of this object be a private person or other legal entity with an unlimited exclusive right to the object that includes the right to dispose of it freely? The object could instead belong to several persons, and thus be common property, while being distributed in such a way that each person comes to possess a limited right to the exclusive use of the whole object or a part of it that is consistent with the exercise of freedom of choice, albeit in a restricted way. Moreover, if an exclusive right to a thing is equated with the absolute or near-absolute right to exclude others from the use or other benefits of this thing and to dispose of it as one pleases, then some people's enjoyment of this right may make another person's exercise of genuine freedom of choice impossible or at least significantly more difficult than it might otherwise be. I shall shortly return to such issues.

Kant's 'real definition' (*Sacherklärung*) of the concept of what is externally mine is stated as follows: 'something external is mine if I would be wronged by being disturbed in my use of it *even though I am not in possession of it* (not holding the object).' The 'nominal definition' (*Namenerklärung*), in contrast, is 'that outside me is externally mine which it would be wrong (an infringement upon my freedom which can coexist with the freedom of everyone in accordance with a universal law) to prevent me from using as I please' (AA 6 [MM]: 248–49; translation modified). The last definition refers to two features of private property: the right to exclude others from the use or some other benefit of a thing and the additional right to dispose of this thing as one pleases, which can be taken to mean according to freedom of choice in a purely arbitrary sense. Yet the real definition

---

[16] See previous footnote.

does not entail an unlimited right to exclude others from the use or some other benefit of a thing, nor the right to dispose of it freely. This definition demands only that one should not be disturbed in one's use of the thing even when one is not in direct physical possession of it. It is only the validity of this real definition of what is externally mine that Kant claims to have established, whereas he would have to establish the validity of the nominal definition if he is to justify private property in a way that excludes the justifiability of other possible forms of property, such as a form of common ownership where goods and resources are distributed on the basis of collective decisions concerning who should enjoy an exclusive but limited right to them. Thus when Kant claims that the real definition of a property right 'would have to go like this: *a right to a thing* is a right to the private use of a thing' (AA 6 [MM]: 261), the term 'private' cannot be equated with an unlimited exclusive personal right to a thing that includes the right to dispose freely of this thing, at least not without an additional argument.

It is relatively easy to conceive of a situation in which the demands that follow from the real definition can be satisfied without a person's freedom of choice being unjustifiably curtailed because he or she lacks an unlimited exclusive right to a thing that includes the right to dispose freely of this thing. For example, one and the same thing could be used by two or more persons without one person's effective use of it unduly interfering with another person's effective use of it, as when the same piece of land is used for two unrelated activities, both of which can be simultaneously performed without preventing or undermining the other activity. A thing would then be an object of free choice, in that it is employed with the aim of realizing an end that an agent has adopted, while this agent's judgement decides how the thing should be employed to achieve this end. Yet no single person would possess the right to dispose of this thing freely, beyond having the right to judge how to make the best use of it in relation to a specific end. Moreover, since the idea of intelligible possession requires that 'abstraction is made from all spatial and temporal conditions and the object is thought of only as *under my control*' (AA 6 [MM]: 253), there are no grounds for appealing to spatial or temporal considerations that are alleged to require private property to the exclusion of other possible forms of property, as if the fact that two persons cannot occupy the same piece of ground or hold the same object at the same time would justify an unlimited exclusive right to a thing even when the person who enjoys this right is not using the thing and shows no intention of doing so in the immediate future.

1.3 Kant's Justification of the Right to (Private) Property

Kant appears to provide a separate argument that denies the possibility of a free and effective use of things based on forms of property other than private property. Although he does not deny that human beings originally possessed land in common, Kant invokes the notion of effective use with the aim of denying that possession of this kind is compatible with the will to use the land. The common ownership of land would undermine the will to use the land because 'the choice of one is unavoidably opposed by nature to that of another', making effective use of the land impossible if the same will to use it 'did not also contain the principle for choice by which a *particular possession* for each on the common land could be determined (*lex iuridica*)' (AA 6 [MM]: 267). On the one hand, this claim could be taken to mean that land may continue to be held in common, but that there must be a principle of distribution that allows the land to be divided among all the people to whom it belongs. On the other hand, the claim could be taken to mean that common ownership of land is simply incompatible with the free and effective use of it. This implies that the division of the land must consist in the dissolution of the original common property and the transformation of the rights associated with it into discrete private rights.

If Kant is making the second claim, however, he is assuming that the absence of fixed patterns of exclusive ownership will inevitability generate conflict between human beings and that such conflict can be prevented only by introducing the private ownership of land. The fact that Kant is indeed assuming this is indicated by the assertion that the choices of individuals are 'unavoidably opposed by nature'. Yet it may be objected that this claim is based on a view of human nature that is conditioned by historical experience and fails to see how the dominance of private property may be regarded as the cause, rather than the effect, of conflict between human beings. In any case, Kant would have to demonstrate that private property, unlike other possible forms of property, tends to prevent conflict, whereas the resources and coercive measures that states employ to protect private property suggest that this is simply not the case.[17]

---

[17] Kant claims that it is not from experience that we learn that human relations are characterized by violent conflict prior to the establishment of a condition of right. Rather, the very idea of a condition in which right was absent implies that human beings would be judges in their own cause in matters of right, and this is sufficient to explain the insecurity of such a condition (AA 6 [MM]: 312). It is questionable, however, that one can draw such a conclusion independently of experience, for it is conceivable that the judgements of human beings in this condition would coincide and continue to do so. Admittedly, part of Kant's point is that such agreement would be contingent. Nevertheless, it is only if some general assumptions about human nature that are allegedly confirmed by experience are introduced that this contingency itself appears self-evident.

An example of the free and effective use of things that does not require private ownership of them is that of books borrowed from a public library. This example also illustrates how access to certain resources can be viewed as a condition of genuine independence and thus meaningful freedom of choice. The object here is not owned by any single person who enjoys the right to dispose of it freely. It is collectively owned and administered in the name of all relevant persons (for example, the residents of a certain area or the citizens of a state) for the potential benefit of all of them. In this respect, it is an example of a form of property that is expressive of a general or common will.[18] The free and effective use of things is here temporally limited and subject to other conditions in such a way that no one can be said to enjoy an unlimited exclusive right to a thing and the right to dispose of it freely. Individuals will nevertheless enjoy intelligible possession of a thing in so far as they have the right to exclude others from the use of the borrowed item for a specified period and this right does not depend on continuous physical possession of this thing. Moreover, this right and the corresponding obligation to respect it presuppose recognition of the norms of an institution that is independent of the private wills of the individuals who make use of it.

How does the relevant form of property help to secure the independence that is a condition of meaningful freedom of choice? To be genuinely independent, individuals require access to resources that enable them (1) to experience themselves as beings with the power to bring about changes in themselves and in the world around them in accordance with ends that they themselves have formed and endorsed and (2) to develop and exercise capacities that are either conditions of genuine independence or ways of enhancing one's independence. These capacities can be thought to include the ability to read about, to understand and to discuss social and political

---

[18] Property of this kind should not be identified with an aggregation of the rights of possession that each person whose will forms a part of this collective will originally enjoyed. This amounts to conceiving of property rights in terms of a right to property whose justification and universal applicability are presupposed. Common property that consists in the right to use objects subject to certain conditions might be said to presuppose a property right akin to that of private property on the part of the state. For example, after using the term 'private property', Ripstein makes the following claim: 'The power of the state to allocate land and chattels based on its priorities, and to determine the ways and terms on which they can be used, is a large-scale version of a property right' (*Force and Freedom*, 89). Yet what if the state administers resources in the name of the people which collectively owns them, though not in the sense that what the state administers is somehow the sum of its citizens' property rights? There is here no original exclusive right to any of these resources, and the state itself is not the owner of them with the right to dispose of them as it pleases. Instead, the state has been entrusted with the task of administering these resources in accordance with the collective will of the people on whose behalf it acts.

1.3 Kant's Justification of the Right to (Private) Property

issues. By their very nature, these capacities are ones whose development requires the proper exercise of them, which is possible only if people are guaranteed regular access to the relevant resources. Only then will individuals be able to think and to judge in the public sphere in such a way as to develop these capacities even further through the exercise of them. Thus public libraries provide an example of how guaranteed regular access to certain resources may require some form of common or collective ownership, whereas private ownership will limit the availability of these resources to those individuals who already happen to possess them or can afford to buy them.

From this example, we can see that there is no necessary connection between private property and a state of genuine independence, unless one assumes that this state consists in being able to do whatever one pleases with a thing, provided one does not thereby violate the rights of others. Moreover, the moment of reciprocity and recognition that is implicit in the demand to universalize the principle that no one would willingly wrong himself or herself would be violated if some citizens were denied access to the material and intellectual conditions of genuine independence because of the property rights of other persons. This moment of reciprocity and recognition entails that for each person the existence of obligations is conditional on the secure possession of rights, as Kant acknowledges when he claims that 'I am therefore not under obligation to leave external objects belonging to others untouched unless everyone else provides me assurance that he will behave in accordance with the same principle with regard to what is mine' (AA 6 [MM]: 255–56). It can then be concluded that no citizen is obliged to respect the property rights of others unless his or her independence is sufficiently secured by his or her own property rights or an equivalent to them. For Kant himself, 'a collective general [*collektiv allgemeiner*] (common [*gemeinsamer*]) and powerful will' that obliges everyone is required to ensure that this reciprocity condition is satisfied (AA 6 [MM]: 256).

Although it has now been shown that there is no necessary connection between genuine independence and private property, and that private property may in fact pose a threat to such independence, the following questions concerning common or collective forms of property then arise: *Who* determines the conditions of use? And *how* are these conditions to be determined? We must, in short, ask who will decide and implement that which the general will demands. Kant's *Rechtslehre* does not rule out a collective decision-making process that determines the allocation of property rights understood in the broad sense of rights of possession and use, while the task of allocating these rights may be the responsibility of the state or another agent that can legitimately claim to act on behalf of the general will of society. Indeed, the following passage concerning the distribution of land may be thought to suggest an arrangement of this kind:

> [T]he law which is to determine for each what land is mine or yours will be in accordance with the axiom of outer freedom only if it proceeds from a will that is united *originally* and a priori... Hence it proceeds only from a will in the civil condition (*lex iustitiae distributivae*), which alone determines what is *right*, what is *rightful*, and what is *laid down as right*. (AA 6 [MM]: 267)

Nevertheless, immediately afterwards Kant states that prior to the civil condition, there is provisionally a duty 'to proceed in accordance with the principle of external acquisition', and he claims that there is '[a]ccordingly ... a rightful *capacity* of the will to bind everyone to recognize the act of taking possession and of appropriation as valid, even though it is only unilateral' (AA 6 [MM]: 267). Kant is here referring to physical, as opposed to intelligible, possession. This physical possession 'has in its favor the rightful *presumption* that it will be made into rightful possession through being united with the will of all in a public lawgiving, and in anticipation of this holds *comparatively* as rightful possession' (AA 6 [MM]: 257).

Presumably, physical possession anticipates rightful possession in that a claim to the right to a thing based on the physical possession of this thing is sufficient to produce a corresponding obligation on the part of others to respect this right, provided the reciprocity condition is satisfied: 'This claim involves, however, acknowledging that I in turn am under an obligation to every other to refrain using what is externally his' (AA 6 [MM]: 255). Thus, although the act of taking possession is a unilateral one, it does not exclude the moment of recognition that makes the right to property more than a relation between a person and a thing. This anticipates the 'collective general' will mentioned earlier. A right of this kind, however, cannot be secured in a pre-legal and pre-political form of society in which there is no reliable way of deciding disputes between competing rights claims and no state capable of protecting rights. If recognition is a necessary moment of the right to property, however, is it really the case that it is only a matter of securing property rights that already exist rather than a matter of deciding what property rights there ought in fact to be?

One might argue that the relation between the right to property and the moment of recognition implied by the reciprocity condition that Kant himself introduces needs to be tighter than this, especially if we reject

1.3 Kant's Justification of the Right to (Private) Property

Kant's distinction between active and passive citizenship by adopting a more robust notion of independence. Kant defines citizenship in terms of the independence that comes from each person's 'owing his existence and preservation to his own rights and powers as a member of the commonwealth, not to the choice of another among the people' (AA 6 [MM]: 314). This implies a deeper and more stringent relation between the right to property and the moment of recognition because securing the independence of all citizens will require a critical assessment of any provisional property rights that are sources of economic and social power that threaten the equality and freedom which define true citizenship. There is a tendency on Kant's part, however, to suggest that the transition from a state of nature to the legal and political order of the civil condition will be one in which provisional property rights achieve legal recognition and are protected by the state, as when he claims that a civil constitution is a rightful condition in which 'what belongs to each is only secured, but not actually settled and determined' (AA 6 [MM]: 256).

Thus, despite the practical difficulties to which the idea of collective democratic scrutiny of property rights in a legal and political order founded upon the principles of equality and freedom gives rise, this idea may be thought to follow from the idea of a state in which its citizens live, to use Kant's own words, 'in accordance with laws of their own independence', and in which 'each is in possession of himself and is not dependent upon the absolute will of another alongside him or above him' (AA 6 [MM]: 317). In the absence of any provisional property rights that entitle a person to the exclusive possession and use of specific things together with the right to dispose of them freely once the civil condition has been established, what is required is a system of property rights whose precise form is the result of a collective decision-making process aimed at securing the genuine independence of all citizens. This independence is a constitutive moment of each citizen's freedom in that it forms a negative condition of meaningful freedom of choice.

From the standpoint of freedom itself, therefore, a presumption in favour of private property cannot be justified. This is not to say that private property cannot be the most appropriate form of property in connection with the free and effective use of certain types of things. Even then, however, it may later be decided that it is no longer so. For example, changes in material conditions, such as an increase in the availability of goods and resources facilitated by technological developments that were inconceivable to earlier generations, may serve to make alternative forms of property more appropriate. If another form of property can be shown to favour the maintenance and enhancement of each citizen's independence more than private property does, then this form of property should be favoured.

I shall now argue that this interpretation of what Kant's *Rechtslehre* truly demands is supported by his concept of enlightenment. I shall again appeal to the idea that there are capacities whose development requires the exercise of them and that people must therefore be guaranteed regular access to the relevant resources, for only then will they be able to think and to act in the public sphere in such a way as to develop these capacities even further through the actual exercise of them. These capacities and the proper exercise of them are conditions of enlightenment as Kant himself describes it.

1.4 Property and Enlightenment

I have argued that Kant should have rejected the idea of provisional property rights because there is no guarantee that rights of this kind will conform to the legal, social and political conditions under which the genuine independence of each citizen can be secured. Indeed, the aim of securing this independence might be more reliably achieved by means of a deliberative process in which citizens collectively determine the form of the property rights that structure the relations between them. I shall now argue that Kant's essay 'An Answer to the Question: What Is Enlightenment?' contains claims and ideas that support these conclusions. In this essay, Kant provides a well-known definition of enlightenment in an attempt to construct a concept of enlightenment that can be employed to identify any genuine instance of enlightenment. This definition is stated as follows:

> *Enlightenment is the human being's emergence from his self-incurred immaturity. Immaturity* is inability to make use of one's own understanding without direction from another. This immaturity is *self-incurred* when its cause lies not in lack of understanding but in lack of resolution and courage to use it without direction from another. *Sapere aude!* Have courage to make use of your *own* understanding! is thus the motto of enlightenment. (AA 8 [E]: 35; translation modified)

This is a negative description of enlightenment in that Kant tells us what enlightenment is not. Yet it can easily be turned into a positive one. Enlightenment consists in the exercise of the capacity to think for oneself. This requires the courage and the resolve to think for oneself. In this respect, Kant's concept of enlightenment implies the necessity of an initial moral act and the need for moral responsibility in the form of the willingness and the determination to make choices in such a way as to become that which one *ought* to be. Enlightenment must, for this reason, be viewed as a process. This process begins with the act of resolving to think for oneself followed by thinking in the appropriate way in relation to specific objects of inquiry. This moral aspect of Kant's concept of enlightenment invites the question as to whether the moral responsibility to think for oneself is limited in any way. Could, for example, the lack of an appropriate education or the fact of being the subject of a despotic ruler absolve individuals of this responsibility, or at least reduce the extent to which they can be justifiably accused of a moral failure if they do not think for themselves? Kant suggests an affirmative answer to such questions when he makes the following claim:

> [I]t is difficult for any single individual to extricate himself from the immaturity that has become almost nature to him. He has even grown fond of it and is *really unable* for the time being to make use of his own understanding, because he was never allowed to make the attempt. (AA 8 [E]: 36; translation modified and emphasis added)

If circumstances of the relevant kind can partly absolve individuals of responsibility for the moral failure of allowing their beliefs and judgements to be governed by an external authority, then both education and liberation from oppressive social and political institutions may be classed as conditions of enlightenment. The existence of these conditions depends on human agency that aims to remove obstacles to achieving an awareness of the capacity to think for oneself and obstacles that prevent or hinder the exercise of this capacity. The following claim concerning a specific social condition of enlightenment is especially relevant in this regard: 'For this enlightenment ... nothing is required but *freedom*, and indeed the least harmful of anything that could even be called freedom: namely, freedom to make *public use* of one's reason in all matters' (AA 8 [E]: 36). This claim implies that enlightenment requires, and is facilitated by, free public debate. The freedom in question is, however, to be restricted to the 'public' use of reason. What does Kant mean by this use of reason? And on what grounds does he restrict free debate to it? I shall now answer these questions in a way that demonstrates their relevance to the issue of property rights.

Kant distinguishes between the public use of reason and the private use of reason. The private use of reason is when human beings employ their reason in ways that do not directly concern their common humanity. This is because the use of reason concerns a specific social role or status (for example, soldier, clergyman, tax-paying citizen) that is associated with a particular identity and particular interests. This identity and these interests are not purely private or personal ones, for they are common to individuals who perform the same or similar social roles. Moreover, in so far as the performance of such a role benefits society, the identity and interests are compatible with general interests. Nevertheless, they fall short of being common to all human beings. The public use of reason, in contrast, is genuinely universal because all determinate identities and interests are suspended, enabling individuals to speak or to write as members of humanity, and thus to address humanity.

Some of Kant's statements concerning the public use of reason indicate that it is restricted to the sphere of educated citizens: 'by the public use of one's own reason I understand that use which someone makes of it *as a scholar* before the entire public of the *world of readers*' (AA 8 [E]: 37). Although one may criticize this restriction, education can be viewed as a condition of enlightenment, in that entering the sphere of the public use of reason demands the possession of sufficient knowledge and the ability to formulate and express coherent arguments. This typically requires being educated in certain ways and being exposed to a certain type of intellectual environment. Moreover, despite its elitist implications, the restriction in question does not, in principle, exclude any human being from the sphere of the public use of reason. If an individual is sufficiently able to engage in public discourse and to abstract from any identities and interests that are not common to humankind, then there are no grounds for excluding him or her from this sphere. Yet if this tells us *who* may enter the sphere of the public use of reason, it does not also tell us *what* would constitute an appropriate object of discussion within this sphere. This object would have to be sufficiently general in nature to apply to every participant in the public sphere viewed as someone who is capable of abstracting from the identities and interests that distinguish him or her from other human beings. Would property rights be one such object? I shall now argue that they would indeed be an object of the right kind.

Kant includes among the appropriate objects of the public use of reason the question of the legitimacy of taxes, laws and military orders, even though, in a private capacity, a citizen is not entitled to refuse to pay taxes, a legal subject is not entitled to violate existing laws and a soldier is not entitled to disobey military orders. The example of taxes and the example of military orders introduce a problem because the contrast between the private use of reason and the public use of reason implies that the identities and interests associated with being a taxpayer or a soldier must be suspended, given that not every adult human being is a taxpayer and certainly not a soldier. The example of critical public debate concerning legal norms is different, however, if it is assumed that all citizens are equally subject to the law and that laws ought to track fundamental human rights and interests. Taxation and the legitimacy of military commands might in consequence of this also fall within the domain of the public use of reason, for they concern the funding and the defence of a legal and political order governed by norms of the relevant kind. Moreover, the requirement to pay taxes typically assumes a legal form. Can property rights be viewed as an appropriate object of the public use of reason on the same grounds? I shall restrict myself to the issue of the type or the form of property rights (for example, private property versus common property) that structure human relations within a society, rather than also discussing the issue of how much property individuals ought to own, though what I say about the first issue may well have implications in relation to the second one.

Property rights structure social relations by establishing entitlements to parts of the world and to objects within it, and by giving rise to the obligation to respect these rights. Property rights can therefore be classed among the general norms that order and regulate human interaction. These norms typically assume the form of laws that are enforced by the state. As we have seen, Kant recognizes how this structuring function has social and political consequences, in that individuals come to possess different degrees of economic and social power relative to one another that may enable one social agent to dominate another social agent. This means that the question of the specific form that the right to property ought to assume is an object of general concern, given how different forms of property may structure society in substantially different ways. The question of the specific form or forms of property that ought to structure a society is therefore one that should be freely and critically discussed on an ongoing basis, so as not to favour one form of property at the expense of proper consideration of other possible forms of property.[19] Moreover, this object of public debate

---

[19] It might be objected that this amounts to deciding the matter of property rights on a case-by-case basis, whereas the task of a *Rechtslehre* is to identify principles according to which a just distribution of goods and resources can be achieved. This is not the case, however. To begin with, a general principle is at work, namely, the principle that parts of the world and external objects within it ought to be distributed and secured in such a way as to establish social conditions that are compatible with the genuine independence of all citizens. Secondly, the way in which the form of property will depend on the application of this principle does not exclude the possibility of general rules based on such considerations as the fact that a specific type of external object generally favours a specific form of property.

applies universally, and thus potentially to the whole of humanity, in that discussions of it can be framed in terms of the question of whether property rights of a certain kind favour the spread of enlightenment by securing and promoting material and cultural conditions that enable individuals to achieve an awareness of their capacity to think for themselves and to exercise this capacity in such a way as to develop it. To illustrate this point, I shall return to the example of the free and effective use of things provided by books borrowed from a public library. This example suggests that any presumption in favour of private property would in fact violate the norms of the public use of reason.

There are here external objects that are not the private property of any single person. They are instead collectively owned and administered in the name of all the relevant persons and for their benefit. The idea that guaranteed regular access to an external object of this kind is a condition of the independence demanded by Kant's concept of enlightenment can be introduced because the capacities that this independence presupposes and the exercise of these capacities in the public sphere may be thought to include the ability to read about social and political issues, to understand them and to discuss them in a suitably informed and coherent way. Private property, in contrast, threatens to restrict access to resources of the relevant kind to those individuals who already own them or can afford to buy them, or it makes access to these resources dependent on acts of charity. Taxation, which is a constraint on the free disposal of property, may fund public institutions that provide wider access to such resources. Yet these institutions may require a form of ownership other than private property that can be justified in terms of how it ensures that the material and cultural conditions of enlightenment are genuinely available to all citizens as a matter of right.

The argument that the specific form or forms of property that ought to structure society should be freely and critically discussed on an ongoing basis nevertheless fails to resolve a specific problem that can be illustrated with reference to Kant's distinction between the private use of reason and the public use of reason. An individual who wants to enter the sphere of the public use of reason is required to suspend those features of himself or herself that limit his or her humanity in the sense of not relating to the common concerns and nature of humanity. As we have seen, these features are not reducible to purely personal and private ones. Instead, they include features that can be traced back to social roles that individuals perform. Because these social roles concern specific occupations, they will tend to correspond to distinctive patterns of ownership, not only with respect to how much a person owns but also with respect to the type of property that he or she owns (for example, the means of production versus ownership of one's own labour power only). The social roles can then be thought to relate to differences in social power whose ultimate source is the right to property. Individuals will therefore have to abstract from their own property rights if they are to enter the sphere of the public use of reason in which property rights form an object of critical discussion. Yet what is to guarantee that an individual's contribution to public debate concerning this specific issue will not be influenced by the property rights that he or she enjoys or lacks when these rights are a source of social power or explain the lack of it? It may therefore be argued that a theory of property that identifies and justifies the most rational form or forms of property is still required.

In Chapter 2, I turn to Johann Gottlieb Fichte's attempt to construct such a theory of property. Fichte denies that the concept of property can be adequately understood in terms of a relation between a person and a thing. It must instead be understood as a relation between persons with respect to things. Fichte stresses the intersubjective nature of property rights by introducing the idea of a series of contracts that not only establishes a legal and political order but also determines the property rights that each person possesses. It is not, however, a matter of what individuals happen to agree among themselves. Rather, it is a matter of that to which they would all consent if they were serious about securing the necessary conditions of their own free agency, and if they acted consistently in relation to this end by accepting the necessary means of achieving it. To this extent, Fichte develops his own version of Kant's notion of 'a will that is *omnilateral*, that is united not contingently but a priori and therefore necessarily, and because of this is the only will that is lawgiving' (AA 6 [MM]: 263). At the same time, however, Fichte adopts a more robust interpretation of Kant's reciprocity condition, by making clear how the appropriate allocation of a specific form of property is a condition of each person's obligation to respect the property rights of others.

In 1796, Fichte reviewed Kant's *Towards Perpetual Peace*, which was published in 1795. This review appeared in the same year as the first part of Fichte's *Foundations of Natural Right* and a year before the publication of Kant's *Metaphysics of Morals*. In his review, Fichte argues that the law of right must go beyond the negative relation between persons that consists in the mutual limitation of their freedom of choice by specifying how far this same freedom extends. He identifies this extension of the law of right with the concept of property:

> The supreme law of right [*Rechtsgesetz*] is provided by pure reason: namely, every person should limit his own freedom in such a way that all others can also be free alongside him. *How far* any one person's freedom should extend, that is, the issue of property in the widest sense of the term, is something that the contracting parties must settle among themselves. The law is purely *formal*; it states *that* everyone should limit his own freedom. It is not *material*; it does not dictate *how far* each person should limit his own freedom. (GA 1/3: 225; RPP, 317)

From this passage, we can see how Fichte does not reduce the concept of property to ownership of external objects. Rather, this concept concerns the extent of a person's freedom. As we shall see, this is because a person's property not only delimits a sphere of freedom of choice but also relates to the conditions of free agency more generally, which include the type of independence from the arbitrary wills of other persons that is required to form and to pursue ends that are genuinely one's own. In addition to introducing this novel concept of property, Fichte attempts to demonstrate how this concept is a specific application of the more general concept of right. Right is purely formal because it tells us only that a person should limit his or her freedom in relation to the freedom of other persons, but not what the limits of each person's freedom ought to be. Right loses its merely formal character and becomes 'material' when it addresses the second issue as well. Therefore, to understand Fichte's arguments concerning the right to property, we need to undertake a systematic reconstruction of the application of the concept of right.

There is another sense in which the concept of right becomes material through its application. Fichte stresses how property rights concern the material conditions of autonomous agency. This is reflected in how he seeks to establish an essential connection between the concept of property and the concept of labour in the *Foundations of Natural Right*, whereas in Kant's *Rechtslehre* labour is a source of domination, in that those who possess only their own selves, bodies and labour lack sufficient productive means and thereby come to depend on others who possess such means or the means to purchase the labour of others. This connection between property and labour leads Fichte to argue for a form of property other than private property in the *Foundations of Natural Right*. Nevertheless, he seeks to accommodate a form of property that exhibits some key features of private property, though, as we shall see, it is questionable that he succeeds in this. Yet there was a fundamental shift in Fichte's thinking about property. In an earlier work, the *Contribution to the Correction of the*

Public's Judgements Concerning the French Revolution, Fichte argues that labour can establish a pre-political right to property that is reducible to the dyadic structure of a relation between a person and a thing. I shall begin with this earlier theory of property because of how it helps to shed light on the later one and especially on what may have motivated Fichte to develop a different theory of property in the *Foundations of Natural Right*.

CHAPTER 2

Fichte on Property and Labour

2.1 Fichte's Early Theory of Property

Fichte's views on the right to property changed significantly between the *Contribution to the Correction of the Public's Judgements Concerning the French Revolution* published anonymously in 1793 and the *Foundations of Natural Right* published in two parts in 1796 and 1797. Given that Kant's *Metaphysics of Morals* was published in the same year as the second part of the *Foundations of Natural Right*, it cannot be said that Fichte is responding directly to Kant's account of property discussed in Chapter 1. Nevertheless, the fundamental change in Fichte's views on the right to property reflects an ambiguity found in Kant's account of the right to property and removes this ambiguity. For this change consists in a decisive rejection of the idea of a right to property that exists prior to the establishment of legal and political norms and institutions to which all relevant agents could agree in favour of the claim that the right to property presupposes both the rational consent of others and the establishment of a legal and political order. The fundamental change in Fichte's views on the right to property can also be explained in terms of a reconsideration of what it is required for the right to property to function as a material condition of free agency.

In his *Contribution to the Correction of the Public's Judgements Concerning the French Revolution*, Fichte seeks to justify the right to property in a way that implies a commitment to what is today known as self-ownership, for he claims that '[o]riginally we ourselves are our property. No one is our master, and no one can become our master' (GA I/1: 266). Fichte explains this right that an individual enjoys in relation to his or her own person in terms of the idea of rational autonomy. Property rights are held to be coextensive with that over which a person, and this person alone, can exercise direct rational control. Ownership of this kind extends beyond a person's body to include any intellectual or bodily powers by means of which a person is able to interact with the world confronting him or her and the things within it, for these powers are likewise things over which only he or she can exercise direct rational control: 'The pure I in us, reason, is the master of our sensuousness, of all our mental and bodily powers; it may employ them as means to any desired end' (GA I/1: 266). This account of the right to property is consistent with the way in which Fichte's defence of the French Revolution is based on the idea of moral autonomy in the following way.

The existence of universally valid norms of action implied by the word 'ought' presupposes a fundamental law or principle that can be employed to judge the moral legitimacy of any action, event or state of affairs. Fichte thinks that his opponents must accept this claim because otherwise they would be in no position to condemn the French Revolution as immoral or unjust. They are therefore also committed to what logically follows from it. Fichte then states a series of arguments designed to demonstrate that the law or principle in question cannot be derived from experience (GA I/1: 212–16). It must therefore be conceded that any standard used to judge a historical event such as the French Revolution will have to be 'independent of all experience and more elevated than it' (GA I/1: 218). Fichte claims that an a priori law of this kind can be discovered only within the pure, original 'I', that is, within one's own self in so far as it remains undetermined by any external influences (GA I/1: 218–19). The only thing that is independent of experience in this way is the 'law of the ought' to which a free but finite rational being finds itself subject in the form of an unconditional command (GA I/1: 219). This is the moral law, of which a finite rational being is immediately conscious.

Voluntary subjection to this law is the highest instance of moral autonomy, in relation to which all forms of civil and political freedom are subordinate because they would not be possible in the absence of the capacity to impose norms of action upon oneself and to act in accordance with these norms. Legal rights concern that which the moral law neither commands nor forbids and is therefore morally permissible (GA I/1: 220). It is a matter of free choice whether one chooses to perform permissible actions. The act of making a contract through which a person agrees to alienate certain powers or goods falls within this sphere of free choice. The moral law here plays the negative role of determining what may form the object of a contract, while the concept of moral autonomy justifies the claim that individuals can be legitimately subject only to legal and political norms to which they themselves have consented, making consent the source of the authority of these norms and thus of their binding character (*Verbindlichkeit*) (GA I/1: 238–39).

Fichte here adopts Kant's idea of moral autonomy, as it is expressed in the following statement: 'the will is not merely subject to the law but subject to it in such a way that it must be viewed as also giving the law to itself and just because of this as first subject to the law (of which it can regard itself as the author)' (AA 4 [GMM]: 431). Fichte understands this moral autonomy in such a way that the law in question does not generate only unconditional moral obligations. Rather, as we have already seen, it also delimits the sphere of permissible actions. Obligations within this sphere are of a conditional nature because their binding character depends on the act whereby an individual voluntarily subjects himself or herself to a law and on whether he or she chooses to continue to subject himself or herself to this law. This implies that individuals have an inalienable right to annul unilaterally any contract into which they have entered, including the one that produces the constitution of the state of which they are citizens, because the laws of this constitution belong to the sphere of that which is permitted rather than commanded by the moral law. Thus the French people's act of collectively and unilaterally freeing itself from its previous obligations by changing the constitution of the French state can be justified in terms of the moral law and the idea of moral autonomy.

On the one hand, Fichte's justification of the right to property is compatible with the grounds on which he defends the French Revolution, not only because it appeals to the idea of moral autonomy but also because there is a liberty right to appropriate raw material and employ it for one's own ends that is explained in terms of how the moral law permits such actions. On the other hand, property rights are not established by mutual consent even though they generate an obligation to respect them on the part of others. Yet the idea of self-ownership alone cannot explain how there can be a right to an object that was originally external to the person who appropriates it and a corresponding obligation on the part of others to respect this right even though they themselves had not consented to it. To fill this gap in his justification of the right to property, Fichte introduces a further argument which concerns the formation of raw material achieved by employing things that a person already owns, namely, his or her own self and body together with any powers immediately connected with them. The argument is stated as follows.

One essential way in which persons employ their intellectual and bodily powers to interact with the world confronting them is by forming things that they encounter within this world with the aim of making these things serve their ends. These things have a fundamentally different status to the one enjoyed by a person because they lack the capacity for freedom and therefore cannot be their own property. Because these things do not belong to themselves in the way that rational agents do, there is no moral prohibition on treating them merely as means to an end and making them fit to serve as such means. Rational agents therefore have the right, in the negative sense of the entitlement to do something in the absence of any moral prohibition that forbids doing it, to employ their powers in such a way as to make these things serve as means to their own ends. The right to a thing is conclusively established when a person makes this thing into a means to his or her own ends to such an extent that another person could not use this thing without either (1) appropriating something that is a result of the application of the first person's powers, thereby indirectly employing these powers themselves for his or her own ends, or (2) destroying the form which the first person had given to the thing, thereby hindering this person's use of his or her powers in so far as the thing serves as a means to his or her ends (GA I/1: 266–67). In both cases, one person would violate another person's freedom because this person's property, in the form of certain powers of which he or she is originally the rightful owner or 'master', would be employed without the owner's consent. If the consent to employ these powers indirectly by appropriating a thing that had been formed by them were given, then the right to this thing would be presupposed, in that this right is what entitles a person to choose how he or she disposes of a thing. It is precisely this prior right to a thing that must be explained, given how it cannot be explained purely in terms of the right that a person originally enjoys in relation to his or her own self and body. It is the act of forming a thing that explains this additional right.[1]

This justification of the right to a thing is said to entail 'the right to exclude everyone else from the use of a thing that we have formed [*gebildet*] by means of our powers, to which we gave our form' (GA I/1: 267). Yet a rather obvious problem emerges in connection with this attempt to justify a pre-political right to property founded on the formation of a previously ownerless external object. For in the course of time, it is bound to happen that the raw material which can be formed in accordance with a rational agent's ends will become so completely permeated by the ends of particular agents that there is eventually nothing left for future generations

---

[1] Despite any similarities with Locke's justification of the right to property, there is no evidence of a direct influence. In his notes to the edition of the *Contribution to the Correction of the Public's Judgements Concerning the French Revolution* edited by him, Richard Schottky provides strong evidence that it was, in fact, Theodor Schmalz's essay 'Das reine Naturrecht' which directly influenced Fichte's earlier account of the right to property. See Schottky, 'Anmerkungen zum Text', 289ff.

to appropriate in a way that would allow them to establish property rights of their own. Given this lack of opportunity to acquire property rights of their own through the exercise of their formative powers for which these future generations cannot be held responsible, many individuals will find themselves in a situation in which they may be considered the innocent victims of the following harsh judgement that is nevertheless an implication of the only possible justification of the right to property that Fichte thinks is compatible with natural right:

> He who does not work may well eat if I want to give him something to eat; he does not, however, possess any legally binding [*rechtskräftigen*] entitlement to something to eat. He may not employ another's powers for himself. If no one is so good as willingly to do it for him, he will therefore have to employ his own powers to find or prepare something, or die of hunger, and do so as a matter of right. (GA I/1: 267)

Fichte's account of the right of children to inherit their parents' property is an attempt to avoid the impression that there could, in fact, be any victims of a situation in which everything apart from air and light – which, according to Fichte, cannot be appropriated in the required way – is already the property of others. His argument for this right is the following one.

The deceased person loses the rights that he or she possessed while living, including any property rights. Despite the form that he or she had previously given it, this person's property becomes equivalent to raw material in that no single person is now the rightful owner of its form. The whole of humankind can therefore be said to inherit this quasi-raw material. In accordance with the general right to appropriate formless things, each person will enjoy the unrestricted natural right to appropriate this raw material until such time as one person has transformed it into a recognizable means to one or more of his or her ends. Nature and the moral law are here in agreement because the former in the shape of the natural physical decay and eventual death of the previous owner cares for those who are born later without violating any rights that derive from each person's moral autonomy. Yet the outcome would be a state of affairs that is suboptimal when viewed in terms of its efficiency because those individuals without property will then be forced to engage in a potentially futile search for things that have become equivalent to raw material as a result of the death of their previous owners. Moreover, this situation is likely to produce social conflict because individuals will find themselves competing with one another to appropriate things that have become ownerless. It must therefore be assumed that once human beings had become citizens by consenting to enter into a political union with one another, they would have agreed among themselves to appropriate only that which was nearest to them, which would typically be their father's property, while renouncing the right to appropriate other things. Fichte goes so far as to speak of 'an inalienable human right' to inherit property of the relevant kind (GA I/1: 274–75).

This solution threatens to perpetuate existing inequalities. Moreover, it assumes that enough raw material was originally available, allowing everyone then alive to establish a property right to at least one thing which could subsequently be inherited. Nor does Fichte provide any grounds for denying the claim that even if a condition in which enough raw material was originally available is presupposed, the process of legitimate transfer would not have eventually been disrupted by acts of deceit or force that deprived people of their rightful property, leaving them unable to pass it on to their children. Since Fichte came to reject his earlier justification of the right to property, these issues need not concern us. I shall instead identify a tension between this justification of the right to property and other claims that Fichte makes in his defence of the French Revolution because of how this tension helps to explain the fundamental change that his thinking about the right to property underwent. This explanation turns on a distinction between the grounds of Fichte's defence of the French Revolution and what motivates this defence.

Fichte's attempt to justify the French Revolution is motivated by moral indignation. This is evident from a passage concerning the fate of those people who lack property rights to such an extent that they are unable to satisfy their basic material needs and how this fate compares to the luxury enjoyed by the members of the unproductive privileged classes, who are incapable of satisfying their alleged needs without commanding the labour of others, and who complain about the privations they suffer now that they can no longer command the labour of others as much as before. Fichte, who himself experienced the evils of poverty,[2] describes the

---

[2] Fichte was the son of a ribbon weaver. This trade was a 'free' one in the sense that it was not subject to guild regulations. Anyone could therefore pursue this trade, resulting in greater competition and significant fluctuations in prices subject to the laws of supply and demand. We can assume that poverty was a constant danger for Fichte's family, which, even if it was not living in abject poverty, would have been by no means wealthy, but can, in fact, be judged to have occupied a place only above day labourers in the social hierarchy of the eighteenth century. Moreover, during his time as a university student and a private tutor (*Hauslehrer*), Fichte suffered acute financial difficulties. At one point, he was forced to ask Kant to lend him some money. Kant declined to do so and instead suggested a publisher for Fichte's *Attempt at a Critique of All Revelation*. Kant also appears to have offered to help find Fichte another position as a private tutor. See Kühn, *Johann Gottlieb Fichte*, 17ff., 62, 137ff.

following situation in connection with how the general attitude towards the fate of the poor differs from people's inexplicable sympathy for the unjustified claims of the unproductive privileged classes:

> It is always a remarkable lack of consistency in our way of thinking that we are so sensitive to the misery of a queen who for once does not have any fresh linen, but find so natural the deprivation suffered by another mother who has also given birth to healthy children for the fatherland, whom she, herself wrapped in rags, sees wandering around naked before her, while in her breasts the source of nourishment, which the most recently born child demands with an enfeebled whimper, has dried up because of a lack of sustenance. (GA I/1: 320)

The moral indignation evident in this passage suggests that it is not the case of someone who lacks the means of subsistence because she is unwilling to work. Rather, the situation in which the mother and her children find themselves can be explained in terms of social structures that deprive some people of the opportunity to engage in forms of productive activity that enable them to support themselves materially and to live in a way that befits a human being, whereas the same social structures enable other people who do not work to get others to work for them, so that only they enjoy the fruits of human labour.

Fichte's justification of the right to property in terms of the formation of things aims to establish a necessary connection between this right and labour. His introduction of the right to inherit property shows that he recognizes that some individuals will be unable to establish property rights in the required way. Yet the solution of a right to inherit property must be said to fail once it is considered in the light of the aim to establish a necessary connection between the right to property and labour for the following obvious reason: there is no guarantee that the person who inherits a thing will use this thing in a productive manner instead of consuming it or letting it go to waste. Moreover, Fichte makes the right to inherit property redundant at the same time as he succeeds in establishing a necessary connection between the right to property and labour when he proposes a way of abolishing the social structures that explain the radical difference between the undeserved fate of the poor and the luxury enjoyed by the members of the unproductive privileged classes. These social structures can be abolished by allowing human beings to dispose of their powers freely in competition with one another. For, according to Fichte, free trade and the 'natural inheritance' of the human being would produce a situation in which 'the income gained from landed property [*Grundeigenthum*] and all property would stand in an inverse relation to its size, the land will of itself, without any violent agrarian laws, which are always unjust, gradually be divided among several people, and your problem will be solved' (GA I/1: 319).

This proposal follows from Fichte's acceptance of the idea of self-ownership, for it rests on the claim that a person's powers, including his or her labour power, are originally his or her rightful property and that only property rights acquired through the employment of these powers are morally justifiable. A person may dispose of this property freely in the same way that he or she disposes freely of other items of property. Fichte himself speaks of property in this sense when he claims that:

> The most immediate property, which is the foundation of all the human being's other property, are his powers. Whoever has the free use of these powers already immediately has in them an item of property [*ein Eigenthum*], and he cannot fail, through the use of them, also to gain property soon in [the form of] things [*ein Eigenthum an Sachen*] outside him. (GA I/1: 315)

It looks, then, as if every human being already has some property. The free exchange of this property will enable a person to acquire other items of property. In the *Foundations of Natural Right*, however, Fichte abandons this position precisely because it cannot adequately explain how each person's right to live from his or her labour can be guaranteed. In this respect, Fichte can be seen to develop a new position that is more compatible with the following claim found in his defence of the French Revolution: 'Every human being must live, that is his inalienable human right' (GA I/1: 315). At the same time, he retains the idea of a contract into which individuals freely enter. This contract makes explicit certain rational demands and what is required to satisfy them, and it shows that there can be no right to a thing based on the formation of a previously ownerless external object that reduces the concept of property to a relation between a person and a thing. Rather, the concept of property necessarily has a more complex structure, whose most basic form is the triadic person–thing–person one. Property rights are nevertheless to be distributed in such a way that an essential connection between the right to property and labour exists. This new theory of property leads Fichte to develop a comprehensive account of the state's role in regulating the economic life of society.

To understand how the concept of property comes to assume the more complex structure identified above, we must turn to Fichte's attempt to demonstrate the rational necessity of the concept of right. As we shall see, although Fichte's *Foundations of Natural Right* may initially appear to develop an argument for private property, the concept of right is subsequently developed in such a way that Fichte must be thought to construct a theory of property that is ultimately incompatible with the existence of private property.

2.2 The Relation between the Concept of Right and the Concept of Property

In the *Foundations of Natural Right*, Fichte seeks to demonstrate that the concept of right is a necessary condition of the practical form of self-consciousness which consists in an awareness of oneself as a rational agent with the capacity to form ends and to 'find' oneself as a free agent by bringing about changes in the world in accordance with these ends (GA I/3: 319–20; FNR, 9). Thus the necessity of the concept of right derives from how it is not possible to comprehend the relevant form of self-consciousness, the existence of which is presupposed, without implicitly thinking this concept. For if a rational agent is to achieve a representation of its freedom, then it must be able to exercise its capacity for self-determination, and this presupposes the reliable, stable conditions of agency provided by right. The philosopher's task is to make explicit this necessary connection between self-consciousness and the concept of right.

Right secures for each person a sphere of action free from external interference. Within this sphere, a rational agent can 'posit itself' as an individual (*Individuum*) (GA I/3: 319; FNR, 9). It can posit itself in this way by choosing from among various possible (that is, permissible) actions, thereby becoming an individual distinct from other individuals: 'no other person is *this person*, i.e. no other person can make choices within the sphere allotted only to him. This is what constitutes the person's individual character: through this determination, the person is *the one* that he is, this or that person, called by this or that name' (GA I/3: 361; FNR, 53). Thus, as with Kant's *Rechtslehre*, right is necessary to ensure that the freedom of choice of one person can coexist with the freedom of choice of other persons. Moreover, there is no reason to restrict the non-interference in question to actual interference. Rather, it may also include the prevention of the kind of possible interference on an arbitrary basis that poses a threat to a person's independence. As we have seen, the state of being independent in this extended sense can be viewed as a condition of the exercise of genuine free choice. Fichte himself acknowledges this, for he claims that a theory of right must explain how this independence can be secured, despite how such a theory equally accepts that persons are not independent in so far as they exercise an influence on one another:

2.2 The Relation between Right and Property 57

Persons as such are to be absolutely free and dependent solely on their will. Persons, as surely as they are persons, are to stand with one another in a state of mutual influence, and thus not be dependent solely on themselves. The task of the science of right [*Rechtswissenschaft*] is to discover how both of these statements can exist together: the question that lies at the basis of this science is: *how is a community of free beings [eine Gemeinschaft freier Wesen], qua free beings, possible?* (GA I/3: 383; FNR, 79).

A person's independence is not threatened by relations of dependence and mutual influence as such. Rather, it is threatened by relations of this kind only in so far as they generate asymmetries in power that allow one agent to dominate another agent. This domination may fall short of actual interference and instead consist in the possibility of interfering in a person's life on an arbitrary basis.

Fichte seeks to demonstrate that the concept of a sphere of freedom which ensures a person's independence entails certain legal and political arrangements to which the term 'right' has traditionally been applied. His theory of right is distinctive, however, because of its explicitly intersubjective character, which is captured by the description of the concept of right itself as 'the concept of the necessary relation of free beings to one another' (GA I/3: 319; FNR, 9). Here, we can see how the claim that persons influence one another is essential to Fichte's theory of right. This understanding of the concept of right leads Fichte to reject the idea that a right to property may exist prior to the establishment of a legal and political order in the sense of being provisionally valid.

In his 'deduction' of this concept, Fichte claims to demonstrate the necessity of both the act of positing other free beings and the relation of right that exists between such beings. To become conscious of itself as free, a rational agent must not only conceive of itself as a being with the capacity to engage in purposive activity in accordance with ends that it itself has formed but also think of something different from itself that is the source of a representation that confirms this self-conception. Although the subject of consciousness is to this extent determined by the object of consciousness, and in this respect limited by it, the subject's self-determining character must be preserved if the consciousness of itself as a free agent is to be achieved.

Fichte identifies the required type of object with a summons or request (*Aufforderung*) that is compatible with the subject's self-determining character because it does not *cause* its addressee to act in any specific way (GA I/3: 345: FNR, 34–35). Rather, it demands only the exercise of the capacity for free choice, which may take the form of choosing *not* to act. This summons presupposes that both the being which is its source and the being to which it is directed are capable of understanding what it means to act freely in the relevant sense (GA I/3: 345; FNR, 35). These beings must therefore be thought to recognize each other as free, rational beings. This recognition finds practical expression in the act of mutually limiting their activity in relation to each other, leaving each of them with a sphere in which they are free to act. The act of summoning another person is accordingly identified with how the other person 'has, in *his* choice, in the sphere of his freedom, taken my free choice into consideration, has purposively and intentionally left a sphere open for me' (GA I/3: 353; FNR, 44).

The 'community among free beings' whose necessity Fichte thinks that he has thereby demonstrated consequently requires that each member of this community adopt 'the rule of right' (*die Rechtsregel*), which finds expression in the following demand: 'limit your freedom through the concept of the freedom of all other persons with whom you come in contact' (GA I/3: 320; FNR, 10). The relation between persons governed by this rule entails that the most basic structure of right is a dyadic person–person relation. The concept of property can be accommodated within a theory of right only if this dyadic structure is extended to become a triadic person–thing–person one. Thus there is already an essential difference between Fichte's earlier and later theories of property because the former was consistent with the reduction of the concept of property to the relation between a person and a thing. Fichte himself identifies how the incorporation of the concept of property into his theory of right entails a triadic person–thing–person structure in the following passage:

> The concept of right [*Rechtsbegriff*] is the concept of a relation between rational beings. Thus, it arises only under the condition that rational beings are thought in relation to one another. It is nonsense to talk about a right to nature, to land, to animals, etc. considered only on their own or in direct relation to a human being. Reason only has power – and by no means a right over – these things, for in this relation the question of right does not arise at all.... Only if another person is related to the same thing at the same time that I am does there arise the question of *a right to the thing*, which is an abbreviated way of talking about – and this is what it should really be called – *a right in relation to the other person*, i.e. a right to exclude him from using the thing. (GA I/3: 360; FNR, 51)

The triadic person–thing–person structure of the concept of property entailed by the concept of right is compatible with different forms of property. Fichte's concept of right might nevertheless be thought to favour private property, if the sphere granted to each person is assumed to include not only the right to exclude others from this personal sphere and whatever lies within it but also the right to dispose freely of that which falls within it. The exercise of the second right may consist in choosing to exchange one thing for another thing, so that a thing leaves the sphere of the person to whom it originally belonged to enter another person's sphere of freedom of choice. Yet in the passage quoted above, Fichte speaks only of the right to exclude another person from using a thing. The significance of this restriction will become evident in due course. We shall see that this restriction follows from the essentially intersubjective character of right and the triadic structure, which represents the most basic form that the concept of property, and thus any specific instantiation of it, possesses. First, however, more needs to be said about the type of sphere that must be allocated to each person in accordance with the concept of right, including why it might be tempting to identify this sphere with private property.

Fichte claims that the sphere in question 'is posited first and foremost as *a part of the world*' (GA I/3: 362; FNR, 54). This suggests that he primarily has in mind the ownership of land and other material objects. Yet Fichte goes on to identify this sphere with a person's body by claiming not only that the body is 'the sphere of the person's free actions' but also that 'the concept of such a sphere is exhausted by the concept of the body' (GA I/3: 363; FNR, 56). Even if these statements imply a commitment to the idea of self-ownership, an argument for extending the right to property to other material objects would still be needed. Fichte appears to provide such an argument in his account of 'original' rights (*Urrechte*). These rights are derived from the concept of a free cause in the world. They include 'the right to the continued existence of the absolute freedom and inviolability of the body' and 'the right to the continued existence of our free influence within the entire sensible world' (GA I/3: 409; FNR, 108).

The right to property can be thought to represent an instance of the second right, given Fichte's claim that, 'The part of the sensible world that is known to me and subjected to my ends – even if only in thought – is *originally* my property' (GA I/3: 407; FNR, 106). Although this claim suggests the existence of an absolute right to parts of the world that a person appropriates in accordance with his or her freely chosen ends, a justification of this right is in fact lacking now that Fichte no longer seeks to explain the right to property in terms of the formation of previously ownerless raw material. A justification of the right in question is nevertheless required by Fichte's description of his theory of right as a 'real science'. A science of this kind must identify and justify the conditions of the application of its object, namely, the concept of right. This application of the concept of right consists in demonstrating how this concept 'is further determined, and the way it must be realized in the sensible world' (GA I/3: 322; FNR, 12).

The demand to apply the concept of right explains Fichte's claim that an original right is 'a *mere* fiction' because '[t]here is no condition in which original rights exist; and no original rights of human beings' (GA I/3: 403–04; FNR, 102). Yet why can no such rights exist beyond the mere thought of them? Fichte's answer to this question leads him to argue for a right to property that is incompatible with a presumption in favour of private property. This answer concerns how, in relation to external things, the idea of an original right abstracts from an essential feature of the concept of right itself, in that it implies that there could be rights independently of any relation to other rights-bearing persons. Fichte, in contrast, explicitly denies this:

> It is possible to talk about rights only under the condition that a person is thought of as a person, that is, as an individual, and thus as standing in relation to other individuals; only under the condition that there is a community [*Gesellschaft*] between this person and others, a community that – if not posited as real – is at least imagined as possible. (GA I/3: 403; FNR, 101).

There are, I think, two related claims at work. The first claim is that if the basis of right is mutual recognition, then the rights that persons possess must reflect this. One person's right to a thing cannot be detrimental to the rights of another person, for this person would then have no rational grounds for accepting the obligation to respect this right. It is precisely this necessary relation to the rights of others from which the idea of an original right abstracts: 'one must abstract from the limitations imposed by the rights of others, an abstraction that free speculation so readily engages in that it does so without even thinking [*unwillkührlich*], and only needs to be reminded of having done so' (GA I/3: 403; FNR, 101).

The tendency to abstract from the rights of others also characterizes theories of property that seek to reduce the concept of property, and thus the right to property, to a relation between a person and a thing. This approach reduces other persons to the bearers of an obligation to respect a right to a thing that has somehow already been established, irrespective of the ways in which the other person's enjoyment of this right may harm their interests. For example, one person's right to a thing that can allegedly be traced back to an act of original appropriation may deny another person the opportunity to appropriate something that is necessary to the achievement of his or her ends, or the property rights enjoyed by one person may threaten the independence of another person who possesses less property or even no property except for his or her own self and body. Such cases are possible once right is reduced to an original right to property that abstracts from the constraints imposed on one person's property rights by the rights of others, for there is then no limit on how far this original right might extend, provided the exercise of this right does not violate the bodily integrity of other persons: 'this concept has no limits at all, but is by its nature infinite, because what is at issue is only that the person is to be free in general, but not the extent to which he is to be free' (GA I/3: 404; FNR, 102–03). This brings me to the second claim.

A situation in which an infinite right of the relevant kind existed, and every person enjoyed this right, would be one in which the freedom of choice of one person could not coexist with the freedom of choice of other persons because of the conflicting claims about ownership of parts of the world and other external objects that would then arise. It should here be borne in mind that persons, as rational beings, are assumed to act not only with a view to the present moment but also with a view to the future. The idea of an original right recognizes this, in that it 'immediately and naturally includes the right to secure the entirety of our rights for all the future' (GA I/3: 409; FNR, 108). Yet it does so in a way that abstracts from the rights of other persons, as if there existed only one rights-bearing person who produces through a series of acts of original appropriation a potentially infinite number of rights to things. All persons, however, have an interest in the establishment of sufficiently stable conditions of free agency. This requires that they coexist peacefully by mutually limiting their rights in relation to one another. Fichte's account of the right to property aims to tell us how persons can come to coexist peacefully in such a way that the conditions of free and effective agency are secured for all of them and by all of them.[3] Fichte's initial approach to the question of

---

[3] This is to assume that they wish to coexist peacefully in a way that secures the conditions of free and effective agency. Fichte claims in the corollary to his deduction of the concept of right that 'we are both *bound* and *obligated* to each other by our very existence', but that the consistency in question concerns only the rules of thinking in general as 'scientifically presented in general *logic*' (GA 1/3: 354–55; FNR, 45). If one were to renounce the end in question, however, one could not be accused of logical inconsistency when one renounces the means to it. The 'community among free beings' entailed by the concept of right is, in this respect, a 'technical-practical' concept, for although the concept of right specifies the principles in accordance with which a community of free beings must be constructed, it 'by no means asserts *that* such a community [*Gemeinschaft*] ought to be established' (GA I/3: 320; FNR, 10). Thus the demand to establish such a community depends not on an unconditional moral demand but only on 'the free, arbitrary [*willkührlichen*] decision to live in community [*Gesellschaft*] with others', whereas 'if someone does not at all want to limit his free choice [*Willkühr*], then within the field of the doctrine of right, one can say nothing further against him, other than that he must then remove himself from all human community' (GA I/3: 322; FNR, 11–12; see also GA I/3: 387; FNR, 82).

the extent of each person's property rights nevertheless suggests that the institution of private property can be justified in terms of the basic triadic structure that the concept of property possesses.

In the case of the right to bodily integrity, the extent of each person's freedom is easy to determine, for it extends only as far as the outer limits of the space occupied by his or her body. Yet it is more difficult to determine the extent of each person's freedom in the case of external objects, the secure possession of which is a condition of producing certain intended effects in the world. So far, we know only that this rightful freedom cannot be infinite because each person's obligation to respect the freedom of other persons is conditional on his or her own freedom being respected. This would not be true of someone who lacked property rights to such an extent that he or she was unable to engage in effective purposive activity within a world consisting of other persons as well as material objects. An account of the permissible extent of each person's property rights is therefore needed, for otherwise it would be impossible to know how far each person's freedom may legitimately extend. Yet how can one person reliably know to which things another person has already established a right? This difficulty arises because Fichte initially suggests that the mere intention to subject an object to one's freedom of choice is enough to establish a right to it. This is compatible with a situation in which an agent intends to take possession of an object but on taking possession of it finds himself or herself confronted with another person who claims that he or she intended to take possession of the same object even earlier. Given the lack of sufficient external evidence of each person's original intention and when it was formed, both persons may in good faith lay claim to the same object.

To avoid the conflict that this situation is liable to generate, each person must declare to the other person what he or she considers to be his or her property. Yet what about those cases in which both persons lay claim to the same object by means of such a declaration? The triadic person–thing–person structure of the concept of property suggests that the only solution would be an agreement in which each person recognizes the other person's claims and agrees to respect them. Only then can possession be transformed into a genuine right to property, as Fichte himself indicates in the following passage:

> As soon as the human being is posited as being in relation to others, his possession is rightful only if it is recognized by the other; and only in this way does his possession acquire an external, *shared* [*gemeinsame*] validity, a validity that – at this point in the analysis – holds only for him and for the other who recognizes it. Only in this way does the *possession* become

2.2 The Relation between Right and Property 63

> *property*, i.e. something individual.... All property is grounded in reciprocal *recognition*, and such recognition is conditioned by *mutual declaration*. (GA I/3: 418; FNR, 117)

As we shall see, however, this is not the end of the story, and so it really does concern only 'this point in the analysis'. There is already a problem to which Fichte alludes in the passage above, namely, that the agreement is binding only on those persons who have entered into this specific agreement ('a validity that … holds only for him and for the other who recognizes it'). Moreover, the agreement in question covers only those external objects to which the parties involved have already laid claim, whereas there are other, perhaps currently unknown, ownerless external objects that they may wish to appropriate in the future. These persons must, therefore, also agree upon a rule governing all future acts of appropriation. The rule that Fichte proposes is that the person who first *declares* the intention to appropriate such an external object acquires the right to it (GA I/3: 420; FNR, 120).

Although this declaration would provide one person with knowledge of another person's intentions, there would still be a gap between the moment in which the intention to take possession of an external object is declared and the moment in which the act of taking actual possession of this object occurs. Thus there needs to be some way in which both acts are united in a single moment. The 'natural' solution is to attach appropriate signs to objects, as when one designates a piece of land as one's own by surrounding it with ditches or fences, thereby separating it from other pieces of land (GA I/3: 421; FNR, 121).[4] If both parties agree to recognize this practice and thus any rights established by means of it, then an exclusive pre-political right to particular objects that conforms to the basic triadic structure of the concept of property appears possible, for, as Fichte himself puts it:

> With respect to the limits of their free actions in relation to each other, both beings have now been completely determined and, as it were, mutually constituted for each other. Each has his own determinate position in the

---

[4] Although the act of marking a thing with a sign might be viewed as a form of labour, if only in the sense that it involves planning, organization and the construction of the sign together with its application to the intended object, there is at least one good reason for not identifying it with the type of act of original appropriation that Fichte had introduced in an attempt to establish an essential connection between property rights and labour in his defence of the French Revolution. For the act in question could be an unproductive one, given how there is no guarantee that the object thus marked will not subsequently be neglected. A person might, for example, have simply wanted to prevent others from establishing a right to a piece of land, as opposed to wanting to secure the piece of land with the aim of being able to cultivate it without suffering any interference by others.

sensible world; and there is no possibility of a conflict of right [*Rechtsstreit*] if they both maintain their respective positions. An equilibrium of right has been established between them. (GA I/3: 422–23; FNR, 122–23)

Yet Fichte is not content with this explanation of the grounds of a pre-political right to property that, unlike an original right, conforms to the triadic structure of the concept of property entailed by the concept of right. Instead, he speaks of a circle in connection with this explanation, thereby signalling that even here there is a failure to explain the possibility of 'a rightful state of affairs', so that the concept of right itself appears 'empty and devoid of all application' (GA I/3: 423; FNR, 123).

The problem concerns how the rules governing property rights are based on agreement, whether it be agreement concerning that which each person already owns or agreement concerning the conventions that will govern the establishment of future property rights. Even if each party enters into the relevant type of agreement in good faith and with the intention of complying with its terms, he or she will lack sufficient assurance that the other party will in fact comply with the same terms. Since the obligation to respect the rights of others is conditional on the expectation that they will respect one's own rights, this obligation ceases to exist once there are grounds for doubting that this reciprocity condition will be satisfied. Thus the circle in question consists in how the explanation of a relation between persons governed by the 'law of right' (*Rechtsgesez*) so far provided presupposes that which it is designed to explain, namely, how each person can be thought to have genuinely subjected himself or herself to this law, not only at the moment of the initial agreement but also with respect to the future (GA I/3: 424; FNR, 123–24). This lack of assurance can be remedied only by a 'law of coercion' (*Zwangsgesez*) that is designed to bring about the opposite of the benefit to himself or herself intended by any agent who violates the law of right in such a way that the rights of all persons are guaranteed (GA I/3: 427; FNR, 127).

As it stands, however, this law of coercion presupposes the conditions of its own application, for the person who violates the law of right can hardly be expected to coerce himself or herself, nor can he or she be expected to allow another person to apply the law of coercion as he or she sees fit. Moreover, even if the person whose rights have been violated possesses enough power to apply the law of coercion in the face of any resistance offered by the guilty party, the danger of a mistaken or excessive application of this law would exist. The law of coercion can therefore be applied only within a state that has the authority and the coercive means required to establish and enforce the legal norms that ought to govern external relations between persons. This raises the question as to how state authority and power can themselves be justified. Fichte's answer to this question is found in his account of the 'civil contract' (*Staatsbürgervertrag*). As we shall shortly see, this contract involves an agreement concerning property rights that is not compatible with unrestricted private ownership. It implies, in fact, some form of common or collective property in the case of certain things.

The idea that it is only by means of the civil contract that property rights can be established is consistent with a conclusion that Fichte has essentially already drawn. Although the way in which property rights can be guaranteed only within and by a state may appear compatible with the idea that the 'fiction' of original rights thereby becomes a reality, Fichte draws a different conclusion, namely, that 'there is no *natural right* at all in the sense often given to that term, i.e. there can be no rightful relation between human beings except within a commonwealth [*in einem gemeinen Wesen*] and under positive laws' (GA I/3: 432; FNR, 132). In the next section, we shall see that this claim can be explained in terms of how Fichte makes property rights conditional on whether the possession of them enables an individual to live from his or her labour, thereby preserving the essential connection between the right to property and labour that he had sought to establish in his defence of the French Revolution. How, though, do the conditions of the application of the concept of right identified above imply this view of property rights? To answer this question, we must turn to the details of Fichte's civil contract.

2.3 Property and Labour

The contract into which each person enters with every other person, and through which a legal and political order in which they all become citizens is instituted, determines the extent of each person's sphere of freedom, not only in relation to the present but also in relation to the future. In accordance with Fichte's rejection of the idea of any pre-political property rights, this contract presupposes a situation in which no person currently enjoys the right to any particular thing. To be more precise, *all* human beings enjoy an *equal* right to *every* thing because prior to this contract 'the only right-based reason [*Rechtsgrund*] anyone can adduce as to why he ought to possess the disputed thing is his free and rational nature; but every free being can adduce this same reason' (GA I/4: 5; FNR, 166).

It may seem inappropriate to speak of an equal *right*, given Fichte's reduction of the idea of an original right to the status of a fiction. The right in question differs from this type of right, however, in that it does not involve a right to any specific thing. This right is unlimited because there are no normative constraints on the exercise of it for which any rational grounds could be provided independently of the terms of the civil contract. In short, everyone has the right to appropriate what he or she desires and possesses the power to appropriate. It is only with the civil contract that this liberty right ceases to exist because renouncing it is a condition of entering into this contract, the terms of which limit the extent of each person's freedom, whereas before 'each of the parties had a complete right to anything that the other party wanted for himself, even those things that – as a result of the contract – were actually allotted to the other party' (GA I/4: 7; FNR, 168). Thus the civil contract tells us both what individuals must be thought to give up on entering into this contract and what they could reasonably agree among themselves would count as sufficient compensation for having given it up.

This echoes Hobbes's account of the right of nature and the act of giving up this right that marks the transition from the state of nature to a condition in which individuals enjoy security and a freedom limited by law. Hobbes defines that 'which Writers commonly call *Jus Naturale*' as follows: 'the Liberty each man hath, to use his own power, as he will himselfe, for the preservation of his own Nature; that is to say, of his own Life; and consequently, of doing any thing, which in his own Judgement, and Reason, hee shall conceive to be the aptest means thereunto'.[5] This definition resembles Fichte's idea of an 'infinite' right of the person 'to extend his freedom as far as he wills and can, and — if he so desires — the right to take possession of the entire sensible world' (GA I/4: 412; FNR, 111). In Hobbes's case, however, the right to extend one's freedom concerns only the right to do all that one judges to be necessary to preserve one's own life. The act of giving up this right must therefore be compensated by a more effective way of achieving the same end if the agent concerned is to act rationally. Fichte's position differs in that he treats the conditions of free agency as such, rather than mere self-preservation, as the basis of rational agreement concerning the extent to which each person limits his or her enjoyment of the liberty right in question.

Fichte's understanding of right as a relation that consists in the mutual limitation of freedom is nevertheless compatible with what Hobbes says about the act of giving up the right to everything that each human being originally enjoys. Although individuals enjoy the right to everything in a

---

[5] Hobbes, *Leviathan*, Ch. 14, 64. Cited by original pagination.

2.3 Property and Labour

condition of natural freedom, they may give up this right or, to be more precise, limit it, by agreeing not to hinder another individual's exercise of the same right. One individual does not thereby grant another individual a right that he or she previously lacked. On the contrary, every individual in the natural condition has a right to all things. Rather, an individual limits his or her enjoyment of this right, so that another individual 'may enjoy his own originall Right, without hindrance from him'.[6] In terms of its function, this act of limiting the natural right to everything that every individual originally enjoys corresponds to Fichte's summons, which reappears at the level of the application of the concept of right in the form of the recognition implicit in the civil contract. By means of this summons, one person signals to another person that he or she is willing to limit his or her freedom and thereby grant the other person a sphere of freedom. There is, then, the difference that Fichte emphasizes how this act of limiting the right to everything is a matter of *mutual* limitation by explaining the relation of right in terms of the concept of recognition.

With respect to the civil contract itself, Fichte initially mentions a contract involving two persons (GA I/4: 5; FNR, 165). Later, however, he speaks of a 'universal relation of right', and he makes clear that he intends a relation between *all* those persons who originally enjoy the infinite right described above, but who then agree with one another to limit their enjoyment of this right: 'each individual must reach agreement with all other individuals concerning the property – the rights and freedoms – he ought to have, as well as those he ought to leave untouched for the others and over which he ought to relinquish all of his natural entitlements' (GA I/4: 8; FNR, 169). Each person must therefore be thought to contract with *all* other persons, making the agreement into which they enter a multilateral rather than a bilateral one. The multilateral structure of the common will generated by the civil contract means that the triadic structure which is the most basic form that the right to property can assume within Fichte's theory of right is not the final one.

Fichte terms the first stage of this multilateral agreement the 'property contract' (*Eigenthumsvertrag*) because it decides each person's property rights. Each person pledges his or her property as a guarantee that he or she will not violate the property rights of others at the same time as these property rights are established by mutual agreement (GA I/4: 9; FNR, 169–70). Thus each person does not pledge property to which

---

[6] Hobbes, *Leviathan*, Ch. 14, 65.

he or she already enjoys the right. Rather, all persons agree to recognize and respect the property rights that others acquire through the property contract and to forfeit the property rights that they themselves acquire if they should ever violate the terms of this contract into which they have freely entered. This stage of the civil contract presupposes the conditions of its own application, which include an agent with the authority and the power to coerce others into giving up their property rights if they violate the property rights of others.

This defect of the citizens' property contract is remedied by the 'protection contract' (*Schuzvertrag*), through which each person promises to all other persons that he or she will employ his or her power to protect their property rights in the event of a violation of them (GA I/4: 10; FNR, 171). This second contract makes the protection of each person's property conditional on whether others can be relied upon to protect it when required to do so. Yet the only guarantee that this condition will be fulfilled is the actual protection of each person's property. Consequently, no person can be certain that the terms of the protection contract will be honoured. This means that each person will lack sufficient grounds for honouring the terms of the civil contract, thereby demonstrating the necessity of a 'unification contract' (*Vereinigungsvertrag*) by means of which a protective power that is independent of each party to the civil contract is established. This unification contract requires agreement on the part of each person to contribute to the maintenance of such a power (GA I/4: 13–15; FNR 174–77). It also requires a guarantee that he or she will in fact do so. This guarantee presupposes a hypothetical 'subjection contract' (*Unterwerfungsvertrag*), through which each person agrees to forfeit all of his or her property (*Vermögen*) if he or she should fail to fulfil this obligation (GA I/4: 17; FNR, 179).

The second, third and fourth contracts concern the application of the terms of the property contract and thus presuppose this contract, which specifies the basic property rights that each person will enjoy. I shall therefore concentrate on the conclusions regarding a person's property rights that Fichte draws from this moment of the civil contract, where each citizen 'acquires a secure portion of property [*ein sicheres Eigenthum*], while the state receives from him a renunciation of all his natural rights to what others possess (which is necessary, if all the state's other citizens are to have rightful possession of their things)' (GA I/4: 18; FNR, 179–80).

In § 18 of the *Foundations of Natural Right*, Fichte constructs an argument that aims to demonstrate what type of property each person *qua* an embodied agent that interacts with a material world with the aim of

2.3 Property and Labour

realizing its ends would seek to secure by means of the property contract. It is here assumed that there is an end that all persons share and that this end provides a sufficient basis for rational agreement among them. They would also be able to agree about the necessary means of achieving this end. The argument consists of the following set of claims:

1. Effective purposive action presupposes the continued bodily existence of the agent who seeks to achieve a freely chosen end through a *series* of actions in which each action occurs in the present and is succeeded by another action.
2. Nature has decreed that human beings are to be free, and since nature necessarily achieves its ends, it must also have willed the means to this end.
3. Given claims (1) and (2), nature must be thought to have willed all the necessary means to the relevant end in a way that is compatible with how that which occurs in the future is always conditioned by an activity occurring in the present, including the activity that is a condition of the continued existence of the agent's body, which is the instrument by means of which he or she interacts with the world in accordance with freely chosen ends in relation to which he or she also wills the means.
4. Yet it is possible to conceive of human beings who did not set themselves ends whose achievement necessarily occurs in the future. This would mean that they would have no desire to *continue* to exist – a desire whose satisfaction immediately depends on their present activity, which would therefore equally be of no concern to them. Given claims (1)–(3), however, we must assume that nature has arranged matters in such a way that individuals are *motivated* to act with a view to the future. Fichte identifies the pain caused by a lack of food and drink as sufficient to motivate individuals to concern themselves with the future and thus also with the activity that is a necessary condition of their continued bodily existence.
5. Given claim (4), securing the means of subsistence, and thus engaging in the activity required to achieve this end, is one that all individuals, as embodied rational agents capable of experiencing hunger and thirst, must be thought to share. It can therefore be said that 'the highest and universal end of all free activity is to be able to live' (GA I/4: 22; FNR, 185).
6. Property serves to achieve this end that all persons *qua* embodied rational agents share.

7. Therefore, the most basic form of property that persons grant to one another through the property contract, and which is then protected by the state, will be the activity by means of which a person can obtain the means of subsistence, that is to say, the activity that enables this person to live from his or her labour.

Although each person must be guaranteed an activity that enables him or her to live from his or her labour, Fichte does not reduce right itself to the legal and political conditions of self-preservation, despite his claim that securing the means of subsistence is 'the highest' as well as the 'universal' end, for his theory of property is fundamentally concerned with the conditions of free and effective agency. The fact that self-preservation is a necessary condition of such agency does not mean that self-preservation is an end in itself. Fichte denies that it is an end in itself when he claims that individuals will to preserve themselves only because self-preservation is a condition of pursuing ends at all: 'All human beings desire life for the sake of something; the nobler in order to go on doing, the less noble in order to go on enjoying' (GA I/3: 408; FNR, 107; see also GA I/5: 119; SE, 117).[7] As this statement shows, the concept of right does not require universal agreement concerning the ends in relation to which the right to property possesses the instrumental value of securing the material conditions of life and basic human functioning. These ends may vary from person to person in so far as right permits this, given how right is not concerned with unconditional moral ends that all rational agents ought to adopt.

In *The Closed Commercial State* from 1800, which is explicitly based on his theory of property (GA I/7: 84; CCS, 129), Fichte constructs a simplified argument in defence of essentially the same conclusion. This argument dispenses with the appeal to natural teleology encountered in premises (2)–(4) of the argument set out above. The argument begins with the idea of a condition of natural freedom in which individuals seek the means of

---

[7] The claim that being able to live is 'the highest and universal end' does not exclude the reduction of self-preservation to a means in the sense of a condition of higher cultural or ethical ends that are external to the sphere of right while being made possible by it. Nor does it exclude a subsidiary criterion which, although not a normative requirement of right itself, may under certain circumstances need to be taken into consideration when distributing goods and resources. See Merle, 'Fichte's Political Economy and His Theory of Property', 215ff. The reduction of the sphere of right to a means to a higher end finds its clearest expression in the *Rechtslehre* from 1812: 'The external ends, however, that nature imposes upon us as conditions of the higher end, are our preservation, and our safety. These must therefore be achieved, and universally achieved, before the moral law [*Sittengesez*] can universally appear' (GA II/13: 214).

2.3 Property and Labour

subsistence and enjoyment. These individuals can claim an equal entitlement to parts of the world, none of which is the exclusive property of any of these individuals. Instead, everyone originally possesses the right to use parts of the world and the things within it as he or she pleases. Why, then, should individuals living in a condition of natural freedom agree to limit the enjoyment of this absolute right that each of them enjoys? The answer to this question is that they have an overriding prudential reason for agreeing among themselves to limit their natural freedom in relation to one another in accordance with the concept of right.

The reason is that it is impossible to achieve one's ends effectively in a condition of unlimited natural freedom. This condition does not allow agents to judge the likely effects of their own actions because they cannot reliably predict the actions of other agents, which may thwart the production of the desired effects. Thus no agent in a condition of natural freedom could be a genuinely free agent, given how becoming conscious of oneself as such an agent requires effective interaction with the world and things within it: 'no one is free, since all are free without limitation. No one can carry out anything in a purposeful fashion and count for a moment on it lasting' (GA I/7: 54; CCS, 92). It is therefore rational for an individual to limit his or her freedom in relation to other individuals on the condition that they agree to do the same in relation to him or her. This requires mutually giving up the natural right to everything that each of them originally enjoys and granting to one another the right to some things but not to other ones. Yet this voluntary act of limiting a right that all human beings originally enjoy by recognizing the right of others to possess and to make use of parts of the world and things within it is insufficient because anyone who chooses not to enter into this agreement will not be bound by its terms.

Fichte claims that this problem can be solved only by accepting the establishment of a state that secures its citizens against the threat posed to their free and effective agency by individuals who have chosen to retain their natural right to everything, or by those individuals who, in effect, seek to reclaim this right by violating the rights of others even though they had previously agreed to respect them. The state must also distribute to its citizens specific parts of the world and particular things. It is therefore only with the establishment of a legal and political order that every individual can be thought to have genuinely consented to subject himself or herself to conditions that secure for each person the right to some things but not to other ones. Conversely, any individual who did not benefit by receiving something that is exclusively his or her own cannot be said to have given up his or her original right to everything. He or she would instead retain 'the rightful claim that was originally his to do whatever he pleases wherever he wants' (GA I/7: 89; CCS, 133). This conclusion agrees with the following passage from the *Foundations of Natural Right*, in which Fichte summarizes the specific demands to which mutual recognition of the right to property gives rise:

> [A]ll property rights are grounded in the contract of all with all, which states: 'We are all entitled to keep this, on the condition that we let you have what is yours'. Therefore, if someone is unable to make a living from his labor, he has not been given what is absolutely his, and therefore the contract is completely canceled with respect to him, and from that moment on he is no longer obligated by right to recognize anyone else's property. Now in order to prevent property rights from being destabilized in this way, all the others must (as a matter of right and in consequence of the civil contract) relinquish a portion of their own property, until he is able to live. (GA I/4: 22; FNR, 185–86)

We have seen how Fichte argues that the common end of being able to live from one's labour is the basis of the contract into which individuals who are willing to give up their natural freedom enter. The allocation and protection of their property must therefore enable each of them to live from his or her labour. Given the state's role in guaranteeing the fulfilment of the terms of this contract, it must ensure that each person is allocated a determinate activity by means of which he or she is able to live. The state must also undertake any specific measures required to achieve this end. These measures will include the distribution of the resources needed to perform this activity effectively.[8] A person will enjoy an exclusive right

---

[8] The state must also determine and regulate the number of people belonging to each occupational group in such a way that the material needs of society can be satisfied. Even if it is logically possible for every person to choose the occupation which enables him or her to live from his or her labour at the same time as the material needs of society are satisfied, in which case the state would only need to endorse decisions that individuals have themselves freely made, the more likely scenario is that the choices of some people, and perhaps many people, will be limited by the material needs of society and an individual's need to earn a living. The occupational group to which an individual belongs will then be determined more, and perhaps exclusively, by natural necessity (that is, by the need to secure the means to life), rather than by free choice. Although this subjection to natural necessity is as much a feature of a free market which is said to accommodate natural freedom in the form of the freedom to sell and to buy goods, including one's own labour, it poses a particular problem for Fichte. This is because he wants to ensure that the freedom which is secured in and by the state is not the freedom of only a minority, or even a majority, of citizens but the freedom of *all* citizens. The measures that Fichte introduces to guarantee this outcome threaten, however, to suppress freedom, not only through the introduction of considerable state control and regulation but also because of his failure to explain how the productive activities of individuals within society will be genuinely chosen by them, rather than being imposed upon them by their own material needs and those of society.

to a thing, however, only in so far as this thing is needed to perform the relevant activity: 'Each person possesses property in objects only insofar as he needs such property to pursue his occupation' (GA I/4: 23; FNR, 187).[9]

In the light of what has been said above, treating the right to property as a pre-political right would amount to an example of the kind of formal thinking that ignores the conditions of the application of the concept of right. Thus, although Fichte does not object in principle to the idea that the state does nothing more than preserve and protect each individual's rights and property, he stresses that this is true only if it is not assumed that property rights can exist independently of the state, whereas it is, in fact, the state that first gives to each person that which is rightfully his or hers and subsequently protects it (GA I/7: 53; CCS, 91).[10] If the state is to allocate the activities and resources by means of which individuals are able to live from their labour and to redistribute them whenever necessary, it must be in the position to exercise effective control over these activities and resources.

[9] Fichte mentions at least one case where not only a productive activity but also the means needed to undertake it are not distributed to the relevant persons, for he claims that 'we can distinguish two classes of artists: those who merely expend their labor but do not own the materials on which they work (*operarii*), and those who do own the materials on which they work (*opifices*)' (GA I/4: 38; FNR, 203). In the first case, it looks as if the workers in question are guaranteed a productive activity at the same time as they are not granted the exclusive right to the relevant means. It is not clear, moreover, in what sense the members of the second group 'own' such means in a way that the members of the first group do not, when in both cases the state distributes these means according to whether the relevant activity requires them. The difference might be that in one case the means are distributed on a case-by-case basis depending on what the object of labour happens to be at any particular time, whereas in the other case, which involves skilled labour, the means (for example, tools) form a constant feature of a person's workplace. For example, a carpenter will always need such implements as saws and lathes. An unskilled labourer, in contrast, may at one time need to employ a specific tool but at another time he or she will perform tasks that require only the use of his or her body. The problem is then how one can meaningfully claim that a *determinate* productive activity is guaranteed to the members of this social group.

[10] This invites the question as to whether Fichte's theory of property implies a strict egalitarian principle of distribution. He himself claims that what is available within a state must be divided equally among all (GA I/7: 56; CCS, 93–94; see also GA I/3: 400; FNR, 98). Evidence that this claim is intended literally is provided by the further claim that in the case of a hundred people living together and working the land, the law of right entails a division of the land into one hundred equal parts, with one part being given to one person (GA I/7: 88; CCS, 132). Yet if this equal division of land concerns only the size of each piece of land, then one piece of land may be more fertile than another piece of land of equal size, so that in qualitative terms the division would be an unequal one. Fichte's theory of property does not, however, demand such a literal interpretation of the equal division of goods and resources. It requires only that each person be guaranteed a productive activity and any necessary means to the effective performance of it. There is no demand for absolute equality with respect to access to specific goods and resources. Indeed, the successful performance of one activity may require some material inequality in that it demands the possession and use of more resources than those needed to perform a different one. Moreover, Fichte himself views different occupations as reflecting and fostering different needs (GA I/7: 67–68; CCS, 106), so that once again the distribution of goods and resources may have to be unequal one both quantitatively and qualitatively.

This does not mean, however, that these activities and resources are the property of the state itself, as opposed to the property of its citizens taken collectively. Rather, the state may exercise control over these activities and resources on behalf of all those individuals who have become its citizens through the series of contracts described in the *Foundations of Natural Right*. Thus these activities and resources would also not belong to the individuals or groups to whom they are allocated. Rather, they would be the property of the legal and political community within which they are distributed in accordance with the fundamental norms governing this community and for the benefit of all its members. The activities and resources would then 'belong' to *every* person who enters into political union with every other person through the civil contract, and they would be allocated to *each* person according to the terms of this contract, that is to say, in so far as a person needs them to live from his or her labour. Although each person will enjoy an exclusive right to an activity and the means of performing it in so far as this activity and these means enable him or her to live from his or her labour, he or she cannot be thought to enjoy the right to dispose of them as he or she pleases. For he or she would not have the right to exchange one activity for another activity without the permission of the relevant authorities. The same would be true of any resources required to perform the relevant activity. Thus a person 'acquires ... objects only for a particular use; and it is only from this use, and from what might hinder such use, that he has the right to exclude everyone else' (GA I/4: 20; FNR, 183–84).

It is difficult to see how one can here speak of private property. Individuals may enjoy the right to exclude others from the use of certain things and even to dispose freely of their property in the sense of exercising judgement in connection with the employment of it. This is sufficient to justify Fichte's use of the term 'exclusive property' (*ausschliessendes Eigenthum*) (GA I/4: 5; FNR, 165). Moreover, certain phenomena associated with the institution of private property, such as fences that mark off a piece of land and designate it as the property of the person who cultivates it, may still be present. Indeed, Fichte treats phenomena of this kind as necessary features of the rational state: 'Under the guarantee of the state, the land is divided up by individuals and designated by boundary markers, so that right can exist with *certainty*' (GA I/4: 26; FNR, 190). This does not itself entail the legal right to dispose freely of one's property in ways that would include neglecting it or exchanging one item of property with a view to obtaining from another person an item of property that one happens to desire.¹¹ Yet the way in which activities and the resources required to perform them effectively must be assumed to be common or collective property does not entail that all property must be of this kind. As it stands, things that do not enable a person to live from his or her labour could be private property without violating the fundamental terms of the civil contract. Fichte himself identifies a form of property that appears to correspond to private property. In the next section, I shall discuss the nature and the possibility of this 'absolute property' (*absolutes Eigenthum*) with the aim of deciding whether a pluralist account of property rights can be attributed to Fichte.

2.4 Absolute Property

Fichte distinguishes between two types of property: 'Property has a double nature: absolute property, which is not subject to state supervision (e.g. money and similar valuables), and property that stands directly under state supervision (e.g. fields, gardens, houses, civil licenses, etc.)' (GA I/4: 55; FNR, 222). Since the first form of property is not subject to state supervision, it cannot concern those activities and resources that the state must distribute so that its citizens are able to live from their labour. Although Fichte speaks of state supervision in connection with the second form of property, he could even then mean private property, the acquisition, exchange and use of which the state regulates, but which does not concern activities or resources over which the state must exercise effective control. An example of this type of state supervision is when a house is a person's private property and for the sake of public safety the state enacts and enforces laws that determine what may rightfully be done with it, thereby limiting a person's right to dispose freely of his or her property without removing this right completely. Fichte himself mentions how the sale of houses must be regulated by the state with the aim of always knowing who the owner is (GA I/4: 47; FNR, 213). The possibility of selling the house entails that it is nevertheless private property, despite any restrictions on what the owner may do with it. Among such restrictions, Fichte includes the impermissibility of disposing of one's property in such a way that one's livelihood is threatened, thereby making one a potential unjustifiable burden on the state (GA I/4: 56; FNR, 223).

---

¹¹ Given how this essential feature of private property is necessarily absent, it is misleading to speak of the protection of private property, as Allen Wood does. See *Fichte's Ethical Thought*, 281f.

As we have seen, the state's duty to allocate and protect the property that each of its citizens requires in order to live from his or her labour implies a significantly stronger form of state supervision, and although a person may exclude another person from the use of this property if two or more persons cannot use it at the same time or within the same period of time,[12] he or she will lack the right to dispose freely of this property. In contrast, property that is not subject to state supervision at all or is subject to a form of state supervision that is compatible with a restricted right to dispose of it freely presupposes a type of ownership that is not conditional on whether a person needs this property in order to live from his or her labour. Yet how is this type of property to be reliably identified?

There are some significant problems with Fichte's main attempt to answer this question. This attempt rests on the following claim: 'My house determines what my absolute property is. If a thing has made its way into my house (obviously, with the state's awareness and consent), then it is my absolute property' (GA I/4: 45; FNR, 211–12). This claim is made in connection with the problem of how to identify items of absolute property destined for future use that do not stand in any immediate relation to their owner in the sense of either being in his or her direct physical possession or being used by him or her in a recognizable way. Fichte argues that an object may have the status of absolute property by virtue of its location in something that is already a person's property, namely, his or her house. This explanation of how it is possible to identify an item of absolute property is insufficient, however, because it is compatible with cases that conflict with the state's duty to distribute and protect property in such a way that every citizen can live from his or her labour. This specific problem can be illustrated by means of the following example. According to this argument, a person would be entitled to claim as his or her absolute property the saw that a carpenter has forgotten to take home with him after working in this person's house, even though this means that the carpenter will be unable to work the next day. This would violate a person's right to be able to live from his or her labour and the state would therefore fail to fulfil its duty to provide a citizen with the means to live from his or her labour if it did not ensure that the saw was returned to the carpenter.

---

[12] Fichte does not exclude the possibility of two or more people making use of the same thing at the same time. He himself provides the example of how the cultivation of land would be compatible with other uses of it, either at the same time (for example, if a mine could be opened beneath it without the ground caving in) or at different times of the year (for example, between the harvesting and reseeding of crops someone may use the same piece of land to graze cattle) (GA I/4: 26; FNR, 190, GA I/7: 86; CCS, 130).

Another problem is that this explanation of how items of absolute property can be identified implies not only that a person's house is his or her property but also that this status is automatically transferred to any objects found within it. Yet the fact that a particular object that is not in the direct physical possession of its owner is found within a person's house is not enough to establish that this object is the absolute property of the person who owns the house. For it could instead be state-administered common or collective property that happens to be located within the house, as indeed the example of the carpenter's saw shows. This would also be true of any implements or tools that the state has allocated to the owner of the house so that he or she is able to live from his or her labour. Moreover, the need for shelter is a fundamental human need on a par with the need to obtain the means of subsistence and other material goods that are necessary to basic human functioning and well-being, which are themselves conditions of free rational agency. If, for this reason, the state must exercise effective control over housing so that it can be distributed according to need, then the house itself cannot straightforwardly be private property, and the status of private property cannot therefore be automatically transmitted to other objects that happen to be located within it. Rather, the more obvious conclusion to draw is that these objects would be items of state-administered common or collective property because they are located within another item of state-administered common or collective property.

There may be other things, however, that neither enable individuals to live from their labour nor are necessary to basic human functioning and well-being in some other way. I shall now argue that Fichte's real justification of absolute property turns on his further claim that 'the fact that I have a house and things within it is sure proof that I have fulfilled my obligations to the state: otherwise, and before I have done so, I have no house; for the state will first take from me what I owe it' (GA I/4: 45; FNR, 212). It is not, then, the location of an object in a person's house that counts. Rather, it is a matter of what the possession of it signifies.

We have seen that it is not only the activity by means of which an individual is able to live from his or her labour that must be allocated and protected by the state. The state must also guarantee access to the means required to perform this activity effectively, such as the fields that the farmer cultivates and the tools that the craftsperson employs. Individuals will then be able to cultivate or produce things that they may exchange for things that they do not cultivate or produce. In certain cases, however, it is unclear to whom a thing would rightfully belong, that is to say, whether it would belong to the state, which must exercise effective control over it on behalf of all citizens, or to the person who has cultivated or produced it. For example, we may assume that the state would provide a dairy farmer with a herd of cows, some fields in which the herd can graze, a building in which to shelter the cows and the equipment needed to milk them. The state would also prevent other persons from interfering with the dairy farmer's possession and use of these things. Yet the dairy farmer will also need to preserve the herd over time if he is to continue to live from his labour in this specific way. This will require replacing the cows that die.

Let us assume, then, that the state allocates to the dairy farmer a bull to ensure the reproduction of the herd. Presumably, the dairy farmer will retain the right to any calves that are born as a result of the bull mating with any of the cows that the state had originally allocated to him, at least in so far as these calves are needed to replace the cows that have died or will soon die. But what if the number of calves that are born exceeds the number needed to preserve the herd? The dairy farmer could make use of this increase in the number of cows to produce more milk, some of which he may want to exchange for other things that he and his family need, such as items of food and clothing, or to fulfil his obligations towards other social groups, given how Fichte advocates a system of distribution whereby all agricultural products, raw materials that have been mined, finished articles and so on are deposited with the state, which allocates them according to its citizens' needs. The providers of these goods are given money in exchange for them. This money may then be used to purchase goods that they need and to pay their taxes (GA I/4: 38–43; FNR, 204–09). Fichte has the following to say about the money that is left to a person once the taxes required to maintain the state and its officials have been paid:

> [T]his money is *absolute, pure property, over which the state no longer has any rights at all*. Every piece of money I possess is simultaneously a sign that I have fulfilled all of my civil obligations. With regard to such money, I am completely free of the state's supervision. Taxes on the mere *possession of money* are completely absurd. All money, by its very nature, has already been allotted to its possessor. (GA I/4: 43; FNR, 209)

Thus, although some of the dairy farmer's money will be spent acquiring things produced or provided by others and paying taxes, he may be left with some money, either because the herd has produced more milk than before or because he chooses to sell the extra calves to someone who is interested in buying them for their meat or their hides. The dairy farmer will be entitled to buy with this extra money, which is his absolute property, other items of property, such as pieces of furniture or items of clothing and jewellery, which are equally his absolute property. He might even be entitled to buy the house in which he lives, provided the state agrees to this, as it may well do if all its citizens are suitably housed because it has ensured that enough houses or apartment blocks have been built and equitably distributed. The permissibility of later selling this house and buying another one in a closely regulated housing market is also not excluded. In this way, an essential feature of private property, the right to dispose freely of a thing that one legally owns, exists. This suggests that Fichte's theory of right can accommodate the institution of private property and thus a free exchange of goods, if only to a limited extent. Yet it will now be shown that a monetized system of exchange, however restricted its scope, cannot be reconciled with Fichte's theory of right and his concept of property once his attempt to spell out their economic implications in *The Closed Commercial State* is introduced.

The main aim of *The Closed Commercial State* is to develop the idea of the rational state (*Vernunftstaat*) in conformity with concepts of right (*Rechtsbegriffen*) (GA I/7: 51; CCS, 87). In this respect, it is a further application of the concept of right and the concept of property whose necessity had been demonstrated and that had already been applied in the *Foundations of Natural Right*. No attention is to be directly paid to existing constitutions or to the legal relations in which individuals happen to stand with one another in existing states. Rather, the principles that determine whether an existing state may be classed as a rational one form the object of inquiry. *The Closed Commercial State* nevertheless also seeks to explain how an existing state can be transformed into a truly rational state with respect to the economic relations that exist between its citizens, the economic relations that exist between its citizens and the citizens of other states, and the economic relations that exist between the rational state itself and other states. *The Closed Commercial State* accordingly consists of three main stages.

First, there is an account of what constitutes right within the rational state in general and with respect to commerce and trade in particular. Second, there is an account of customary commercial relations both within existing European states and between them. These states are products of history and thus the result of a spontaneous, unregulated process, as opposed to a process guided by the normative demands of a rational state. Third, there is an account of how an existing state can be transformed into a truly rational one. My initial focus will be on how the state regulates the economic relations between those of its citizens who engage in some form of productive activity, either directly through the extraction of raw materials, the cultivation of land and the production of objects with a use value, or indirectly by facilitating the exchange of goods, products and resources. I shall then turn to the way in which this regulation of economic life ultimately requires the commercial closure of the state, which is to be achieved by means of currency reform.

In many cases, the activities that the state allocates to its citizens so that they can live from their labour will be ones that produce or provide not only the means of subsistence but also goods and resources that allow people to live as agreeably as possible, given the state's current level of economic development. Regulation of the economic life of society must guarantee that the relevant goods and resources are available to all who need them, either to perform the activity that enables them to live from their labour or for consumption purposes. This will require state supervision of how many people belong to each key occupational group or 'estate', each of which enjoys the exclusive right to pursue a particular type of economic activity. There will otherwise come a point at which there is too much or too little of the same good or too many or too few of the same item in circulation. To prevent such an outcome, the state must achieve sufficient oversight of the type and the quantity of each good or item in circulation at any given time. Moreover, since people are not permitted to exchange their products or goods directly, the state must not only prevent any violations of this law of the rational state but also oversee the activity of the members of the estate of traders and merchants, to which the task of exchanging goods is entrusted. This oversight will require the fixing of prices. Prices are to be fixed also to ensure that they cannot be increased in such a way as to prevent people from obtaining the goods and resources to which they are entitled. The fixing of prices will in turn require some way of measuring the objective value of the goods and items in circulation, as opposed to their value being left to depend on what individuals happen to think they are worth and are willing to pay for them, or what they are forced to pay for them, thereby allowing the prices of goods to be determined by their market value.

Fichte explains the objective value that determines the relative value of goods and services in terms of the possibility of living from an activity or, to be more precise, in terms of the amount of time during which one could live from this activity. There is here an objective form of value because the value of any productive activity and its products is determined by an end that all individuals share. This objective form of value needs to be represented by something other than itself. Fichte proposes that it be represented by that which is universally recognized by a nation as its staple food. In the case of the European nations, this happens to be bread, the most basic ingredient of which can therefore represent the relative value of all things. For example, the value of something that nourishes an individual for a whole day would correspond to the value of the amount of grain that would nourish an individual for a whole day (GA I/7: 65–67; CCS, 104–05). Fichte seeks to extend this model to all the basic activities, products and services found within the rational state. Since grain cannot serve as both the medium of exchange and a staple food, there must be a purely symbolic expression of its value, namely money. In this way, Fichte justifies the introduction of a national currency (*Landesgeld*) (GA 1/7: 78–81; CCS, 122–24).

The amount of money in circulation at any given time must correspond to the total value of the goods in circulation at the same time if prices are to remain pinned to the objective measure of value, as they must be if the state is to fix prices in accordance with a law of value. The money supply must therefore be increased or decreased in response to any increases or decreases in the total value of the goods in circulation at any given time. Economic relations between the citizens of the rational state and the citizens of other states would introduce unforeseeable, destabilizing and potentially uncontrollable factors that pose an existential threat to the equilibrium of this economic system that the government ought to create and seek to maintain. Therefore, the state must '*close itself off entirely to all foreign trade*, forming from this point on an isolated commercial body, just as it had already previously formed an isolated juridical and political body' (GA 1/7: 114; CCS, 163). To achieve this end, the state must prevent its citizens from entering into commercial relations with the citizens of other states by denying them access to the world currency (*Weltgeld*) of gold and silver that serves as the medium of exchange in international commerce and trade (GA 1/7: 120; CCS, 173). This shows how the commercial closure of the state and the measures associated with it are not ends in themselves. They are instead necessary means of securing the property rights of all the citizens of the rational state, and they therefore belong among the conditions of the full application of the concept of right.

Since money is claimed to be a person's absolute property in the *Foundations of Natural Right*, the introduction of money into the internal economy of the closed commercial state suggests some limited recognition of private property within a state that is otherwise structured by common or collective forms of property administered by the state. The right to property is nevertheless subject to significant restrictions in so far as the right to dispose freely of one's property is concerned. In addition to the obligation to use part of one's absolute property to pay taxes, it follows from the economic organization of the rational state that its citizens are not permitted to engage in commercial transactions that involve the exchange of their absolute property for items of property possessed by the citizens of other states. This would require exchanging the domestic currency for gold or silver. Even acts of unregulated exchange between citizens of the rational state using the domestic currency would threaten to disrupt the carefully constructed equilibrium between the amount of money in circulation and the total value of the goods in circulation at any given time. Thus the details of Fichte's account of the internal economy of the rational state imply that even if there is absolute property in the form of money within this state, the right to dispose of this property freely is ultimately incompatible with the state's duty to regulate the economy in such a way as to guarantee that each citizen is able to live from his or her labour. This feature of private property would have to be restricted to such an extent that the right in question becomes essentially meaningless.

One example of the extent to which this defining feature of private property is restricted concerns the estate of merchants or traders. There is the question of how the members of this estate can live from their labour when the moment at which they buy something and the moment at which they sell it do not coincide. There will instead typically be a significant interval between these two moments, leaving the members of this estate without the means to purchase that which they need. Fichte's response to this problem is to claim that a prospective member of this estate must establish a reserve fund sufficient to cover the interval between the purchase and the sale of the goods in which he or she intends to trade and provide proof of it to the government (GA I/7: 64–65; CCS, 103).

Although this measure implies an acceptance of the legitimacy of a prior process of capital accumulation, once the members of this estate are granted the right to a commercial activity, they are not entitled to decide according to their own judgement, desires and interests alone if and when they should buy or sell something. They must instead purchase and sell specific goods as and when necessary, so as to honour the agreements concerning the exchange and distribution of goods into which they and the members of the other estates have entered. If the merchants were entitled to dispose freely of their money and the goods that they buy and sell, they could choose to buy only when the members of the other estates find themselves compelled to sell their products at prices lower than those stipulated by the state and to sell only when the members of the other estates are compelled to buy goods at prices higher than those stipulated by the state. The legitimate expectations of others would then be disappointed, thereby undermining the foundations of the state. There would also be price fluctuations that are incompatible with the state's task of fixing prices in such a way that it is able to adjust the money supply according to the total value of the goods in circulation at any given time. The right to accumulate property is therefore not accompanied by the right to dispose freely of the property that has been accumulated.

Another example of the accumulation of property accompanied by strict limits on the permissible free disposal of it concerns the citizen who saves or hoards money. On the one hand, Fichte permits such practices in the case of a 'skilled and industrious worker' who 'does somewhat more work than one had counted on him doing, and thus also draws more than his share of money', but who then restricts himself to purchasing necessities or even seeks to do without them so as to save the money (GA I/7: 82; CCS, 125). On the other hand, the state needs to prevent, or at least restrict, such practices because of how they threaten to undermine its attempt to establish and maintain an equilibrium between the amount of money in circulation and the total value of the goods available in society at any given time. Yet Fichte claims that any coercive measures would 'limit the fitting and rightful freedom of the citizen' (GA I/7: 82; CCS, 126). He thinks, in fact, that there would not be a problem in the long term because the only genuine reasons for accumulation of this kind are to support oneself when one is too ill or too old to work, or to use this wealth in connection with the upbringing and education of one's children. Thus the money accumulated will eventually enter into circulation again (GA I/7: 82–83; CCS, 126).

There is nothing, however, to prevent the illicit use of money that has been accumulated in this or some other way, such as using it to buy something directly from a producer at a price that is cheaper than or exceeds the price stipulated by the state in relation to goods of the relevant kind. A dual economy would then develop: the official economy, in which the prices of goods are fixed by the state, on the one hand, and an informal economy akin to a black market, in which prices fluctuate depending on the prices at which people are willing or forced to buy and to sell goods, on the other. Although an informal economy restricted to non-essential goods and services might be tolerated, it is difficult to see how this informal economy would not eventually contaminate the official one.[13]

---

[13] It is therefore not the case that '[t]here is no reason why one person, in Fichte's rational state, could not perform services for another in exchange for payment' because this is 'a private and voluntary matter' (Wood, *Fichte's Ethical Thought*, 285). A non-monetized exchange of goods or services that

The right to dispose freely of one's absolute property would therefore have to be restricted to such an extent that there would be no private property in the genuine sense of the term.

The restrictions to which private property is subject in Fichte's rational state, assuming that there is any room for this form of property at all, make it difficult to describe his theory of property as a genuinely pluralist one that can accommodate the idea that the specific form or forms that the concept of property assumes within a society must be decided by the public use of reason guided by the aim of securing for all citizens the conditions of their own free and effective agency. In his *Rechtslehre* from 1812, Fichte himself acknowledges that the economic arrangements demanded by the application of his concept of property impose significant constraints on freedom. He claims that all citizens who can labour must labour, not only to provide themselves with the means to live but also to fulfil their obligations to the state. Given this subjection to necessity, it can be said that human beings have 'no freedom at all under these conditions' (GA II/13: 223). The problem is stated as follows.

The property contract is meant to guarantee that each person has a determinate sphere in which he or she may exercise freedom of choice. Yet the application of the concept of right, through which this sphere of personal freedom is delimited, implies that one *must* work and fulfil one's obligations to others and to the state, despite how individuals accept the terms of the property contract and agree with one another to establish a condition of right for the sake of their freedom (GA II/13: 224). Then there are the measures required to ensure that individuals can live from their labour that significantly restrict their freedom of choice, especially in the form of the right to dispose freely of their property. This invites the question as to the sense in which the citizens of Fichte's rational state can still be described as free.

Fichte's answer is that all individuals are nevertheless left some freedom for the pursuit of their own freely formed and chosen ends once they have obtained the necessities of life and human well-being through their own labour and fulfilled their duties as citizens, which include paying taxes (GA II/13: 224). In other words, leisure time is the sphere of freedom that the rational state secures for all its citizens. Fichte accordingly identifies the absolute right to property with the 'free leisure for arbitrary ends'

has no significant negative effects on the system of distribution and pricing that the rational state must construct and maintain might be permitted. Yet it is then difficult to see how one can meaningfully speak of 'a *market economy* highly regulated by the state to guarantee that every citizen's labor should earn a livelihood' (Wood, *Fichte's Ethical Thought*, 286; emphasis added).

(*freie Muße zu beliebigen Zweken*) that is guaranteed to every person by the state (GA II/13: 229).[14] The state's task of protecting its citizens' property will therefore involve guaranteeing them as much leisure time as possible. The more leisure time a state can allocate to its citizens, the more it will secure their property in the sense of providing them with a sphere of freedom of choice that other persons are obliged to respect. Conversely, a state that fails in this regard would be one in which individuals are subject to necessity alone, so that one can no longer speak of right but only of 'mere coercion and subjugation' (GA II/13: 226).

It is, however, difficult to see what would be gained by describing this type of property as *private* property. Individuals may possess an exclusive right to their leisure time in that one person is not entitled to interfere with the leisure time of another person by seeking to control what this person does during it or by forcing him or her to work instead of enjoying time free from work. The state can guarantee this right by ensuring not only that the private life of each agent is something in which other agents are unable or disinclined to interfere but also that individuals possess the means required to make sufficiently meaningful use of their leisure time. Yet we may ask if individuals would also have the right to dispose freely of their leisure time by exchanging it for other things that they happen to desire more than time free from work. Might a person not choose to work longer in order to earn more money or for the sake of something else that he or she desires? Leisure would then itself become a commodity that can be exchanged in an informal economy. Yet for the reasons identified above, this type of economy poses an existential threat to the official economy described in *The Closed Commercial State*. We must therefore assume that Fichte would not want to permit this type of free disposal of the leisure time that the state secures for its citizens.

In Chapter 3, we shall see that Hegel attempts to justify private property because he considers the right to dispose freely of things to which one possesses the exclusive right to be integral to the consciousness of oneself

---

[14] Although Fichte makes clear that when he speaks of 'free leisure for arbitrary ends', he means arbitrary in the sense of freely chosen, he also views leisure time in terms of a moral teleology by treating it as the means of achieving a higher, moral freedom, whose ends are found neither in nature nor in given desires, but in a higher world, which reveals the human capacity to adopt supersensible ends (GA II/13: 223–24). Fichte praises the Jewish Sabbath because it compels people who, driven by greed, would otherwise never stop working, and who would force the people working for them to labour continuously, to stop working in the hope of enabling them to discover that they possess spirit (*Geist*) and to reflect upon it (GA II/13: 225). This suggests that, from a moral standpoint, individuals do not possess the right to use their leisure time in any way that they please, provided their use of it does not violate the rights of other persons. Rather, they ought to employ it in ways that satisfy the demands of morality and promote moral ends.

as free. This consciousness is made possible by the recognition accorded to one person by another person that is implicit in any act of exchange regulated by a contract into which both persons have freely entered. Thus Hegel draws a very different conclusion from premises that are central to Fichte's theory of right. This conclusion might appear more palatable in that it promises to avoid the extensive state regulation that Fichte introduces in an attempt to apply the concept of property. Hegel criticizes the lack of freedom found in Fichte's rational state in connection with the police's role in ensuring public security by keeping track of what all the citizens are doing, which requires that they are always easily identifiable (GA I/4: 87–93; FNR 257–63). For Hegel, this is characteristic of a police state (*Polizeistaat*) with the appearance of a galley (PR 1819/20, 190–91).[15] Hegel presumably means that individuals, like galley slaves, here lack any freedom and are subject to the constant oversight of those people who have been entrusted with the task of commanding and supervising them.

The repressive character of Fichte's rational state to which Hegel seeks to draw our attention may be said to follow from the economic proposals presented in *The Closed Commercial State*. To illustrate this point, we might consider how a speech that Maximilien Robespierre gave in a sitting of the National Convention in December 1792 accords with Fichte's intentions in that it asserts the right to live and demands state intervention to guarantee this right.[16] In this speech, Robespierre emphasizes that the right in question is the most fundamental of all the human being's inalienable rights and that the first 'law of society' is therefore to ensure the availability of the means of subsistence for every member of society. He then makes the following series of claims:

> If human beings were just and virtuous, if greed [*cupidité*] were never tempted to devour the people's substance, if, obedient to the voice of reason and nature, all the rich people viewed themselves as the treasurers of society, or as the brothers of the poor, it would undoubtedly be possible to recognize no law other than the law of the most unlimited freedom. But if it is true that greed [*avarice*] may speculate on the people's poverty, and tyranny itself on their despair, if it is true that all the passions declare war on suffering humanity, then why should the laws not repress these abuses? Why should they not stay the murderous hand of the monopolist, as they

---

[15] This criticism is one-sided in that it fails to acknowledge the more liberal features of Fichte's theory of right and the state's role in guaranteeing them. For a summary of these liberal features, see Wood, *Fichte's Ethical Thought*, 275f., 287.
[16] See Manfred Buhr, 'Die Philosophie Johann Gottlieb Fichtes und die Französische Revolution', 43f.

do that of the common murderer? Why should they not concern themselves with the subsistence [*existence*] of the people after having so long concerned themselves with the pleasures of the great and the power of despots?[17]

Law and its application are here viewed as necessary because of a moral failure on the part of one social group that cannot be trusted to do what reason and justice demand. If, in contrast, humanity consisted of genuinely moral beings, then law would be unnecessary. There would, in effect, be a condition of natural freedom in which individuals assert their inalienable right to the means of subsistence while recognizing that others enjoy the same right, leading them to modify their behaviour to make it compatible with this recognition of the rights of others.

In the *Foundations of Natural Right*, Fichte similarly claims that right is necessary because one cannot rely on the morality of human beings. One must instead assume the existence of 'universal egoism' (GA I/3: 433–34; FNR, 134). Right is therefore concerned only with the legality of actions. This requires ensuring that individuals behave *as if* they possessed a good will, even though they may not, in fact, do so (GA I/3: 425; FNR, 125). Because the application of the concept of right cannot presuppose the existence of a morally good will, we are confronted with the possibility of such moral shortcomings as greed and the practice of seeking to monopolize essential goods with the aim of increasing the prices of them. It is then conceivable that the state's attempt to apply the concept of right in the form of law will encounter determined and persistent resistance on the part of certain sections of society. Robespierre appears quite optimistic in this regard, in that he counters the objection that the measure he proposes are impractical with the claim that they present 'no difficulty to common sense [*bon sens*] and to good faith' and that they would harm neither the interests of trade nor property rights.[18] Yet what would happen if common sense and good faith did not prevail? Would state violence not then be needed to ensure that the relevant laws are obeyed and that the appropriate measures are implemented?

Questions of this kind are pertinent to the measures proposed in *The Closed Commercial State* because some of these measures clearly do pose a threat to certain forms of trade and to private property, while the 'universal egoism' on which Fichte bases his theory of right means that we cannot assume that individuals will subordinate their private interests to the

---

[17] Robespierre, 'Sur les subsistances', 113f.
[18] Robespierre, 'Sur les subsistances', 114.

interests of society. The monopolist who aims to maximize his or her profits at the expense of the satisfaction of other people's basic material needs condemned by Robespierre provides a clear example of the potential need for repressive measures in Fichte's rational state. For the monopolist seeks, for his or her own benefit only, to inflate prices artificially by controlling the circulation of goods. This is achieved by removing goods from circulation until such time as people are compelled to pay more than they ought to pay for them, that is, at a higher price than the one fixed by the state on the assumption that goods will circulate freely. The state would then be justified in coercing this person to sell his or her goods at the price that it has stipulated or in punishing him or her for failing to do so.

A freedom-based justification of private property may, in contrast, seek to demonstrate how there is an exclusive right to things that demands that the legal owner is entitled to dispose of them freely. This right to property would limit the state's right to interfere in the lives of its citizens. Although Hegel will be shown to attempt to provide an argument for private property that incorporates the moment of recognition that is an integral feature of Fichte's theory of right, he does not ignore the threat that this form of property poses to society, and he accordingly seeks to situate private property within a larger social and political whole that limits it. This invites the question as to how successful this attempt to integrate private property into a larger social and political whole is. Hegel also explicitly acknowledges the historical character of property rights. I shall argue that his acknowledgement of their historical character generates a problem in relation to the claim that private property is superior to other forms of property, which is a claim to which Hegel will be shown to be committed. For Hegel's idea of 'ethical life' (*Sittlichkeit*) implies not only that a different form of property ought to be recognized alongside private property within a state that embodies this idea but also that this form of property is superior to private property because it is more expressive of this idea.

CHAPTER 3

Property and Ethical Life
Hegel's System of Right

3.1 Property and the Science of Right

Hegel's 'science of right' (*Rechtswissenschaft*) aims to demonstrate the rational necessity of each moment of the concept of right. This requires observing 'the proper immanent development' of the concept of right, whose rational necessity is presupposed (PR § 2). The concept of property is one such moment of the concept of right. Hegel's justification of the concept of property will therefore consist in showing how it is one way in which the concept of right *must* articulate itself. Hegel's attempt to demonstrate the rational necessity of the ethical, legal, social and political concepts, norms, practices and institutions that are essential moments of the concept of right is accompanied by an attempt to derive an internally articulated *system* of such concepts, norms, practices and institutions from the initially abstract concept of right. Hegel describes this system as 'the realm of actualized freedom, the world of spirit produced from within itself as a second nature' (PR § 4).

This idea of a system of right which actualizes freedom implies that each moment of the concept of right cannot be properly understood if it is viewed independently of the other moments of this concept. Rather, the moments of the concept of right form an interconnected whole that constitutes a 'world' in which individuals relate both to one another and to the institutions that mediate and regulate their relations with one another in such a way that their freedom is actualized. Moreover, the moments of the concept of right are hierarchically ordered. Hegel defines this hierarchical ordering in terms of how a later moment of right 'possesses a higher right, for it is the *more concrete* sphere, richer within itself and more truly universal' (PR § 30). Hegel's attempt to demonstrate the rational necessity of the concept of property belongs to the first sphere of right, which is called 'abstract' right. Thus the following question arises: how does this moment of the concept of right relate to the later, and 'higher', moments of the same concept?

The features of Hegel's science of right identified above mean that his account of property faces two key challenges. The first challenge is to provide a justification of the concept of property and any specific form of it by demonstrating that this concept and this specific form of property are essential moments of the concept of right. The second challenge is to locate the concept of property and any specific form of it within a system of moral, legal, social and political concepts, norms, practices and institutions in which the validity of property rights may be limited by their subordination to a higher moment of the concept of right. In this way, Hegel's science of right promises to provide an account of both how concepts, norms, practices and institutions are interrelated and their correct ordering. There is, then, the task of *justifying* each moment of the concept of right, on the one hand, and the task of *integrating* each of these moments into the system of right, on the other. The accomplishment of one of these tasks does not entail the accomplishment of the other one. If one task were to be accomplished while the other one was not, Hegel's science of right would have to be said to fail when judged in accordance with its own internal standards. Therefore, to remain true to the intentions of his science of right, Hegel must seek to meet both challenges.

As we shall see, Hegel seeks to demonstrate the rational necessity of *private* property. The rational necessity of private property leads Hegel to accord historical importance to the increasing recognition of the rights associated with this form of property. Although 'the *freedom of personality*' on which the right to property is based began to be recognized by a part of humanity already with the emergence of Christianity, 'the *freedom of property*' has been recognized only in more recent times. This is 'an example from world history of the length of time which the spirit requires in order to progress in its self-consciousness' (PR § 62R). The second form of freedom refers not only to an exclusive right to the possession and use of things but also to the right to dispose freely of that which is rightfully one's own. This general, if belated, recognition of a right that is rational accords with Hegel's understanding of the retrospective character of philosophy, which comprehends the rationality of what already is, and can, therefore, appear 'only at a time when actuality has gone through its formative process and attained its completed state' (PR Preface, 28 [23]). The last claim implies that Hegel's justification of private property has become possible only during the historical period to which he himself belongs, that is, in an age characterized by increasing recognition of private property and the rights that define it. Hegel will seek to make explicit the rational grounds of this recognition.

3.1 Property and the Science of Right

This relation between philosophy and history helps to explain Hegel's remarks on Plato's failure to acknowledge the rationality of private property. Private property and the principle of personality from which it derives were not recognized in the ancient Greek form of ethical life. Consequently, Plato was not prompted to seek to discover the grounds of the rational necessity of this specific form of property, though his attempt to exclude private property form the state reflected an awareness of the threat that it posed to the existing form of ethical life because of how it was expressive of a new principle that was already beginning to undermine this form of ethical life. The principle in question is 'the *self-sufficient particularity and inherently infinite personality* of the individual, the principle of subjective freedom'. In this respect, Plato's hostility to private property represented a natural attitude rather than a case of philosophical blindness. Recognition of the rights associated with private property and the consequent need to justify them presuppose a principle that is historically later than the one that shaped the ancient Greek form of ethical life, so that 'the philosophical reflection which can fathom these depths is likewise later than the substantial Idea of Greek philosophy' (PR § 185R). In Hegel's own time, in contrast, increasing recognition of private property and the rights that define it demands the philosophical comprehension of the rational grounds of this recognition.

If increasing recognition of private property and the rights that define it is evidence of a rational historical process that philosophy must comprehend, then the task of situating this institution and these rights within the social and political context designated by the term 'ethical life' cannot be accomplished in such a way as to make this recognition appear unjustified. Two key points here need to be emphasized: (1) *increasing* recognition of the rationality of private property is claimed to be a sign of historical progress, and (2) Hegel does not provide an explicit defence of any other form of property, even though, as we shall see, he subjects the rights of private property to some constraints in accordance with the demands of ethical life. When taken together, these points imply that private property must be the *dominant* form of property within the *modern* form of ethical life. This is not to say that other forms of property must be excluded. Nevertheless, it does mean that if a form of property other than private property can be shown to be more rational, in the sense of being more appropriate to the higher moment of right that Hegel terms 'ethical life', then this form of property ought to be the dominant one, the extension of which would be a sign of historical progress.

On the one hand, the subordination of private property to the higher moments of right is compatible with Hegel's understanding of how the various moments of right relate to one another. Indeed, he himself mentions the possibility of having to subordinate this form of property to higher demands, though only when genuine rational necessity is involved:

> [T]hose determinations which concern private property may have to be subordinated to higher spheres of right, such as a community [*Gemeinwesen*] or the state ... Nevertheless, such exceptions cannot be grounded in contingency, private arbitrariness, or private utility, but only in the rational organism of the state. (PR § 46R)

On the other hand, the dominance and extension of a different form of property would be incompatible with the claim that increasing recognition of the institution of private property is a sign of historical progress.

It should be noted that in the passage quoted above Hegel speaks of 'exceptions'. This implies that private property will be the dominant form of property whose rights can be limited or suspended only for exceptional reasons and in clearly specified ways. Thus it remains a matter of accommodating private property within the modern form of ethical life in such a way as to ensure that it is still the dominant form of property. Therefore, even if not all property would have to be private property, most of it would have to be so. I shall argue that there is, however, a form of property that can be considered *more* compatible with the idea of ethical life than private property because it is more *expressive* of this idea. This entails limits to the extent to which increasing recognition of private property and the rights that define it can be said to provide evidence of a rational process at work in history. Yet we first need to turn to Hegel's argument for private property, beginning with the relation between the concept of property in general and the specific sphere of right to which it belongs, namely abstract right.

3.2 Property and Abstract Right

Each moment of the concept of right in some way concerns 'the *existence* of the *free will*' (PR § 29). Since property is a moment of the concept of right, it must be an essential way in which the free will exists. Yet what does it mean for the free will to exist in the form of right? Hegel's account of abstract right, which includes the concept of property, indicates what this means and why it is necessary for the free will to 'exist' in the form of property.

3.2 Property and Abstract Right

Abstract right is the most 'immediate' form in which the free will exists. Its abstract character is reflected in the subject of this form of right, which Hegel terms the 'person'. The concept of the person involves two essential features. On the one hand, the subject is 'finite' because of its specific desires and ends, the specific objects of its willing and its specific characteristics and circumstances. On the other hand, and more importantly at the stage of abstract right, the same subject can conceive of itself in abstraction from all such determinate features of itself. It is, in fact, only in this way that an individual becomes a person:

> Personality begins only at that point where the subject has not merely a consciousness of itself in general as concrete and in some way determined, but a consciousness of itself as a completely abstract 'I' in which all concrete limitation and validity are negated and invalidated. In the personality, therefore, there is knowledge of the *self* as an *object*, but as an object raised by thought to simple infinity and hence purely identical with itself. (PR § 35R)

The capacity to become conscious of one's independence of any specific, given features of one's own self and circumstances is a condition of 'abstract and hence *formal* right' (PR § 36). This is because this stage of right is concerned with rights that apply to *all* persons. The universal applicability of the norms of abstract right presupposes the capacity to conceive of oneself as equal to, and identical with, other persons, despite the real differences that distinguish one individual from other individuals in a way that goes beyond the formal self-identity of numerically distinct subjects. This consciousness of both oneself and others as equal rights-bearing persons ultimately requires conceiving of oneself and others as independent of any determinate features, including ends, motives and interests: 'In formal right ... it is not a question of particular interests, of my advantage or welfare, and just as little of the particular ground by which my will is determined' (PR § 37).[1] The relevant form of consciousness enables individuals to recognize one another as persons and thereby address both to themselves and to others the command to '*be a person and respect others as persons*' (PR § 36). Thus the formal nature of the norms of abstract right corresponds to the formal nature of the person that is the subject of abstract right. Already, then, it looks like the right to property cannot be

---

[1] This corresponds to the first moment of the concept of the will, the 'universality' which consists in 'the element of *pure indeterminacy* or of the "I"'s pure reflection into itself, in which every limitation, every content, whether present immediately through nature, through needs, desires, and drives, or given and determined in some other way, is dissolved' (PR § 5).

reduced to a relation between a person and a thing, for abstract right and the rights that follow from it presuppose a specific type of recognition. Yet how does the right to property and the obligations that it entails follow from the command to be a person and to respect others as persons?

The abstract, rights-bearing person finds itself confronted with a world that remains external to it and limits its activity. In order to maintain the consciousness of itself as free that has been achieved through becoming aware of its independence of any given features of itself, the person must act in such a way as 'to overcome this limitation and to give itself reality – or, what amounts to the same thing, to posit that existence as its own' (PR § 39).[2] The limitation in question is overcome by appropriating parts of an external world that would otherwise confront a person as something independent of his or her will that, by virtue of its brute existence, is an absolute constraint on his or her willing. At this stage, the immediate object of the person's will is a 'thing' that necessarily lacks rights of its own because it lacks the capacity for abstraction presupposed by the type of self-consciousness that defines personality (PR § 42). The legal expression for things that have been appropriated by the will of a person is 'property'.

This shows that the rational necessity of property does not consist in how items of property serve as the means to ends that remain external to freedom. Rather, a person's power and control over things enables him or her to achieve and to preserve a consciousness of the relevant type of freedom in the face of a material world that would otherwise limit his or her self-activity to such an extent that this consciousness of freedom could not be maintained: 'the circumstance that I, as free will, am an object to myself in what I possess and only become an actual will by this means constitutes the genuine and rightful element in possession, the determination of *property*' (PR § 45). Thus Hegel's argument for the rational necessity of the concept of property turns on the idea that property is a necessary condition of the freedom of persons and the type of self-conception associated with this freedom. Indeed, Hegel identifies the rational necessity of property with how it confirms a person's conception of himself or herself as free, not only by removing the constraints on a person's free activity generated by a world and objects within it that confront this person as external things but also by giving a person's will 'existence' in the sense that it embodies or objectifies itself in things over which it exercises effective control and employs in accordance with freely chosen ends.

---

[2] This corresponds to the second moment of will, 'the absolute moment of the *finitude* or *particularization* of the "I"' (PR § 6).

We have so far encountered only the concept of property as such. One interpretation of Hegel's argument for *private* property implies that the concept of property can ultimately be reduced to a relation between a person and a thing, from which an obligation on the part of other persons to respect the right to property follows. This interpretation can be called the 'embodiment' interpretation because it focuses on how individuals embody their personality in things in such a way as to turn a purely subjective conception of themselves into something concrete and recognizable both to themselves and to others.[3] This interpretation captures some key elements of Hegel's argument for property in general. Moreover, recognition is a feature of it, though only as something that is elicited through the possession and the exercise of a right to a thing that has already been established. Yet I shall identify some significant problems with this interpretation of Hegel's argument for private property and show how these problems can be overcome by another interpretation of it that reduces the stage of embodiment to a necessary but not sufficient condition of the consciousness of oneself as a person. This is what can be called the 'recognition' interpretation because of how recognition this time forms a constitutive moment of the concept of property. It is only at the stage of contract, however, that this moment of recognition becomes explicit and Hegel's argument for private property is completed. At this stage, it is less a matter of embodying one's will in a thing than a matter of disengaging one's will from a thing.

3.3 The Embodiment Interpretation of Hegel's Argument for Private Property

The embodiment interpretation of Hegel's argument for private property is compatible with the statement that 'I, as free will, am an object to myself in what I possess and only become an actual will by this means', and how this way of becoming an object to oneself 'constitutes the genuine and rightful element in possession, the determination of *property*' (PR § 45). The embodiment interpretation takes this to mean that private property is the most immediate objective condition of the development and maintenance of the type of self-conception that characterizes personality.

The idea of the development and maintenance of a self-conception implies that this self-conception is, to some extent, already present. Hegel's

---

[3] See Waldron, *The Right to Private Property*, 353.

account of personality relies on the prior existence of the relevant self-conception in that the act of abstracting from all given features of oneself presupposes some awareness of the capacity to do this. This presupposition is nevertheless compatible with the idea that an external confirmation or verification of the relevant self-conception is necessary and that this external confirmation or verification takes the form of the right to property. Indeed, this is Hegel's position. The transition from the concept of property in general to private property requires more than this, however, for the rational *necessity* of this specific form of property must be demonstrated by showing how it is the *only* way of achieving such a confirmation or verification of the type of self-conception that characterizes personality. We have already seen how Fichte develops a theory of property rights that concerns the same type of practical self-consciousness, but that entails only the right to the exclusive possession and use of parts of the external world and objects within it. The effective control that a person is nevertheless able to exercise over parts of the world and external objects within it means that this world and these objects are not an absolute constraint on this person's self-activity. Thus the relevant form of property may serve to confirm a person's conception of himself or herself as a free agent, as may the moment of recognition that is implicit in the civil contract.

One attempt to supply the missing step in Hegel's argument for private property in such a way as to preserve the embodiment interpretation of this argument involves the introduction of a temporal condition. An action that a person performs on or with an object is likely to constrain or determine any subsequent actions that he or she may perform on or with the same object. Thus the successful embodiment of the will in an object presupposes the possibility of acting on or with the same object in ways that are consistent and stable over time. A person must, therefore, be in the position to act with a view to how changes in the object at one point in time determine what changes are possible at a later point in time. This would not be possible, however, in the absence of the exclusive right to the possession and use of one and the same object because other persons would then be entitled to perform actions on or with the object that may change it in ways that are incompatible with the first person's plans and ultimate ends.[4] Private property, in contrast, removes this constraint on a

---

[4] See Waldron, *The Right to Private Property*, 373f. Fichte might be thought to employ a similar argument when he claims that 'it is necessary that *everything remain* as it was once known by the free being and posited in his concept (regardless of whether it is now specifically modified by him or not)' (GA I/3: 406; FNR, 105). One attempt to provide the missing argument for the claim that private property is a necessary condition of the development and maintenance of the self-conception and

person's control over an object. Therefore, only private property can secure the 'beneficial effects' of embodiment.[5]

This type of argument at most establishes that an exclusive right to the possession and use of the same external object regulated by certain conventions or rules is necessary in so far as effective control over this object is required to develop and maintain the conception of oneself as a free, purposive agent. It does not, therefore, entail a form of property that is essentially different from the one found in Fichte's *Foundations of Natural Right*, for it does not also establish the rational necessity of the right to dispose freely of a thing. This right can, in fact, be considered incompatible with the argument presented above, in so far as this argument treats *continual* possession and use of the same external object as a condition of successful embodiment. For the right to dispose freely of one's property would entitle a person to discard items of property in such rapid succession that he or she is unable to exercise the exclusive right to the possession and use of the same object long enough to embody his or her will successfully in this object. Moreover, the embodiment argument, as presented above, does not acknowledge the possibility of successful embodiment that is achieved by acting on or with a *series* of *different* objects. Although recognition of this possibility would make the embodiment interpretation of Hegel's argument for private property more compatible with a person's right to dispose freely of his or her property, it would also challenge this interpretation's key premise that successful embodiment is possible only by means of the possession and use of the *same* object for an extended period of time, from which the claim that there must be an exclusive right to the possession and use of this object is held to follow.

---

capacities that constitute free personality appeals to such statements as this one. See Patten, *Hegel's Idea of Freedom*, 150ff. Yet the statement in question belongs to Fichte's discussion of original rights, which he considers to be fictional ones, and, as we know, his further development of the concept of right does not represent an attempt to justify private property, but is, in fact, thought by Fichte himself to require a different form of property.

[5] Waldron, *The Right to Private Property*, 374. This appeal to the production of beneficial effects is problematic because Hegel's argument is not meant to be of a consequentialist kind, as is shown by such statements as the following one: 'In relation to needs – if these are taken as primary – the possession of property appears as a means; but the true position is that, from the point of view of freedom, property as the first *existence* of freedom, is an essential end for itself' (PR § 45R). The necessity of each moment of the concept of right must be explained in terms of how it follows from the concept of the will, which for Hegel necessarily means a free will (PR § 4, including A). As one moment of the concept of right, property must be justified in terms of how it is an instance of objective or 'actualized' freedom: 'The rational aspect of property is to be found not in the satisfaction of needs but in the superseding of mere subjectivity of personality. Not until he has property does the person exist as reason' (PR § 41A).

Another issue concerns the duration of the period of time in which the exclusive possession and use of the same object are required for successful embodiment. It is assumed that the process of embodiment is capable of completion. The exclusive right to the possession and use of an object would therefore need to extend only to the point in time at which the process of embodiment is completed. This is logically compatible with a situation in which a person is granted an exclusive right to the possession and use of an external object for a limited period of time and for a specific purpose, while lacking the right to dispose freely of this object beyond being entitled to judge how to employ it in relation to the specific end for which it has been allocated to him or her. This right is also compatible with the consumption or using up of a thing, which may be unavoidable consequences of the effective use of this thing. Fichte can be thought to conceive of the property rights that the state grants to persons so that they can live from their labour in precisely this way. I shall now argue with reference to the role of the body in Hegel's account of the right to property that the embodiment interpretation of his argument for private property does not, in fact, correspond to his own argument for this specific form of property.

Hegel introduces the concept of private property in the following way: 'Since my will, as personal and hence as the will of an individual, becomes objective in property, the latter takes on the character of *private property*' (PR § 46). From this statement, the rational necessity of private property appears to rest on two key claims: (1) the will of the person is necessarily the personal will of an individual distinct from other individuals, and (2) the will of this individual must therefore be objectified or 'embodied' in a form of property that adequately reflects this fact. The relevant form of property is private property. The first claim can be taken to mean that the actual or potential bearer of a property right is always a *particular* person, despite the way in which the legal concept of personality presupposes the capacity to abstract from all determinate features that distinguish one individual from other individuals. The second claim would then consist in the assertion that being *this* person requires the corresponding form of property, which is private property, because only it can adequately reflect the personal character or 'singular individuality' of the specific will that takes possession of a thing.[6]

---

[6] See Nuzzo, 'Freedom in the Body', 119. Since legal personality itself requires abstracting from the determinate features that distinguish individuals from one another, we might think of the person as an individual only in the sense of a single person who is numerically distinct from other persons. The argument could then be reduced to the claim that the object of any private right enjoyed by a self-identical person must itself be an individual entity that is numerically distinct from other such

The subject of right is here understood to have personal ends and projects that can be realized only by means of the unlimited right to possess, use and dispose of specific external objects as he or she pleases. Yet, as we have already seen, this type of argument begs the question, in that it assumes that more restrictive forms of property are incompatible with the pursuit of personal ends and projects. The fact that Hegel is not relying on an argument of this kind is shown by how he does not attempt to construct an argument that is any less question-begging in this regard. Instead, he attempts to justify the claim that property must take the form of private property in a way that directly relates to the idea that a person can become conscious of his or her freedom only in this form of property. The freedom in question is the type of freedom that is characteristic of abstract right. Understanding the grounds of this argument for private property requires turning to the various moments of property, which are the possession, the use and the alienation of things. I shall argue that it is only in connection with the alienation of things that Hegel's full argument for private property is found.

It is not clear how the relations between these three moments of property are to be understood. Possession and use might be thought to represent successive and increasingly adequate ways in which a thing is appropriated by a person. There is here a process through which the right to a thing is established. Alienation, in contrast, does not involve the act of appropriating a thing, whether by taking possession of it or by using it, for it consists in the voluntary act of relinquishing a thing to which one already has a legal right in exchange for another thing as part of a contract. Does this mean that possession and use explain how the right to a thing is established, thereby suggesting the kind of dyadic person–thing model of the right to property that Kant and Fichte have been shown to reject? I do not intend to address such interpretative questions at this stage. I shall instead restrict myself to demonstrating the limited effectiveness of possession and use as ways of justifying private property, before going on to show how Hegel's account of the alienation of a thing fills the gap in his argument for private property in such a way as to favour a triadic person–thing–person model of the right to property because of the moment of recognition that this right presupposes and incorporates.

---

entities. Yet this would be true of any single thing, including a person's body, so that it remains unclear why the embodiment of personality requires that things that are external to a person's body also be the object of a private right.

Hegel asserts that a thing belongs to the first person who happens to take possession of it. This claim is described as 'self-evident' (PR § 50). By possession Hegel means more than the mere intention to make a previously ownerless thing one's own (PR § 51). Nor does he reduce the act of appropriation to the physical seizure of a thing, which is always limited in terms of its scope (PR § 55). Rather, as with Fichte's earlier account of the right to property, it consists in giving form to a thing until it is penetrated by a person's will in such a way as to be evident to other persons even when the first person is no longer in physical possession of the thing (PR § 52R, § 56). This type of possession may include designating a thing as one's property by means of a sign (PR § 58). Hegel then presents an argument for private property. This argument rests on the claim that to separate ownership from the full use of a thing would result in a contradiction, for the full use of a thing entails exclusive ownership of it. This means that the owner of the thing cannot be a person other than the person who possesses the right to the thing in question.

The limitations of this argument are reflected in the hypothetical terms in which Hegel formulates it: 'if I have the whole use of the thing, I am its owner; and beyond the whole extent of its use, nothing remains of the thing which could be the property of someone else' (PR § 61). In other words, a person who enjoys the whole use of a thing would penetrate this thing with his or her will to such an extent that only his or her will would exist in the thing. For this argument to work, however, Hegel would have to demonstrate the impossibility of a situation in which one person exercises effective control over a thing by using it at the same time as another person exercises effective control over the same thing by using it. Although there may well be cases in which the nature of a thing makes the effective use of it by two or more persons impossible, Hegel must demonstrate that there cannot be any cases in which the possibility of common use of one and the same thing is conceivable. In addition to what has already been said concerning this issue, the challenge that Hegel faces can be illustrated by applying his own reasoning. If one and the same thing could be worked upon or used in different ways by several people and there was no reliable way of determining which changes to the thing were to be attributed to each person, then the thing in question would have to be viewed as their common property. For the thing would have been penetrated by the wills of all of these persons in such a way that it has become impossible to divide it into parts that have been penetrated by the will of only one of them. Yet this is precisely the conclusion that Hegel must avoid because it is incompatible with the conclusion that he himself draws, namely, that '[p]roperty is therefore essentially *free and complete* property [*freies, volles Eigentum*]' (PR § 62; translation modified).

Hegel's argument works better in the case of a person's own body. A person's body has the status of a thing. Although the body cannot literally be separated from the person whose 'undivided external existence' it is, this person can adopt a reflective and volitional attitude in relation to his or her own body: 'as a person, I ... possess *my life and body*, like other things, only *in so far as I so will it*' (PR § 47). Hegel cites the example of choosing to destroy or to mutilate one's own body (PR § 47R). We may assume that an individual has no natural inclination to treat his or her body in this way. He or she may nevertheless will to treat it in this way because of a principle of action to which he or she has committed himself or herself. For example, a soldier may choose to mutilate himself or herself with the intention of not having to fight in a war in which he or she will be ordered to perform acts that are contrary to certain moral beliefs and values that he or she strongly endorses, such as the belief that it is impermissible to endanger the lives of innocent people unless absolutely necessary, whereas he or she judges that this particular war is far from necessary. The body is also a thing of which a person may will to take possession through the act of forming it, in the sense of actively seeking to develop the powers associated with it (PR § 48, § 52R, § 57). From the standpoint of persons other than the person whose body it is, however, this 'thing' is inseparable from this person's will. Each person is therefore obliged to respect the right to bodily integrity of other persons (PR § 48R).

Even if the case of a person's own body shows that there is at least one thing that could not be anything other than private property because it necessarily belongs to the only person who is genuinely capable of willing or not willing it, the embodiment interpretation of Hegel's argument for private property would then work only with respect to a person's relation to his or her own body. One might identify certain things that are in some way so intimately connected with a person's body that they are or become figuratively a part of it. It is difficult, however, to see how one could extend the range of such things without stretching the notion of identity so far that it becomes essentially meaningless.

Although Hegel's account of possession and use suggests that he is attempting to demonstrate the rational necessity of private property in a way that relies on explaining property rights purely in terms of a relation between a person's body and things that are external to it, his argument for this specific form of property will be shown to depend on his account of the alienation of property. There is here a relation between two persons mediated by things. These persons demonstrate their freedom in relation to each other in a way that its not possible through the appropriation and use of their own bodies or other things. This brings me to what can be called the 'recognition' interpretation of Hegel's argument for private property.

This interpretation is compatible with the embodiment interpretation of Hegel's argument for private property in so far as the relevant type of recognition presupposes that a person has previously placed his or her will in a thing. Yet it provides the missing justification for the claim that a person must possess the right to dispose freely of his or her property. This right involves the act of disengaging one's will from a thing rather than the act of placing one's will in it. The embodiment interpretation focuses on the second type of act, and it can therefore be criticized on the grounds that it ignores how personality is not reducible to the consciousness of the capacity to choose ends. Rather, it is equally a matter of being able to detach oneself from any ends that one has chosen.[7] Moreover, it is not only a matter of the ends themselves but also a matter of the means that one employs to achieve them, which may include items of property. A person can, in fact, retain the same end while willing new means to it, thereby choosing to withdraw his or her will from an item of property in which he or she had placed it.

Even if, for the sake of argument, it is granted that the embodiment interpretation of Hegel's argument for private property demonstrates the necessity of the right to dispose freely of one's property because embodying one's will in a thing requires the arbitrary use of this thing, it would still be a matter of the arbitrary employment of only a single object in which a person has placed his or her will. In this respect, the person's will would remain bound to this one thing in which it seeks to embody itself. Yet this dependence on a thing is incompatible with the freedom of the person because this freedom consists in the consciousness of oneself as 'a completely abstract "I" in which all concrete limitation and validity are negated and invalidated' (PR § 35R). Thus the embodiment of a person's will in a thing is ultimately a constraint that must be removed if a person is to become fully conscious of his or her freedom.

We can here see how Hegel's idea of the type of independence enjoyed by a genuinely free will is a demanding one, in that it concerns more than freedom from the influence of natural or psychological drives and independence from the choices of others. Rather, it concerns the will's independence

---

[7] See Mohseni, *Abstrakte Freiheit*, 80f.

of anything external to itself, and thus a state of being in which the will is 'completely *with itself* [*bei sich*], because it has reference to nothing but itself, so that every relationship of *dependence* on something *other* than itself is thereby eliminated' (PR § 23). The confirmation or verification of personality nevertheless requires more than an immediate consciousness of this type of freedom. How, then, can a relationship of dependence on something other than the person's will be eliminated? Hegel's description of alienation as 'the reflection of the will from the thing back into itself' (PR § 53) indicates where the answer to this question is to be found.

3.4 The Recognition Interpretation of Hegel's Argument for Private Property

As we have seen, a thing necessarily lacks a will of its own. It may therefore become subject to the will of a person who appropriates it. This person may then choose not to continue to subject this thing to his or her will: 'It is possible for me to *alienate* [*entäußern*] my property, for it is mine only in so far as I embody my will in it' (PR § 65). Common or collective forms of ownership would restrict this right to dispose freely of a thing because each person would be required to seek the permission of others, whether it be the permission of all other owners or the permission of a single entity which acts as their representative, before being entitled to transfer this thing to another person. It is therefore in Hegel's discussion of the alienation of things that we should expect to find his justification of private property, given how the right to dispose freely of a thing of which one is the legal owner distinguishes this form of property from other forms of property. How, then, does Hegel seek to justify private property in terms of the alienation of things? So far, we know only that his argument appeals to the inadequacy of the consciousness of freedom that a person achieves when he or she enjoys nothing more than the exclusive right to the possession and use of a thing in which he or she objectifies his or her will.

A person's effective control over a thing and the penetration of this thing by his or her will through the consumption and use of it are sufficient to demonstrate to others that this person has made this thing into an expression of his or her own will by employing it in accordance with ends that he or she has formed, thereby generating the demand that others recognize him or her as a free rational agent and treat him or her as such. Yet this is compatible with remaining bound to a single thing or set of things in which one has chosen to embody one's will. This would also be true of a person's body when it is viewed from the standpoint of other persons, if not from the standpoint of the person whose body it is. Although we may conceive of ways in which one person attempts to demonstrate to other persons that he or she has withdrawn his or her will from his or her body, such as extreme bodily neglect, Hegel distinguishes between a first-person perspective and a third-person perspective. An immediate relation to another person's body *qua* object of this person's will is not available from the third-person perspective, for one person necessarily lacks direct access to the thoughts and intentions of another person, and an interpretation of any signs that a person has withdrawn his or her will from his or her body can be mistaken. For example, the reason behind the lack of interest that a person shows in his or her body might be explained in terms of how the neglect of it is intended as a moral or political statement, such as a protest against a society in which a person's physical appearance has become a commodity, rather than in terms of how this person no longer wills his or her own body, which is, in fact, being willed as an instrument by means of which he or she seeks to achieve an end that he or she has adopted.

For Hegel, a person's independence of things becomes fully explicit only when he or she freely enters into a contract with another person with the aim of exchanging things. A relation between one person and another person is here established by means of a voluntary act on the part of each person. This relation demonstrates each person's independence of the thing that he or she chooses to exchange for another thing. Importantly, it also implies recognition of the other person's capacity to withdraw his or her will from any specific thing in which he or she had previously placed it and thus to enter into a voluntary agreement of the relevant kind. As with Fichte's summons, then, the persons in question implicitly recognize each other as persons.

This extends the structure of the concept of property beyond a dyadic person–thing model to a triadic person–thing–person model, for each person's consciousness of freedom is achieved through a relation to another person that is mediated by an exchange of things. While contract has the moment of mutual recognition built into it because it requires that both parties conceive of themselves and each other as free in the relevant sense and treat one another as such,[8] recognition is not a constitutive feature of

---

[8] The importance of the idea of recognition to Hegel's account of property, including contract, has been noted and even stressed. See Chitty, 'Recognition and Property in Hegel and the Early Marx', Patten, *Hegel's Idea of Freedom*, 158ff., Waldron, *The Right to Private Property*, 375ff. and Williams, *Hegel's Ethics of Recognition*, Chapter 7. Only Chitty, however, genuinely identifies the important role played by contract in Hegel's argument for *private* property. See 'Recognition and Property in Hegel and the Early Marx', 688ff. My reconstruction of this argument differs from his, however, in that I seek to explain this role in a way that makes more explicit how it seeks to justify a defining feature of private property, namely, the right to dispose of a thing freely.

the embodiment interpretation of Hegel's argument for private property. For although a person may signal to others that he or she is a person by embodying his or her will in a thing, the moment of recognition is reduced to a supplement to this objectification of a person's freedom. The transition from a person–thing relation to a person–thing–person relation in contract is necessary because it is a more adequate way in which a person's freedom comes to exist in the other person's recognition of it. Hegel himself refers to this understanding of the rational necessity of the alienation of property as part of a contract in the following passage:

> It is not only *possible* for me to dispose of an item of property as an external thing ... I am also *compelled* by the concept to dispose of it as property in order that *my* will, as *existent*, may become objective to me. But according to this moment, my will, as externalized, is at the same time *another* will. Hence this moment, in which this necessity of the concept is real, is *the unity* of different wills, which therefore relinquish their difference and distinctiveness (PR § 73).

In this passage, a person is said to be '*compelled* by the concept' to dispose of his or her property. At the stage of abstract right, the only explanation of this necessity is that the free disposal of property is a condition of becoming fully conscious of oneself as a person, in that only it can explain the possibility of an external confirmation of a person's conception of himself or herself as being independent of any specific thing in which he or she chooses to place his or her will. As we know, the consciousness of this independence requires abstracting from any given, determinate features of oneself, which explains why Hegel claims that the two wills 'relinquish their difference and distinctiveness'.

The necessity of contract is therefore not explained in terms of how it enables objects to be bought and sold. Rather, its necessity consists in how it is a condition of the objectification (*Objektivierung*) of personality, whereas taking possession of things and using them are not enough: 'In immediate property the free will has not become truly objective to me' (PR 1821/22, § 71). A person can then be thought to be motivated to enter into a contract with another person by his or her drive to encounter an objectification of his or her personality in the recognition accorded to him or her by this other person, whose own personality likewise encounters its objectification. This is an example of '[t]he absolute determination or, if one prefers, the absolute drive, of the free spirit ... to make its freedom into its object' (PR § 27). The object here is the recognition of oneself as a person provided by another person, whereas the thing exchanged is reduced to the middle term of this relation between two persons. Thus we have the beginnings of a 'truly infinite' will whose 'object is itself, and therefore not something which it sees as *other* or as a *limitation*; on the contrary, it has merely returned into itself in its object' (PR § 22).

Hegel emphasizes the moment of mutual recognition implicit in the relation between persons who freely enter into a contract with one another: 'Contract presupposes that the contracting parties *recognize* each other as persons and owners of property [*Eigentümer*]; and since it is a relationship of objective spirit, the moment of recognition is already contained and presupposed within it' (PR § 71R). Contract presupposes recognition of the other person as the legal owner of the thing that he or she alienates. Hegel's argument for private property can then be understood in the following way. Only in contract can a person become truly conscious of his or her freedom. Contract presupposes the right to dispose freely of one's property, and this right is a defining feature of private property. If contract is a necessary condition of the consciousness of the type of freedom that characterizes personality, and the right to dispose freely of one's property is a presupposition of contract, then private property must be considered rationally necessary.

This shows how Hegel adopts a two-stage argumentative strategy. The first stage seeks to demonstrate the exclusive right to the possession and use of a thing. This is not enough, however, to justify private property in preference to other possible forms of property. The second stage consists in demonstrating what is required for a person to become fully conscious of his or her freedom by not remaining dependent on the things in which he or she chooses to place his or her will.[9] This condition is satisfied by the act of alienating such things as part of a contract that presupposes that the contracting parties recognize each other as persons and thus as the rightful owners of items of property that they are entitled to dispose of freely. In this way, private property is shown to be a condition of personality itself. Therefore, to be a person, one must enjoy not only the exclusive right to the possession and use of things but also the right to dispose of them freely, and recognizing others as persons will, therefore, consist in ascribing to them these same rights. The second stage of the argument demonstrates

---

[9] Taken together, these two stages explain how right in the form of property is 'the *existence* of the *free will*' (PR § 29). For while the person's embodiment of his or her will in a thing corresponds to the second moment of the will, in which the 'I' achieves determinacy, the abstract universality of the first moment of the will is confirmed by the recognition of each person as someone who is independent of any single thing or set of things in which he or she chooses to place his or her will, which, in this respect, remains indeterminate. Thus there is the unity of these two moments of the will that Hegel associates with the higher moment of 'individuality', and which he identifies with the freedom of the will (PR § 7).

the validity of a claim that had until then remained problematic. This is the claim that '[s]ince my will, as personal and hence as the will of an individual, becomes objective in property, the latter takes on the character of *private property*' (PR § 46).

The question arises as to whether Hegel demonstrates that private property is the only possible way in which a person can demonstrate that he or she is free by withdrawing his or her will from a thing in which he or she had placed it. If it is not the only possible way of demonstrating to other persons that one is free, then the rational necessity of private property alone would not have been conclusively shown. Some alternative ways of demonstrating to others that one is a person by withdrawing one's will from a thing in which one had previously placed it cannot satisfy key conditions of the relevant type of consciousness of freedom. One example is the giving of gifts.[10] Although this might qualify as a case of a person withdrawing his or her will from a thing in which he or she had placed it, allowing the giver to be recognized as someone with the capacities that define a person, and even making mutual recognition possible if there is an exchange of gifts, the contingency of this practice means that it cannot be classed as a moment of right. Contract, in contrast, involves a type of a necessity that is lacking in the case of the practice of giving and receiving gifts. This is evident from Hegel's account of how the contingency of contract is removed.

Contract involves a type of identity in difference. Each person is identical to the other one as a legal person because he or she not only alienates an item of property but also receives a different item of property in return: 'each party, in accordance with his own and the other party's will, *ceases* to be an owner of property, *remains* one, and *becomes* one' (PR § 74). Since this contractual relation between persons consists in their mutual agreement to exchange items of property, it depends on the arbitrary will of each of them and it is thus an ultimately contingent relation, despite its

---

[10] Another example is subletting. A person is here not the legal owner of the property even though he or she is entitled to dispose freely of parts of it by renting them to other persons. Although the person in question may sublet a room in the apartment or house that he or she is renting and, in this way, withdraw his or her will from a thing in which he or she had placed it, he or she is still subject to the will of the legal owner of the apartment or house because the permissibility of subletting the room depends on the owner's prior agreement to such an arrangement. If the person also owned the apartment or house, he or she would be free of this constraint. He or she would also be entitled to dispose of the apartment or house itself by leasing all of it or selling it as part of a contract. The person in question would then be more independent of things, and thus able to achieve a more adequate confirmation of his or her personality through the alienation of his or her property as part of a contract.

rational necessity as a moment of the concept of right: 'the identical will which comes into existence through the contract is only *a will posited by the contracting parties*, hence only a *common* [*gemeinsamer*] will, not a will which is universal [*allgemeiner*] in and for itself' (PR § 75). The arbitrary and contingent nature of this common will means that the common will must assume the form of a coercive will whenever the terms of a contract are violated. In other words, although any act of exchange that satisfies the norms of abstract right entails a moment of recognition, this recognition must be secured in the form of laws that govern contracts and by means of a coercive power capable of enforcing these laws, for only then does the common will become independent of the arbitrary, contingent acts through which specific contracts come into being. Hence Hegel's designation of abstract right as '*coercive right*' (*Zwangsrecht*) (PR § 94). This model would be incompatible with the practice of giving and receiving gifts because this practice by its very nature presupposes the absence of actual or potential coercion.

The importance of the alienation of property and contract in my reconstruction of Hegel's argument for private property implies a necessary connection between abstract right and a specific conception of freedom. A person has the right to dispose freely of parts of the world and things within it subject to the single restriction that he or she does not thereby violate the personality and the property rights of others. This right is expressive of the person's capacity to exercise free choice in relation to any potential object of the will. The choice is, however, an essentially arbitrary one. To treat this form of freedom, and thus the form of right in which it achieves 'existence', as the highest form of freedom would be to ignore how Hegel characterizes the freedom of personality as an inadequate conception of freedom, as when he states the following about it:

> The commonest idea [*Vorstellung*] we have of freedom is that of *arbitrariness* [*Willkür*] – the mean position of reflection between the will as determined solely by natural drives and the will which is free in and for itself. When we hear it said that freedom in general consists in *being able to do as one pleases*, such an idea can only be taken to indicate a complete lack of intellectual culture; for it shows not the least awareness of what constitutes the will which is free in and for itself, or right, or ethics [*Sittlichkeit*], etc. (PR § 15R)

This arbitrary form of freedom is an essential moment of the concept of the free will because it enables individuals to demonstrate their independence of things and to achieve recognition of themselves as free agents. It must, therefore, be accommodated within Hegel's system of right if the following statement is to hold true: 'Whatever the will has decided to choose ... it can likewise relinquish' (PR § 16). Contract is nevertheless not the final stage of the process in which the free will comes to exist 'for itself' in the form of right. We should therefore not lose sight of the limitations of abstract right.

These limitations include not only a partial understanding of freedom but also an impoverished relation between individuals. This relation is a purely external one because it is not necessary for the parties to a contract to recognize one another as anything more than abstract legal entities and to concern themselves more directly with each other's freedom. Thus the common will generated by contract requires only that both parties recognize each other as abstract legal persons. This reflects the way in which abstract right more generally ignores any determinate features of both the subject and the object of right or, at most, accords them only a secondary importance.[11] This ultimate indifference to others is captured by Kant's claim that right governs the external actions of persons and the external relations between them in such a way that one person is indifferent to another person's freedom and may, in fact, wish in his or her heart 'to infringe upon it' (AA 6 [MM]: 231). Indeed, this is the only form of right that Hegel discovers in Kant's *Rechtslehre*, leading him to claim that it rests on an inadequate conception of freedom precisely because the idea of the limitation of each person's arbitrary will in accordance with a universal law reduces right to an *external* limitation on the free choice of each person (PR § 29R). The abstract and external character of the relevant form of recognition means that the particularity of individuals and the concrete ethical, social and political relations in which they stand with one another have yet to be integrated into Hegel's system of right.

Hegel's attempt to justify private property, on the one hand, and his need to situate this moment of right within a larger ethical, legal, social and political system, on the other, result in the demand to accommodate the right to dispose freely of one's property within such a system in a way that is compatible with the other moments of the concept of

---

[11] The parties to a contract may be motivated by the desire to satisfy their own specific needs and thus to obtain things to consume or use. Yet the act of exchanging things is governed by a conception of value that must abstract from the specific useful properties of things if qualitatively different things are to be compared with one another in such a way that their relative value can be determined and represented by a third thing that itself lacks any utility and can therefore serve as an appropriate medium of exchange, namely money (PR § 63) In Chapter 4, we shall see that Marx also associates the way in which abstract legal persons engage in acts of exchange governed by the abstract value of the things that are exchanged with merely contingent, external relations between persons.

right.¹² As we shall see, these moments concern a more adequate understanding of freedom and a correspondingly different type of relation between individuals. It is therefore to be expected that the relations that are constitutive of ethical life will be characterized by norms and values that are different in kind from those of abstract right. I shall now identify some ways in which Hegel seeks to limit private property in the face of the demands and values of other, higher moments of his system of right.¹³ In each case, the right to property is subject to restrictions but private property is not replaced by a different form of property. I shall nevertheless argue that Hegel's idea of ethical life implies the rational necessity of a different form of property.

3.5 The Integration of Private Property into Ethical Life

One example of a constraint on private property is encountered in Hegel's brief discussion of a right of necessity (*Notrecht*) in the section on morality. The right to property is here overridden by the right to be a person in a specific situation. Whenever an individual's life is genuinely at risk, the violation of another person's property rights can be justified by the necessity of preserving it, for there is a radical choice between suffering the 'infinite injury' of no longer being a rights-bearing person and acting in a way that violates only a single right of another person, thereby leaving intact the rights-bearing status of this person (PR § 127).

---

[12] The claim that this right must be accommodated within Hegel's system of right is different from the claim that a proper understanding of Hegel's argument for private property requires looking at the place of this form of property within this system, as argued in Duncan, 'Hegel on Private Property'. As we have seen, Hegel's full argument for private property is already found at the stage of abstract right. Duncan argues that the role of private property in civil society is of key importance because of how it is the source of benefits whose value derives from how they promote freedom. Yet Hegel's account of civil society presupposes the rightful nature of private property, even if civil society provides the social context within which the right to property is exercised in ways that are beneficial to those who enjoy it and to society.

[13] I shall ignore the status of private property in times of war. Hegel clearly thinks that the government has the right to do all that it judges to be necessary to protect the political independence of the state in the face of the actual or merely perceived military threat posed to it by other states and that its citizens may be required to sacrifice their property for the sake of this greater good (PR §§ 323–24). Although Hegel suggests that war and the sacrifices that it demands are an expression of the subordination of one moment of the concept of right (that is, abstract right) to another, higher one (that is, the state), and that this subordination of one moment of the concept of right to another one reflects some kind of metaphysical truth ('[i]t is *necessary* that the finite – such as property and life – should be *posited* as contingent, because contingency is the concept of the finite' [PR § 324R]), war concerns external relations between different states that, to varying degrees, embody the concept of ethical life. It does not, therefore, promise to tell us anything about the status of private property *within* the normative framework of a single state that successfully instantiates the concept of ethical life.

3.5 The Integration of Private Property into Ethical Life

From this distinction between the complete loss of the capacity for rights and the violation of a single right, Hegel derives a specific right that represents an application of the right of necessity. The object of this right is 'the benefit of competence, whereby a debtor is permitted to retain his tools, agricultural implements, clothes, and in general as much of his resources – i.e. of the property of his creditors – as is deemed necessary to support him, even in his accustomed station in society' (PR § 127R). This specific right shows that a right of necessity exists not only when a person's life is directly and immediately threatened but also when it is indirectly threatened, as when someone would be unable to perform the activity that is his or her livelihood if he or she were deprived of the means of doing so. We are here reminded of Fichte's argument that the right to property must be compatible with the demand that individuals are able to live from their labour. Unlike Fichte, however, Hegel does not extend this demand to property rights more generally. Although the right of necessity may justify occasional violations of the right to property in exceptional circumstances, it does not suspend this right completely. Appeals to a right of necessity cannot, therefore, become so frequent and widespread that a right of this kind becomes the rule instead of an exception to the rule. As we shall shortly see, Hegel attempts to explain how the welfare of individuals is guaranteed within ethical life in such a way that the right of necessity would remain an exception that does not threaten the right to property understood in terms of private property.

Another constraint on private property emerges in the first stage of ethical life, which is the family. The constraint is not this time justified in terms of exceptional circumstances. Rather, the right to property does not apply to this sphere of ethical life in so far as the distinctive ethical attitude (*Gesinnung*) and type of ethical relationship that characterize the family are concerned. The ethical attitude has its source in an emotion, namely love, while the ethical relationship that exists between the members of the family concerns how within the family 'one is present ... not as an independent person but as a *member*' (PR § 158). The family can then be seen to exhibit two essential characteristics that are absent at the stage of abstract right. First, its members relate to one another in a way that is not based on their arbitrary wills, for they do not *choose* to love one another. Second, it is not a relationship between persons who recognize one another as abstract legal subjects with the relevant capacities and rights, but who otherwise remain indifferent to one another.[14] The relevant type of relationship is instead rooted in the emotional lives of the members of the family in such a way that they relate to one another as concrete individuals, each of whom values the others because of their specific characters and other features. Abstract right, in contrast, requires conceiving of oneself and others in such a way as to abstract from those features that distinguish individuals from one another.

The legal recognition associated with abstract right and private property begins to apply to the family only with its dissolution (*Auflösung*), which occurs as a result of divorce or death (PR § 159), and when the children have been raised and educated to become self-sufficient persons, at which point they 'are recognized as legal persons and as capable both of holding free property [*freies Eigentum*] of their own and of founding their own families' (PR § 177). This claim shows how it is only outside the family that recognition of oneself as a person is achieved through the ownership and alienation of property. Within the family itself, the appropriate form of property is 'common property' (*gemeinsames Eigentum*), where 'no member of the family has particular property, although each has a right to what is held in common' (PR § 171). This property is to be administered in accordance with the needs and ends of the family. Hegel grants effective control over this common property to the husband and father, who acts as the family's representative in civil society, in which the family possesses the legal status of a person. The demand to dispose of the family's property with a view to the needs and interests of its members limits the right to property, whereas the only constraints on the right to dispose freely of property at the stage of abstract right derive from the nature of personality and the rights that follow from it, which neither the right to property itself nor the exercise of this right may violate.

Leaving aside Hegel's account of who exercises control over the family's common property, his recognition of this form of property commits him to the claim that the right to property enjoyed by the person of abstract right must be supplemented by another form of property within the framework of ethical life because this form of property is a more adequate

---

[14] The founding act of the modern family, namely the marriage ceremony, involves an act of consent by means of which each of the marriage partners freely surrenders his or her independence as a person (PR § 164, § 168). Although the moment of consent makes this act appear similar in kind to a contract, the consent this time establishes an ethical bond that is different from the common will established by means of a contract: 'the precise nature of marriage is to begin from the point of view of contract – i.e. that of individual personality as a self-sufficient unit – *in order to supersede it*' (PR § 163R).

3.5 The Integration of Private Property into Ethical Life

expression of the relevant type of ethical attitude and relationship. Private property is nevertheless integrated into ethical life rather than completely suspended, for each family constitutes a legal entity with the status of a person, from which its right to the exclusive possession and use of its property and the right to dispose of it freely subject to the ethical norms of the family follow. In other words, the family's property is common property in so far as it remains *within* the family, whereas it is private property in relation to other legal entities that exist *outside* the family. Moreover, a key function of the modern family is to instil and to develop in children the ways of thinking and the capacities required of a legal person and independent social agent. In this respect, the modern family aims at its own dissolution. It can therefore be described as 'an *inherently dissolvable* community' (*eine*[*r*] *an sich auflösbare*[*n*] *Gemeinschaft*), if not one 'in which it is in itself a matter for the arbitrary will whether or not I retain my share in it' (PR § 46). Hegel is here describing a type of common property (*gemeinschaftliches Eigentum*) that is owned by separate individuals and can therefore acquire the exclusive form of private property (*Privateigentum*).

This brings me to the next sphere of ethical life, civil society, and to the question of how it accommodates abstract right and the right to property, not only by providing a legal and institutional framework within which rights are actualized but also by establishing in this way the conditions in which individuals can recognize one another as persons. In civil society, the individual is a 'concrete person who, as a *particular* person, as a totality of needs and a mixture of natural necessity and arbitrariness, is his own end'. This individual 'stands essentially in *relation* to other similar particulars', each of which 'asserts itself and gains satisfaction through the others'. Thus individuals relate to one another 'through the exclusive *mediation* of the form of *universality*' (PR § 182). From these statements taken from a single paragraph, we can identify the following defining features of civil society:

1. Individuals are viewed in terms of their specific needs and ends, whereas abstract right ignores such needs and ends and must ignore them if there are to be rights and legal norms that apply to all persons.
2. Individuals relate to one another in such a way that they come to satisfy their needs and achieve their ends through forms of social cooperation that arise from the condition of material interdependence in which they find themselves. This condition is the result of an increasingly diverse set of natural, artificial and social needs (PR §§ 190–94). It

is also the result of a growing division of labour aimed at producing the means of satisfying these needs more efficiently, and which makes individuals even more dependent on one another with respect to the satisfaction of their needs (PR § 198).

3. The relations of material and social interdependence that exist between individuals possess a universal dimension in the following ways: (i) in their attempts to obtain the means to satisfy their needs and those of their families, individuals unintentionally contribute to the satisfaction of the needs of others, and thus to their welfare, by producing and exchanging specific means of satisfying increasingly particularized needs; (ii) there arises a set of social norms, practices and ideas to which individuals feel themselves compelled to conform; and (iii) civil society is structured by laws and institutions that provide the kind of legal and social framework that makes effective agency possible within a condition of material and social interdependence.

Since the members of civil society are subject to the legal norms of abstract right, the right to property must be integrated into civil society. The integration of private property into this sphere of ethical life can be illustrated with reference to two passages from the *Elements of the Philosophy of Right*. Both passages are relevant to the claim that private property is necessary to maintain and to develop the self-conception and capacities associated with personality, which is integral to the embodiment interpretation of Hegel's argument for private property. This appeal to the development of the relevant self-conception and capacities is, however, misleading if it is identified as Hegel's justification of private property,[15] for the rational necessity of private property has been demonstrated at the stage of abstract right on other grounds. Hegel is nevertheless seeking to explain how the exercise of this right within the broader legal and social context of civil

---

[15] For criticisms of the argument that private property is a necessary condition of the development of the capacity for self-discipline, see Patten, *Hegel's Idea of Freedom*, 141f. This does not stop Patten endorsing a version of the embodiment interpretation even if he criticises this feature of Waldron's version of it, whereas Duncan criticizes the embodiment interpretation while endorsing a modified version of the argument that private property promotes self-discipline that focuses on civil society. See 'Hegel on Private Property', 279. This line of argument is susceptible to counterexamples that show that private property does not, in fact, necessarily foster self-discipline but, rather, tends to produce its opposite, such as the example of the reckless behaviour of investment bankers who acquire and dispose of items of private property in the form of shares on the financial markets in ways that contribute to the creation of economic crises, or the compulsion to buy things exhibited by some individuals in societies that are characterized by a rampant consumerism which threatens to destroy the conditions of human life itself.

3.5 *The Integration of Private Property into Ethical Life*

society can foster the development of the self-conception and capacities that define personality.

In connection with a person's relation to his or her own body, which we have seen Hegel assimilates to a property right, it is stated that 'it is only through the *development* of his own body and spirit, *essentially* by means of *his self-consciousness comprehending itself as free*, that he takes possession of himself and becomes his own property as distinct from that of others' (PR § 57). The language that Hegel uses in this passage suggests a process of self-development through which an individual becomes conscious of himself or herself as free. This process is identified with the act of taking possession of one's body and the act of exercising control over it. By means of this act of self-appropriation, the person, who is only implicitly or subjectively free, becomes objectively free in accordance with the concept of the 'free spirit', which 'consists precisely in not having its being as mere concept or *in itself* ... but in overcoming this formal phase of its being and hence also its immediate natural existence, and in giving itself an existence which is purely its own and free' (PR § 57R). This act of self-appropriation presupposes the ability to exercise rational control over one's body. It is therefore a matter of maintaining and developing the relevant self-conception and the capacities associated with it through such acts as training one's body with the aim of transforming it into 'spirit's willing organ and soul-inspired instrument' (PR § 48).

Hegel returns to the role of private property in maintaining and developing the self-conception and capacities associated with personality in connection with the type of education that individuals undergo in civil society. Individuals are constrained to produce things or to provide services with a view to the needs and opinions of others. This subjection to constraint develops in them the ability to exercise the self-control that is a condition of genuine autonomous agency, leading Hegel to speak of a form of 'liberation' (PR § 187R). Moreover, successful participation in civil society requires gaining the necessary forms of theoretical knowledge and developing practical skills as well as the appropriate attitudes (PR § 197). This is again a matter of maintaining and developing a self-conception and certain capacities, rather than coming to possess them, because for Hegel the family already performs the function of 'raising the children out of the natural immediacy in which they originally exist to self-sufficiency and freedom of personality' (PR § 175). Although the confirmation of oneself as person is more fully achieved in civil society, where individuals confront one another as the legal owners of property that they are entitled to dispose of freely, the disciplining effects of participation in a society in which goods and services are freely exchanged cannot be used to justify private property because this form of property is in fact presupposed.

The social context in which private property is embedded and the non-legal as well as legal norms that structure civil society restrict the exercise of the right to property, whether in relation to the exclusive right to the possession and use of things or in relation to the right to dispose freely of things by alienating them. Other constraints include how human relations are established by voluntary acts whose source is the arbitrary will or power of choice of others. In civil society, there is not only the exchange of products of labour but also the exchange of labour itself, for a person may treat his or her physical and mental powers as something external that he or she is entitled to dispose of freely. As with the exchange of products of labour, the exchange of physical and mental powers depends on whether others view these powers as an appropriate means of satisfying their own needs or achieving other ends and choose to pay for them. To this extent, the free disposal of one's property is constrained by the needs and intentions of others. This brings me to one way in which non-legal norms constrain a person's right to dispose freely of things to which he or she enjoys the legal right, namely, the moral demand to guarantee the welfare of individuals.

There is so far no guarantee that individuals will be able to satisfy their needs by exchanging their labour power or its products. Moreover, acts of production and exchange within the system of needs are governed by economic laws that operate independently of the wills of the agents who are subject to them, such as the law of supply and demand. Thus 'the satisfaction of both necessary and contingent needs is itself contingent' (PR § 185). This contingency can be removed by securing 'the livelihood and welfare of individuals' (PR § 230). Hegel identifies two institutions in connection with this goal. The first institution is the police, which not only guarantees public order and safety (PR §§ 231–34) but also deals with matters of common concern and utility such as the maintenance of infrastructure and regulation of the economy (PR §§ 235–36). The regulation of economic life may require imposing constraints on the free disposal of property, such as food standards and environmental regulations. Yet it does not extend to guaranteeing the right to live from one's labour as in Fichte's rational state. This is the task of the second institution, which is the corporation. A corporation is a trade or professional association whose character and functions are outlined in §§ 252–55 of the *Elements of the Philosophy of Right*. I shall now explain the relevance of this institution to Hegel's attempt to integrate private property into ethical life.

3.5 The Integration of Private Property into Ethical Life 117

An individual must demonstrate that he or she possesses the aptitudes and skills required by a specific trade or profession if he or she is to become a member of a corporation. In this way, something that a person has the right to alienate, namely, his or her labour and that which he or she produces by employing it, must meet socially recognized standards. Thus an individual who is acknowledged to possess the relevant aptitudes and skills achieves social recognition. This type of recognition differs from the legal recognition of abstract right, in that it concerns social characteristics and roles that distinguish one individual from another individual, if not from all other individuals. These characteristics and roles concern the specific type of productive activity that enables an individual to provide for himself or herself and his or her family. Moreover, the free disposal of one's property, in the form of the exchange of one's labour and its products, is no longer only a matter of individual choice, for it is now subject to the norms of the corporation.

The right to property understood in terms of private property remains, however, because 'the so-called *natural right* to practise one's skill and thereby earn what there is to earn is limited only to the extent that, in this context, the skill is rationally determined' (PR § 254). In other words, a person who is suitability qualified remains free not only to choose to become a member of a corporation but also to leave one that he or she has joined. This person is thereby able to demonstrate his or her right to dispose freely of something to which he or she already enjoys a right, though the costs of exercising this right may well prove costly. In this respect, a corporation can also be described as 'an *inherently dissolvable* community in which it is in itself a matter for the arbitrary will whether or not I retain my share in it' (PR § 46), for a person has the right to leave it and, we may assume, the accompanying right to withdraw from it those things of which he or she remains the legal owner, such as tools or capital. In this respect, the members of a corporation would be more like the shareholders of a company than the members of a commune, even if their property has an ethical meaning and value in so far as it contributes to the achievement of the ends of the corporation and these ends limit the rights of any individual who remains a member of a corporation.

The corporation provides its members with a secure livelihood and protects them and their families from such contingencies as the inability to work because of ill-health or a temporary lack of demand for their skills and the products of their labour. In this way, the corporation assumes 'the role of a *second* family for its members' (PR § 252), and 'particular welfare is present as a right and is actualized within this union' (PR § 255). Thus the constraints that membership of a corporation imposes on the right to dispose freely of one's property are offset by clear benefits. These benefits are likely to motivate the members of a corporation to remain part of it even though they enjoy the right to leave it and to take with them anything of which they remain the legal owner. This welfare function requires that certain resources be held in common and distributed according to need. This implies further constraints on the free disposal of property. The resources in question are nevertheless the private property of each corporation viewed as a legal entity. Moreover, in accordance with each member's right to leave a corporation and to take with him or her that of which he or she remains the legal owner, these resources can be thought to correspond to the type of common property owned by separate individuals that Hegel associates with 'an *inherently dissolvable* community'. Thus it remains predominantly a matter of constraints on private property, rather than the replacement of this form of property by another form of property.

This reflects how the ethical nature of the corporation's property is limited, both in the sense that it is founded on what individuals consider to be in their best interests and in the sense that it concerns the property of specific corporations whose interests cannot straightforwardly be identified with the interests of society as a whole. Indeed, Hegel will attempt to identify ways in which the interests of different corporations can be made to harmonize not only with one another but also with the interests of the state. Moreover, the corporation and its common, if ultimately private, property fulfil a significant ethical function in society. For the corporation fosters a common identity and a sense of solidarity among its members, so that they come to think of themselves as members of a greater whole and to develop an ethical disposition that prevents them from acting in arrogant and extravagant ways aimed at eliciting social recognition from others. In this respect, membership of a corporation places moral constraints on how much property and what kinds of property individuals ought to seek to possess and to accumulate. The members of a corporation will not, or so Hegel assumes, be disposed to acquire luxury items that are inappropriate to their station in life, either because acquiring such items would manifest the wrong type of attitude or because acquiring them would endanger their material security. Private property nevertheless retains its rights because individuals continue to enjoy not only the exclusive right to the possession and use of things that are appropriate to their station in life but also the right to dispose of them freely in so far as the exercise of this right is compatible with the effective performance of their trade or their professional activities and it is not detrimental to the reputation of the corporation to which they belong. Moreover, if an individual chooses to renounce his or her membership of a corporation, these moral constraints on the acquisition and disposal of property would cease to apply to him or her.

Hegel does not limit himself to showing how private property can be integrated into ethical life by subjecting it to moral and social constraints as well as legal ones. He also identifies ways in which private property may restrict the freedom of those individuals who do not benefit from the existence and protection of private property because of contingent circumstances. From the fact that individuals must demonstrate that they possess the aptitudes and skills required to become a member of a corporation, it follows that anyone who cannot satisfy this demand will be denied the benefits that membership of a corporation brings. A person in this position is then unlikely to develop the relevant type of ethical disposition. Hegel himself acknowledges that there are such people, who belong to one of the following social groups.

There is the social group comprised of those individuals who have only their labour to exchange and this labour, by virtue of its general and unskilled character, does not entitle them to be members of a corporation. Hegel accordingly distinguishes between the tradesman who 'is a member of an association not for occasional contingent gain, but for the *whole* range and universality of his particular livelihood' and the day labourer whose livelihood is subject to contingency because the sale of his labour remains irregular and uncertain (PR § 252R). The day labourer's livelihood depends on whether others happen to recognize the value and utility of his or her labour, have the desire to purchase it and possess the means to purchase it in the form of money. As we have seen, this element of contingency is reduced, if not altogether eliminated, by membership of a corporation. Yet it is precisely the possibility of becoming a member of a corporation that is denied to those individuals who cannot demonstrate possession of the relevant aptitudes and skills.

The contingency in question can be explained in terms of how '[t]he *possibility of sharing* in the universal resources' of a society is '*conditional* upon one's own immediate basic assets (i.e. capital) … and upon one's skill', which are in turn subject to 'contingent circumstances whose variety gives rise to *differences* in the *development* of natural physical and mental aptitudes which are already unequal in themselves' (PR § 200). In other words, the failure to develop the necessary aptitudes can be explained in terms of lack of access to the resources required to develop them or in terms of other circumstances, such as poor health. This shows that Hegel accepts that natural, economic or social factors for which individuals cannot reasonably be held responsible tend either to produce outcomes that do not accurately reflect natural inequalities, in that someone who possesses a natural talent or aptitude is unable to make effective use of it, or to amplify the effects of such inequalities. Society itself, through its protection of property rights, not only limits the possibilities available to individuals who find themselves in this situation but also deprives them of access to resources that are the property of other individuals. Thus these individuals 'are more or less deprived of all the advantages of society, such as the ability to acquire skills and education in general, as well as of the administration of justice, health care, and often even of the consolation of religion' (PR § 241).

The contingency to which the livelihood of the day labourer is subject means that he is in constant risk of falling into the second social group, which Hegel terms 'the rabble'. A rabble develops when poverty leads to the loss of 'that feeling of right, integrity, and honour which comes from supporting oneself by one's own activity and work' (PR § 244).[16] Within the corporation, in contrast, 'the help which poverty receives loses its contingent and unjustly humiliating character' (PR § 253R). Even if the right of necessity identified earlier suggests that some action on the part of the state aimed at alleviating the suffering of this social group is demanded, it will concern only strict necessity. This suggests that state intervention will be limited to the provision of the means of subsistence. Yet civil society generates needs that extend beyond basic material ones. These needs can generally be satisfied only by exchanging private property in the form of money. The members of the social group in question are therefore still likely to suffer from a sense of '*dependence* and *want*' and 'an inability to feel and enjoy the wider freedoms, and particularly the spiritual advantages, of civil society' (PR § 243). Their extremely limited property rights, which are reducible to their own labour power and some personal belongings, will not sufficiently compensate their obligation to respect the property rights of others. Instead, they will be disposed to view the private property of others as a constraint on their own freedom that appears 'absolutely unyielding' (PR § 195).

It is therefore not the case that Hegel fails to acknowledge the freedom-endangering consequences of private property. He is nevertheless reluctant

---

[16] This type of disposition is not restricted to those without much property. Hegel speaks of a rich rabble because a rabble mentality can be produced by the possession of too much wealth and thus too much private property. This rabble mentality arises because people tend to come to believe that they are independent of society when their wealth enables them to buy almost anything, including social recognition (PR 1819/20, 196).

to endorse state intervention as the means of guaranteeing the freedom and welfare of all citizens. This reluctance may in part be explained in terms of the undesirable effects that he thinks would result from such intervention, including the creation of a culture of dependency in which 'the livelihood of the needy would be ensured without the mediation of work … contrary to the principle of civil society and the feeling of self-sufficiency and honour among its individual members' (PR § 245).[17] Yet this attitude towards state intervention also reflects the extent to which Hegel is committed to the idea that private property must retain its rights within civil society. Moreover, we have seen that although Hegel suggests that forms of common ownership are appropriate to the family and the corporation, in both cases the common property is ultimately a type of private property. Thus private property remains the dominant form of property in modern ethical life. In his account of the political state, however, Hegel is willing to suspend the right to property in so far as it consists in a person's right to dispose freely of a thing that he or she legally owns. This suspension of a defining feature of private property is justified in terms of the need for political stability and the need for society to be governed by appropriate laws. In the next section, I shall identify the grounds of this constraint on the right to property.

3.6 Inalienable Property

It is by voluntarily alienating things that one person demonstrates to another person his or her independence of any single thing or set of things. Yet already in the section on property in the *Elements of the Philosophy of Right*, Hegel signals that a suspension of the right to dispose of one's property freely can be justified in terms of the demands of a higher sphere of right, especially the state. In this connection, he mentions one institution that he associates with the state, namely landed property. Hegel makes clear that this institution is not fully compatible with private property: '*Entailed family property* [*Familienfideikommissarisches Eigentum*] contains

---

[17] Hegel considers solutions to the problem of poverty other than charity and welfare provision administered by the state. The last solution that he proposes is state-directed colonization. His presentation of this solution in one of his lectures implies that private property must be respected and that the ultimate solution to its undesirable social effects is to increase the opportunity to acquire property by means of colonization. For he claims that the establishment of colonies would enable those individuals who are currently the victims of poverty to obtain some property (PR 1819/20, 198). For the argument that this solution is problematic because it is incompatible with the type of freedom that is meant to characterize ethical life, see James, *Practical Necessity, Freedom, and History*, 140ff.

a moment which is opposed to the right of personality and hence of private property' (PR § 46R). What justifies this partial suspension of the rights of private property?

Hegel's justification of the suspension of the legal owner's right to dispose freely of land concerns the role of the legislative power (*die gesetzgebende Gewalt*). The decisions of this institution whose task is to make laws and modify existing legislation are subject to the monarch's approval. The monarch's decisions are in turn based on the expert advice provided by high-ranking civil servants who form part of the executive power. The legislative power itself consists of two 'estates' that perform a mediating function in that they 'stand between the government at large on the one hand and the people in their division into particular spheres and individuals on the other' (PR § 302). To perform this mediating function effectively, the estates must reflect the division of society into distinct groups whose members have common interests and a common identity rooted in a shared way of life.

There are two such estates: the agricultural estate, whose 'substantial disposition in general is that of an immediate ethical life based on the family relationship and on trust' (PR § 203), and the estate of trade and industry, which is comprised of individuals involved in such activities as manufacture and commerce (PR § 204). A third estate, the 'universal' estate, consists of the members of the state bureaucracy (PR § 205). Since it is part of the government, this estate belongs to one of the terms that requires mediation. It cannot, therefore, form part of the mediating institution that unites the sphere of government and the sphere of civil society. This mediating institution is instead made up of members of the landed nobility, who are entitled by birth to belong to it and therefore do not need to be elected, and deputies elected by the social groupings of civil society, including the corporation (PR §§ 307–08). Yet these two estates are not of equal importance with respect to the mediating function performed by the legislative power.

The estate of 'natural ethical life', whose 'basis is the life of the family and, as far as its livelihood is concerned, landed property [*Grundbesitz*]', is, Hegel claims, better suited to perform this mediating function because it stands closer to the monarch, who embodies the moment of sovereignty. This closeness to the monarch is explained in terms of how this estate 'shares that independent volition and natural determination which is also contained in the moment of sovereignty' (PR § 305). In other words, like the monarch whose final decisions are not subject to any higher authority, the members of the estate of natural ethical life possess an independence that the members of the estate of trade and industry lack because of how they are subject to the dynamic, shifting relations of material and social interdependence that characterize civil society and make it inherently unstable. Hence Hegel's reference to 'the *changing* element in *civil* society' (PR § 308). The greater independence enjoyed by the members of the estate of natural ethical life derives from how they are 'equally independent of the resources of the state and of the uncertainty of trade, the quest for profit, and all variations in property' (PR § 306). The ultimate source of this greater independence is nature, not only viewed as that which is the basis of a more predictable and stable livelihood but also in the sense that the ownership of land is determined by the natural event of being born the eldest son of someone who is already the legal owner of the land. This corresponds to how the monarch's status and independence are determined by birth. Thus, if they are to retain their independence, the members of this estate cannot 'have the same right as other citizens either to dispose freely of their entire property or to know that it will pass on to their children in proportion to the equal degree of love that they feel for them'. Instead, 'their resources become *inalienable inherited property*, burdened with primogeniture' (*ein unveräußerliches, mit dem Majorate belastetes Erbgut*) (PR § 306).

The independence that the members of the estate of natural ethical life enjoy cannot be directly identified with independence from the freedom of choice of others. Rather, the basis of this independence is a secure form of property that is not subject to market and social forces whose existence and operation depend on choices that find expression in voluntary acts of exchange regulated by contracts. Thus the disadvantage of not having the right to dispose freely of one's property is outweighed by the benefits of secure access to resources that ensures that the owner of these resources is not obliged or forced to act contrary to his own views and to adapt them to the interests of others. He may instead judge and act in a genuinely independent and impartial manner. This is not to say that the members of the landed nobility will not be legal persons with the right to dispose freely of their property in other ways. They may, for example, engage in commercial activities that involve the exchange of the products of the land that they have inherited.[18]

---

[18] Hegel draws attention to how feudal arrangements have been superseded by modern developments when he mentions how the increasing mechanization of agriculture has resulted in farming becoming more factory-like, thereby reducing the differences between the two estates (PR § 203A). We may also assume that practices such as the inheritance of feudal subjects as well as estates, as if persons were items of property, are forbidden by how abstract right is an integral element of the modern form of ethical life.

From the fact that the members of the landed nobility are more like the monarch with respect to the type of independence that they enjoy and because nature is the ultimate source of this independence, it does not follow that the landed nobility is better suited to perform the mediating political function that Hegel assigns to it. On the contrary, it can be argued that the landed nobility is less suited to perform this function precisely because of its closeness to the monarch. For this closeness is liable to generate shared interests that the landed nobility and the monarch will seek to pursue in opposition to the interests of the estate of trade and industry. Despite such issues, the political function performed by the landed nobility entails a restriction on a person's right to dispose freely of any property of which he or she is the legal owner that is greater than the ones that we have previously encountered. This shows Hegel's willingness to suspend this right for the sake of political stability.

Private property still exists, however, in that the members of the landed nobility continue to enjoy an exclusive right to the possession and use of their land. Moreover, the restriction on the right to dispose freely of their property concerns only certain things, namely land and the estate connected with it, including such things as buildings and farming equipment. Thus, although the independence enjoyed by the landed nobility requires limiting a right that is a presupposition of contractual relations, this suspension of an integral feature of private property does not prevent the members of the landed nobility from being persons and being recognized as such by others through the free disposal of items of property other than those things to which their wills remain bound as the price of their social and political independence.

The inalienability of land and the estate connected with it nevertheless represents a significant constraint on the right to property when viewed from the standpoint of modern private property. This invites the question as to whether Hegel in any way commits himself to limiting private property more radically by showing that a different form of property is more appropriate to ethical life. In the next section, I shall argue that there are grounds for regarding a type of common or collective property as more appropriate than private property because it is more expressive of the idea of ethical life. Although this opens the way for a pluralist theory of property rights, it presents a significant challenge to Hegel's claim that increasing general recognition of private property is a sign of historical progress measured in terms of the consciousness of the concept of freedom and how this concept exists in the form of right.

3.7 Ethical Property

In the remark to § 64 of the *Elements of the Philosophy of Right*, Hegel speaks of 'national property' (*Nationaleigentum*), and he mentions public memorials and works of art as examples of such property. Hegel acknowledges that this type of property can satisfy the condition of 'the subjective presence of the will', in the absence of which the form given to an object or the sign that designates it as a person's property become 'mere externals' (PR § 64). In this respect, national property satisfies the 'embodiment' condition that is considered to be central to Hegel's argument for private property. This time, however, it is a *collective* embodiment of the will. Moreover, Hegel implies that the initial act of embodiment is not sufficient, for the will of the nation must *continue* to express itself in a thing. The continuing subjective presence of the will in a thing can be taken to mean that those individuals whose wills form a collective will continue to invest the thing with a cultural, ethical or political significance, and thereby still identify themselves with it. This significance with which a thing is invested implies the transcendence of the personal beliefs and values of individuals.

The genuine embodiment of a collective will in items of national property explains how they are objects of the will whose 'indwelling soul of remembrance and honour ... gives them their validity as living and self-sufficient ends' (PR § 64R). The description of items of national property as 'self-sufficient ends' indicates that they have value in themselves, as opposed to a value that derives only from their usefulness in relation to ends that remain external to them. National property has this value because it is expressive of the fundamental beliefs, memories, sentiments and values of a nation, which find expression in this form of property in such a way that what is expressed and that in which it finds expression are so intimately bound up with each other that they cannot be separated except in thought. If an item of national property continues to perform this expressive function, then it ought to remain the property of the nation for which it performs this function, and of which it thereby forms an integral part. The fact that an item of national property continues to perform this expressive function will be demonstrated by the nation's attitude towards it, as when it demands the careful preservation of a founding document or a monument of historical significance to it.

In the course of time, however, items of national property may cease to perform this expressive function. They then become purely external things. The fact that the collective will of a nation has withdrawn itself from the object is shown by how this object is neglected or how it is preserved merely as a matter of habit rather than from a genuine sense of devotion or reverence. The now purely external object may then become the exclusive property of a person who values it on other grounds, such as for its aesthetic or commercial value: 'if this soul abandons them, they are then in this respect ownerless as far as the nation is concerned and become contingent private possessions, as, for example, the Greek and Egyptian works of art in Turkey' (PR § 64R). Yet so long as a collective emotional and psychological attachment to and identification with an object persists, this object ought not to be treated as a thing to which any private person is entitled to establish a legal claim.

Although the subjective presence of the collective will of a particular nation in a specific item of national property is liable to become less powerful and less evident in the course of time because of changes in the nation's core beliefs and values, the concept of national property as such retains its validity. In this section, I shall argue that objects other than national monuments and works of art can satisfy the conditions that Hegel identifies in connection with the concept of national property. The objects are this time institutions that are the source of a public good or secure a public good and that in some cases may themselves be classed as public goods. Although an object of this kind may not be as easily identifiable as an artefact or a building, there is a sense in which it is a distinct entity. It is an entity made up of specific roles and specific relations between the individuals who occupy these roles. The roles and relations are shaped by the norms, goals and values of the institution, and they are accompanied by forms of authority and obligation. An institution may also be defined in terms of specific types of buildings and equipment. Moreover, individuals may experience specific sentiments, including a sense of national pride or unity, in relation to the relevant type of institution. By showing how such institutions can be thought to exemplify a form of property that resembles national property, I intend to demonstrate that a common or collective form of property is, in fact, more compatible with the idea of ethical life than private property. I shall therefore begin with Hegel's idea of ethical life.

Hegel defines ethical life in the following way:

> Ethical life is the *Idea of freedom* as the living good which has its knowledge and volition in self-consciousness, and its actuality through self-conscious action. Similarly, it is in ethical being that self-consciousness has its motivating end and a foundation which has being in and for itself. Ethical life is accordingly the *concept of freedom which has become the existing world and the nature of self-consciousness*. (PR § 142)

From this description of ethical life, three essential features of it emerge.

First, there is a subjective element. This element concerns the way in which ethical life requires knowledge of it and the disposition to will it on the part of individuals because it can become actual and 'living' only by means of the conscious goal-directed activity of individuals and the social groups to which they belong. Second, the object of knowledge and volition is ethical life in the form of institutions that are conditions of the existence of freedom. These institutions are the sources of norms that identify what individuals ought to do independently of whatever they happen to desire to do at any given time (PR §§ 144–45). In other words, ethical life is the source of an individual's duties (PR § 148). At the same time, the effective functioning of these institutions requires that individuals, if not any particular individual, act in accordance with the relevant norms. Third, there is the unity of the subjective moment and the objective moment of ethical life.

This unity of the subjective and objective moments of ethical life is achieved when each participant in ethical life performs his or her duties with the appropriate ethical attitude because he or she genuinely identifies himself or herself with the institutions of ethical life, which are thereby 'not something *alien* to the subject', but something to which 'the subject bears *spiritual witness* … as to *its own essence*, in which it has its *self-awareness* and lives as in its element which is not distinct from itself' (PR § 147). Individuals would otherwise obey the norms of ethical life in a mechanical fashion that is incompatible with the idea of ethical life as a 'living good'. Thus, although an individual's given desires may not conform to the demands of ethical life, which is precisely why the relation between the subjective moment and the objective moment of ethical life expresses itself in the form of an obligation, a genuinely successful instantiation of the concept of ethical life requires sufficient alignment between the desires of individuals and the norms of ethical life. It is this unity of the subjective moment and the objective moment of ethical life, rather than factors such as race or a specific culture, that binds individuals together so that they form a people in a normative, as opposed to a merely descriptive, sense (PR § 156).

The features of ethical life identified above taken together indicate a different conception of freedom to the one associated with abstract right. For there is a stronger identification with the norms to which one is subject combined with an awareness of how these norms, and thus the institutions from which they derive, unify and sustain the society of which one is a member. These norms and institutions are therefore not merely external, if necessary, limits on the exercise of freedom of choice that structure the relations between legal persons who may otherwise remain completely indifferent to one another. Instead, there is a harmony between the individual and 'universality' in the form of the general norms that govern the relations between the members of the same society and unify them into a single whole. Individuals encounter themselves in the norms to which they are subject in part because they themselves, in cooperation with others, reproduce the institutions that are the sources of these norms by fulfilling their duties for the right reasons. This identification with institutions and the norms to which they give rise is possible, however, only because these institutions and norms are expressive of what the individuals who are subject to them essentially are and take themselves to be, that is, free and rational agents who depend on one another. Thus, although 'the ethical substance and its laws and powers' possess an 'absolute authority' (PR § 146), there is an identification with them that can be explained in terms of how the institutions of modern ethical life are recognized to be conditions of free agency, both one's own and that of other members of society. This helps to explain Hegel's claim that 'the individual liberates himself so as to attain substantial freedom' (PR § 149).

From this, it follows that a genuinely 'ethical' institution must somehow instantiate the following three moments of the concept of ethical life:

1. The subjective moment which concerns the knowledge and volition required of an agent who actualizes an institution, in the sense of ensuring that it functions effectively and maintains itself over time, and who thereby plays a role in the actualization of the concept of ethical life within the society of which he or she is a member.
2. The objective moment which concerns how the same institution is the source of ethical demands on the agents who contribute to its effective functioning and thus to the actualization of the concept of ethical life. Acting in conformity with these demands is, in fact, required to ensure the effective functioning of the relevant institution and the maintenance of it.
3. The unity of the subjective moment and the objective moment of ethical life which is explained in terms of how an agent genuinely identifies himself or herself with the institutions that form the object of his or her knowledge and willing and are the sources of his or her ethical duties. This identification with institutions disposes individuals to act in ways that facilitate the effective functioning and maintenance of these institutions. This requires acting in conformity with institutional norms and the ends embodied in institutions. This unity of the subjective and the objective moments of ethical life is therefore essential to the actualization of the concept of ethical life.

Consequently, any form of property that instantiated all three moments of the concept of ethical life would be 'ethical' in the full Hegelian sense of the term. Is it possible to identify a form of property that does so, but is different from private property and closer in kind to national property? As we have seen, even the 'common' property of the family and the corporation must ultimately be viewed as private property. The entailed property of the landed nobility is also private property, albeit subject to a constraint that distinguishes it from private property in the full modern sense. Before seeking to answer the question posed above, two points should be emphasized.

The first point is that Hegel states that the subjective presence of the will may take the form of the 'use, employment, *or some other expression of the will*' (PR § 64; my emphasis). This shows that he does not limit the subjective presence of the will in a thing to such obvious examples as the actual use of a thing, either as an object of consumption or as an instrument employed in relation to an end. What matters is only that there is a meaningful way in which the will of an agent can be said to express itself in the object. As Hegel's remarks on national property show, this may include investing an object with a meaning and value whose ultimate source is a deep-seated collective human need, as when the members of a nation are motivated to preserve and to respect an object because they consider it to be expressive of a common identity and history that binds them together.

The second point concerns the question of who, if anyone, owns institutions and items of infrastructure. Does the monarch own them, given that Hegel endorses the idea of a constitutional monarchy? Or does the state own them? Hegel mentions public poorhouses, hospitals and streetlighting (PR § 242R). These examples indicate his acceptance of the need for at least some state-owned property, as does the distinction that he draws between what individuals can hope to achieve and what society can achieve in a 'universal' manner found in the same remark. To this extent, Hegel already adopts a pluralist model of property, though the role of forms of property other than private property so far looks minimal and peripheral to his account of property.

The following question then arises: why not regard the institutions of the state and items of infrastructure as a form of 'ethical' property, in the sense that they belong to the whole people in such a way that the essential moments of the concept of ethical life are all present? Rather than being the owner of public goods, the state itself would then be reduced to the administrator and protector of such goods in the name of their real owner, the people, whose unity is established and maintained through the participation of individuals in the reproduction of the 'living' whole of a common ethical life. The reproduction of ethical life will require direct participation in institutions, or at least an endorsement of them that finds expression in practices that contribute to their functioning and maintenance, such as the paying of taxes. Moreover, individuals must act with the appropriate ethical disposition. This disposition is characterized by a sense of commitment and responsibility accompanied by a concern for the common good.

The state would be responsible for deciding such matters as the most effective use of the available resources, how certain functions within an institution are to be performed and by whom, how the relations between individuals within an institution are to be structured and what equipment and resources are still needed or are no longer necessary. The state may decide such matters directly, or it may delegate the decisions to others whom it considers sufficiently qualified to make them. The state will nevertheless be constrained by the views of its citizens concerning the importance of an institution, as reflected in their attitudes towards it. For example, although the state may enjoy the right to purchase land and equipment, and even to sell it, it ought to do so with a view to ensuring the effective functioning of an institution and the achievement of the common good that is the fundamental goal of this institution. Although the state may then need to be the legal owner of buildings, pieces of land and items of equipment,[19] it would not be entitled, in an ethical sense, to treat them as commodities that it may exchange with a view to making a profit that can subsequently be distributed among a particular social group, such as wealthy people whose tax burden is reduced. Moreover, although it is possible for ethical property to become private property, I shall shortly argue that this change in status would, in fact, reflect the dissolution of ethical life itself.

Hegel does not directly endorse this view of the status of institutions and items of infrastructure. Nevertheless, he himself objects to certain ways in which elements of the state can be treated as private property, as when he claims that 'the functions and powers of the state cannot be *private property*' (PR § 277), whereas certain offices have been, and continue to be, bought and sold in some countries (PR § 277A). Statements of this kind imply that there are limits to the extent to which the rights associated

---

[19] In contrast, the state would not need to be the legal owner of things such as buildings, pieces of land or items of equipment in relation to its own people, even if it must enjoy this status in relation to companies, individuals or other states with which it enters into commercial or other legally binding agreements. This would be especially true of a state that successfully embodies the concept of ethical life, in which the levels of trust that exist between the citizens and the state may be assumed to be sufficiently high that one party would not need to assert its authority and rights in relation to the other party, unlike at the stage of abstract right and at the stage of civil society in so far as it is structured by the legal norms of this form of right.

with private property are appropriate to ethical life. Yet Hegel's remarks on common property suggest that the ethical form of property identified above would be incompatible with the demands of reason:

> The idea of a pious or friendly or even compulsory brotherhood of men with *a community of goods* [*Gemeinschaft der Güter*] and a ban on the principle of private property may easily suggest itself to that disposition which misjudges the nature of the freedom of spirit and right and does not comprehend it in its determinate moments. (PR § 46R; translation modified)

Despite such claims, I intend to argue that forms of common or collective property to which no single person or other legal entity enjoys the exclusive, unlimited rights of possession and use accompanied by the right to dispose freely of items of property are compatible with the idea of the subjective presence of the will in a thing. Moreover, such forms of property are compatible with this idea in a way that can explain the presence of all the essential moments of ethical life. I shall develop this argument in connection with institutions and infrastructure that provide citizens with benefits that not only concern generally recognized human needs but also require that citizens directly or indirectly contribute to the maintenance and effective functioning of these institutions and this infrastructure, examples of which may include a publicly owned and funded health or transport system.

The availability of resources and access to them are here based on either the collective interests of society as a whole or interests that are common to all members of society. For example, there is the collective interest in having healthy and contented citizens who, through their close identification with the social and political whole of which they are members, are sufficiently motivated to will its existence and flourishing even when this involves significant costs to themselves. There is also each individual's interest in having secure access to resources and services that satisfy needs that are either natural ones (for example, good health) or a result of the way in which society is organized and how it functions (for example, being able to get easily from one part of a city to another one). This shows how collective interests and common interests may overlap and demand the same mode of allocation and corresponding form of property. As we shall see, this does not mean that the value of the relevant type of property is reducible to how it serves as a means of satisfying society's needs and the material and social needs of individuals. Rather, like national property, this property also possesses a symbolic value that consists in how it expresses and embodies an idea of solidarity and unity which cannot be reduced to a matter of mutual interest. Let us now turn to how all the essential moments of ethical life are present.

The subjective presence of the will in a thing can be thought to exist in the following way. Individuals tend to identify themselves with an institution or a public good when it provides them with tangible benefits that they believe would not be available to them, or not available to them to the same extent, if different arrangements were in place. The level of identification may nevertheless be even stronger than this, in that an institution or public good is invested with a symbolic meaning and value. This has partly to do with how the institution or public good contributes to the citizens' welfare. Yet it may also have to do with how an institution or public good is expressive of commonly held attitudes and values that imply a transcendence of the standpoint of self-interest and mutual advantage. The object of these attitudes and values may include the idea of social solidarity. The attitudes and values may then manifest themselves in an interest in the well-being of others as well as one's own well-being, while this sense of social solidarity finds concrete expression in a common endeavour to secure the institutional conditions of the welfare of all citizens, even if it means forgoing certain advantages or benefits that one might have otherwise enjoyed.

This is consistent with Hegel's characterization of the individual's relation to the state, for he describes this relation as one in which '[u]nion as such is itself the true content and end', and he claims that 'the destiny of individuals is to lead a universal life' (PR § 258R). The state is here regarded as an object of the will in such a way that what unites its citizens is not mutual advantage alone. Rather, political union possesses a significance and value of its own. This significance and value derive from how political union is expressive of a genuinely 'universal life'. A flourishing form of ethical life will therefore require a concrete expression of the idea that 'union as such' is 'the true content and end'. Direct or indirect participation in institutions may satisfy this demand, in that the act of making union as such the object of one's willing could then be identified with the willingness to contribute to the effective functioning and maintenance of an institution and acting with a sense of commitment and integrity in relation to it. This type of attitude is more likely to be encountered when individuals genuinely identify themselves with an institution, not only because it serves their own interests but also because of the symbolic meaning and value that they and their fellow citizens invest it with. The subjective and the objective moments of ethical life would then be present and unified.

The subjective moment, which concerns an agent's knowledge and willing, would be present not only in the form of each citizen's consciousness of the benefits that an institution provides, his or her knowledge of how it produces these benefits and what is required to produce them, but also in the form of the willingness either to participate directly in this institution or to bear indirectly the costs associated with the effective functioning and maintenance of it, such as through the payment of taxes. Although this willingness is partly to be explained in terms of self-interest, it can also be explained in terms of the higher meaning and value that citizens attach to an institution that embodies a public good.

The objective moment, which concerns the way in which the institutions of ethical life are the source of certain duties, would be present because institutions that embody or serve a public good are not only independent of the contingent desires and opinions of individuals but also expressive of shared concerns and values. In this way, an institution that embodies or serves a public good may symbolize a form of association in which 'union as such' has become an end, if not the only end. There are consequently grounds for claiming that a common or collective form of property is more compatible with the idea of ethical life, and thus more 'ethical' in Hegel's sense of the term, than private property. The relevant form of property can therefore be called ethical property.

Common or collective property is incompatible with private property because no single person or other legal entity has the right to the exclusive, unlimited possession and use of a thing accompanied by the right to dispose freely of this thing without considering the needs and views of others. As we have seen, the second right is integral to Hegel's argument for private property because it is only by exercising the right in question that individuals can conclusively demonstrate to one another that they are persons and ought to be treated as such. This invites the question as to whether Hegel's theory of ethical life is compatible with a pluralist model that relegates private property to only one form of property whose rational necessity is demonstrated by his science of right.

A model of this kind is compatible with how the rational necessity of private property is established at the stage of abstract right rather than at the stage of ethical life. There is, moreover, a sense in which individuals can withdraw their wills from items of ethical property and thereby demonstrate their independence of them. For they may signal to others that they no longer identify themselves with an institution and thus now regard it as something purely external to themselves. Examples of how this lack of identification might manifest itself include expressing opposition to how the taxes that one pays are being used to fund an institution that one no longer considers to be an effective provider of the relevant public good and a careless or indifferent attitude when performing a role within an institution. Although this possibility of withdrawing one's will from ethical property threatens to reduce the unity of the subjective and the objective moments of ethical life to a matter of what individuals happen to believe and desire at any given time, Hegel acknowledges that individuals can cease to identify themselves with the institutions of ethical life on objective grounds. This lack of identification may then find expression in such attitudes as the longing for a better constitution even before a sense of alienation and the attitudes in which it finds expression have become more widespread. He cites Socrates as an example of this phenomenon (PR § 274A).

If certain attitudes and actions can be viewed as symptoms of a lack of genuine identification with an institution and there are objective grounds for this alienation, then the subjective *absence* of the will in an object of the relevant kind would be evidence of a *failed* form of ethical life. Conversely, widespread identification with the institutions of ethical life or, more minimally, the inability to provide objective grounds for not identifying oneself with them will be evidence of a successful instantiation of the concept of ethical life. The absence of any genuine identification with an institution that was previously invested with significance and value by a collective will would correspond to how the soul may 'abandon' items of national property, leaving them 'in this respect ownerless as far as the nation is concerned', and thus as things that may become private property (PR § 64R). Even in the case of ethical property, then, it is possible to speak of 'an *inherently dissolvable* community' (PR § 46). Yet there is a fundamental difference between the dissolution that this form of property may undergo and the dissolution that the 'common' property of the family and the corporation may undergo.

The common property of the family and the corporation can be viewed as an aggregate of the legal rights of their members. The tendency to view this property in this way becomes dominant, however, only when the bonds that unify the members of a family or a corporation begin to dissolve and the moral constraints on private property are correspondingly weakened or disappear completely. Nevertheless, this process only makes explicit the status of the relevant form of property rather than marking a change in the form of property. Ethical property, in contrast, *becomes* the potential private property of one or more persons, and this change entails that it is *no longer* ethical property.

3.7 Ethical Property

An extension of the rights associated with private property to public goods and the institutions that embody or serve them must therefore be interpreted as a sign of the *disintegration* of ethical life itself, as opposed to evidence of the progressive actualization of the idea of ethical life in the course of history. The actualization of the idea of ethical life requires the subordination of abstract right to ethical life, and thus the transition from the standpoint of property-owning persons who are externally bound together in civil society by legal norms to the standpoint of the citizen who identifies himself or herself not only with the state but also with institutions that embody or serve a public good, and who leads a 'universal' life by participating in these institutions or supporting them with the right ethical attitude. Thus there is a tension between the form of property that is most compatible with the idea of ethical life and Hegel's claim that recognition of private property and the rights that define it is a sign of historical progress measured in terms of an increasingly adequate consciousness of the concept of freedom, for this claim implies that private property ought to be the dominant form of property in modern ethical life. The tension between this claim and the way in which a form of common or collective property is more consistent with the idea of ethical life can be illustrated in the following way.

The extent to which the rationality of private property and the rights associated with it is recognized in modern ethical life and this recognition is justified may vary. If 1 indicates the point at which there is universal recognition of the rationality of private property and justifiably so and 0 indicates the point at which there is no recognition of it, then *increasing* recognition of the rationality of private property and the rights associated with it in the course of history will consist in a movement from some point after 0 towards 1. Since Hegel regards entailed landed property as rationally necessary by virtue of its political function and it is not private property in the full modern sense, while also appearing to accept the necessity of some state-owned property, this movement cannot be thought to reach 1, that is, the point at which only the rationality of private property in the full modern sense is recognized and justifiably so. The privileged status of private property nevertheless significantly limits the extent to which any other form of property may figure in a pluralist theory of property that is appropriate to modern ethical life. This constraint that the rational necessity of private property imposes on history is reflected in the fact that Hegel does not seek to demonstrate the rational necessity of any other form of property, even if he limits the rights of private property in its distinctively modern form and indicates a peripheral role for state-owned property. If the system of right provides the model of a rational legal, social and political order rather than a description of an existing state of affairs, as it is indeed meant to do, then this constraint must be thought to apply to the future as well as to the present.

The privileged position that private property must be thought to occupy in Hegel's system of right entails that recognition of the rationality of this form of property and its existence in the form of legal rights must extend beyond 0.5 in the case of modern ethical life, for otherwise at least one other form of property would be equally justified and therefore deserving of equal recognition, unless one assumes the justifiability of more than one other form of property, each of which enjoys less justified recognition than private property. Recognition of the rationality of private property is, however, likely to approach even more closely to 1, given (1) Hegel's statements concerning how the extension of the rights associated with private property is a sign of historical progress; (2) the limited extent to which entailed landed property is needed for the 'substantial' estate to fulfil its political function and how this property, like the 'common' property of the family and the corporation, ultimately remains a form of private property; and (3) the absence of any explicit attempt to justify other forms of property. Thus Hegel is committed to the claim that *most* property ought to be private property in modern ethical life, even if he must, at the same time, reject the claim that *all* property ought to be private property.

Yet the justifiability of common or collective property, on the grounds that it is more compatible with the idea of ethical life, implies a movement in the opposite direction with respect to the justified recognition of private property and the rights associated with it, that is, a movement towards 0 rather than towards 1. In other words, in conformity with the way in which abstract right is reduced to a subordinate moment within Hegel's system of right, it is now recognition of this ethical property that ought to increase in the course of history because it is more expressive of the idea of ethical life, whereas private property is reduced to a subordinate moment within Hegel's system of right. Indeed, for the reason identified earlier, ever closer approximation to 1, and thus to the absolutist claim that private property in the full modern sense is the only justifiable form of property, would signal the disintegration of ethical life.

Thus, even if Hegel's argument for private property and his integration of the rights associated with it into modern ethical life are enough to limit the extension of ethical property in the direction of 1, there are sufficient grounds for challenging the claim that increasing recognition of the rationality of private property is a sign of progress measured in terms of the consciousness of the concept of freedom, if this is taken to mean that private property ought to be the dominant form of property in modern ethical life. For it now looks as if the only way of upholding this claim would be to argue that in Hegel's own time recognition of the rationality of private property and the rights associated with it did not extend much beyond 0, and so only a modest increase in the recognition of private property and the rights associated with it would reflect the rational necessity of this form of property. Yet this empirical claim is hardly a plausible one. The correct conclusion to draw may therefore be the following one: we should remain open to the idea that different forms of property are equally justifiable in terms of the idea of freedom. This will require not privileging any single form of property, whereas Hegel commits himself to the claim that only the extension of private property in its full modern sense is evidence of progress measured in terms of the consciousness of the concept of freedom and its actualization in the form of right.

In Chapter 4, I turn to Marx's theory of property. This theory appears diametrically opposed to Hegel's because the abolition of private property is viewed as one of the main goals of history. Marx's position is unique among the ones that I consider because it is the only one to reject this form of property completely, whereas Fichte attempts to leave at least some room for it in the form of absolute property. This invites the question as to why Marx advocates the abolition of private property. One answer to this question that has been proposed centres on another fundamental difference between Hegel's and Marx's views on property. This difference concerns the way in which Hegel considers private property to be a condition of a 'rich' individuality, whereas Marx thinks that this individuality requires the abolition of private property.[20]

This statement is misleading because Hegel's argument for private property appeals to the conditions of personality and personality is abstract rather than concrete.[21] I shall nevertheless construct an argument that shows that the statement is essentially right in so far as it applies to Marx's critique of private property. The precise grounds of the claim that private property stifles individuality must therefore first be identified. This will require making clearer what type of individuality is at stake. I shall also show that Marx's demand that private property be abolished does not amount to a rejection of property as such. Marx follows Kant, Fichte and

---

[20] See Stillman, 'Property, Freedom, and Individuality in Hegel's and Marx's Political Thought'.
[21] Only in civil society does a genuinely 'concrete' and 'particular' individual become the subject of right. See PR § 190R.

Hegel in that he understands the concept of property in terms of a triadic structure. Moreover, he argues for a form of property that performs the type of expressive function that I have attributed to the ethical property that, or so I have argued, Hegel should have endorsed more than private property. This form of property is meant to make possible a genuinely free individuality within a social context in which individuals are concerned with the freedom and the needs of other individuals as well as their own freedom and needs.

CHAPTER 4

Equality, Exchange Value and Individuality
Marx's Critique of Private Property

4.1 Property and Equality

For Marx, property is a constant feature of human society. He identifies property both with the appropriation (*Aneignung*) of nature and with specific material elements of human productive activity (MEGA II/1.1: 25, MEGA II/1.2: 389–96; 25; G, 87, 485–92). Any productive activity presupposes the appropriation of nature in some form. Yet the concept of property cannot be reduced to a relation between human beings and nature. The relations that exist between human beings in society are structured by forms of property that determine the place of individuals and social groups within a system of production and exchange founded on the appropriation of nature. The relations between human beings within society, as structured by property relations, change in the course of history because the forms of property, and thus the relations that they structure, vary according to specific material conditions. Thus '[t]o try to give a definition of property as of an independent relation, a category apart, an abstract and eternal idea, can be nothing but an illusion of metaphysics or jurisprudence' (MP, 153; PP, 197).

The concept of property can nevertheless be viewed as transhistorical in that any form of property possesses the triadic person–thing–person structure that Marx, like Kant, Fichte and Hegel, identifies. Yet this concept ultimately tells us little about the institution of property and its role in society. Instead, the historical forms of property are what really matter. Among these historical forms, there is the one that is a presupposition of capitalist society, namely private property. The right to property here has a different character according to the type of social agent that possesses this right, with each type of social agent being defined in terms of ownership of a specific type of property: 'Private property, as the antithesis to social, collective property [*Privateigenthum, als Gegensatz zum gesellschaftlichen, kollektiven Eigenthum*], exists only where the means of labour and the external conditions of labour belong to private individuals. But according to whether these private individuals are workers or non-workers, private property has a different character' (MEGA II/8: 711; Cap. 1: 927).

Private property is one among a constellation of concepts in capitalist society, in which the right to property assumes a different character depending on whether the possessor of this right is a worker or a non-worker (that is, a capitalist). The other concepts are freedom and equality. Private property must therefore be related to these other concepts if we are to fully understand Marx's critique of it. In the following passage, Marx himself alludes to the interconnectedness of the concepts of property, freedom and equality within the same social totality with reference to the exchange of commodities, especially the commodity of labour power, that is a defining feature of the capitalist economic and social system:

> The sphere of circulation or commodity exchange, within whose boundaries the sale and purchase of labour-power goes on, is in fact a very Eden of the innate rights of man. It is the exclusive realm of Freedom, Equality, Property and Bentham. Freedom, because both buyer and seller of a commodity, let us say of labour-power, are determined only by their own free will. They contract as free persons, who are equal before the law. Their contract is the final result in which their joint will finds a common legal expression. Equality, because they relate to each other only as the owners of commodities and exchange equivalent for equivalent. Property, because each disposes only of what is his own. And Bentham, because each looks only to his own advantage. The only force bringing them together, and putting them into relation with each other, is the selfishness, the gain and the private interest of each. (MEGA II/8: 191; Cap. 1: 280; translation modified)

From this passage, we can see that Marx associates the property rights that structure the capitalist economic and social system with the equal legal recognition accorded to rights-bearing persons. These persons are motivated by self-interest to enter into contractual relations with one another. Since these contractual relations rest on the voluntary agreement of both parties, they are held to be compatible with the idea of freedom. Thus, as with Hegel's account of property and the way in which he locates it at the stage of abstract right, we have legal persons who, implicitly at least, recognize one another as bearers of the right to dispose freely of their property. In the case of the worker, this property is reducible to his or her own labour power. It should therefore come as no surprise that, as we shall see, Marx's reasons for advocating the complete abolition of private property concern private property's function within an economic and social system structured by contractual relations that exist between allegedly free and equal rights-bearing persons who exchange commodities.

4.1 *Property and Equality*

Some of Marx's statements concerning property are nevertheless compatible with the idea that he does not, in fact, advocate the complete abolition of private property. Communism's aim is said not to be the abolition (*Abschaffung*) of property in general, but the abolition of the 'bourgeois property' which 'is the final and most complete expression of the production and appropriation of products which rests on class conflict, on the exploitation of individuals by others' (MEW 4: 475; MCP, 13). Immediately afterwards, Marx mentions the *Aufhebung* of private property. This may suggest that private property is somehow preserved in communist society rather than being abolished altogether, given the Hegelian provenance of the term *Aufhebung*.[1]

Hegel draws attention to the various meanings of the verb *aufheben*. This word can mean to preserve (*aufbewahren*) or to maintain (*erhalten*). Yet it can also mean to cause to cease (*aufhören lassen*) or to put an end to (*ein Ende machen*). Hegel compares this double meaning of the verb *aufheben* favourably with that of the Latin verb *tollere*, because of how the affirmative element found in the latter concerns only the raising or lifting up of something, whereas something is *aufgehoben* by being unified with its opposite, thereby becoming a moment of a greater whole (WL1: 114; SL, 107). Although this additional sense of the term *Aufhebung* is compatible with the idea that private property is preserved at the same time as the limitations of 'bourgeois' property are overcome in the transition from capitalism to communism, the question of how it can be unified with its opposite, which is 'social, collective' property, then arises.

One possible answer to this question is that private property is limited in some way, which may include restricting it to certain types of things. There are statements concerning the incompatibility of private property with the free individuality of the worker that suggest that only the abolition of private property in the form of the means of production is required. Marx claims, for example, that the property to be abolished is the 'modern bourgeois private property' that 'creates capital, i.e. property which exploits wage-labour, which can increase only on condition that it produces new wage-labour to be exploited afresh' (MEW 4: 475; MCP, 14). He also claims that 'capitalist' private property 'rests on the exploitation of alien, but formally free labour' (MEGA II/8: 712; Cap. 1: 928).

---

[1] For the argument that Marx should have adopted a Hegelian approach by seeking to preserve liberal ideals and rights, which might include the right to private property, while rejecting certain aspects of them that can be explained in terms of the form that they assume in capitalist society, and that he did, in fact, to some extent endorse this approach, see Neuhouser, 'Marx and Hegel on the Value of "Bourgeois" Ideals'.

This exploitation can be explained in terms of the capitalist's ownership of the means of production. Common ownership of the means of production might nevertheless coexist with private property in the form of an individual's right to dispose freely of an object that he or she has produced and any object that he or she receives in exchange for this object. Yet what if the 'bourgeois' property that communism is to abolish essentially means private property?

We shall see that the relevant distinction is, in fact, one between property in general, which concerns the appropriation of nature and the different historical economic and social relations corresponding to it, and private property, which is one historical form of property among others. My account of the grounds on which Marx attempts to justify the abolition of private property and its replacement by 'social, collective property', to use his own description of the antithesis of private property, will explain why he is committed to the stronger claim that private property in so far as it concerns the right to any commodity that can be produced and exchanged primarily with a view to its exchange value must be abolished. This makes it difficult to see how private property, as Marx himself understands it, and the specific rights that characterize this form of property would survive the abolition of capitalist society.

The first stage of my reconstruction of Marx's argument, or rather arguments, for the abolition of private property will concern the self-conception of legal persons who, implicitly at least, recognize one another as bearers of the right to dispose freely of that which is legally theirs. This self-conception and the corresponding understanding of social relations are determined by an abstract exchange value that finds its legal and political expression in a purely formal notion of equality in such a way that individuals are unable to relate to others, and through this relation to others to relate to themselves, as 'real' and genuinely free individuals. The complete abolition of private property is required to eliminate abstract exchange value and its psychological, social and political effects, including the way in which a necessarily formal notion of equality has come to govern society. The complete abolition of private property is also necessary because it and the corresponding conception of freedom are presuppositions of a system of exchange that has become independent of the agency of those individuals who are caught up in it, thereby dominating them.

In accordance with the claim that property is a constant feature of human society, Marx identifies a form of property that will structure social relations in communist society. If, as I shall argue, a key element in Marx's argument for the complete abolition of private property concerns

4.1 Property and Equality

the self-conception and relation to others demanded and fostered by the capitalist economic and social system, a different self-conception and relation to others may become possible in communist society by means of the abolition of private property and the introduction of a different form of property. For individuals may then be able to relate both to themselves and to others as 'real' and genuinely free individuals. In the final section of this chapter, I shall consider whether Marx successfully explains the possibility of this alternative self-conception and relation to others in terms of the abolition of private property and its replacement by the communist form of property. First, though, we must turn to Marx's account of the essential role played by the idea of equality in a society characterized by acts of commodity exchange into which rights-bearing persons freely enter, that is, a society structured by the rights associated with private property, and in which these rights are protected and enforced by the state.

Marx's vision of a classless society might be thought to signal a commitment to the idea of equality, for if all class distinctions were abolished, then it seems that individuals would have to be viewed as essentially equal and be treated as such, which is to presuppose the value of equality. There are nevertheless reasons for denying that Marx considers equality to be valuable, either in its own right or because it promotes another human good.[2] These reasons include the claim that equality is an essentially bourgeois concept that serves as a vehicle of oppression by concealing relations of domination. Another reason concerns Marx's rejection of the application of an equal standard with the aim of determining what would count as a just distribution of goods in communist society. Although I do not intend to address the issue of whether Marx completely rejects the idea of such a standard, his criticisms of this idea will be shown to be relevant to identifying the precise grounds on which he advocates the abolition of private property.

In the *Critique of the Gotha Programme*, Marx associates the attempt to apply an equal standard with the first phase of communist society. This is communist society 'not as it *has developed* on its own foundation, but on the contrary, just as it *emerges* from capitalist society, hence in every respect – economically, morally, intellectually – as it comes forth from the womb, it is stamped with the birthmarks of the old society' (MEGA I/25: 13; CGP, 213; translation modified). During this phase of communist

---

[2] See Sayers, *Marx and Alienation*, 120ff., 126ff. and Wood, *The Free Development of Each*, 252ff.

society, each worker is provided with a receipt which specifies the amount of labour that he or she has contributed. After deductions for a common fund have been made, the worker is entitled to take from society's stores consumption goods equal in value to the value of the remaining amount of labour. This arrangement presupposes that labour possesses a value that is equivalent to the value of such goods. Abstract labour time is the measure of both the value of labour and the value of the goods received in return for it. Thus for each producer, the 'same quantity of labour he puts into society in one form comes back to him in another' (MEGA I/25: 14; CGP, 213).

An equal standard is being employed because the same principle of distribution is applied to each producer and every producer is formally entitled to the same benefits in so far as he or she fulfils the same obligations. The obligations condition the benefits because that which each producer receives depends on how much he or she contributes. Marx argues that this attempt to apply an equal standard would, in fact, produce outcomes that are incompatible with the idea of equality because 'one person is physically or mentally superior to another, and hence contributes more work in the same time or can work longer' (MEGA I/25: 14; CGP, 214). In other words, the mode of distribution found in this phase of communist society entitles the person who can contribute more because of his or her greater strength or superior aptitudes to more consumption goods than those members of society who can contribute less, irrespective of whether the first person needs more consumption goods than these other members of society. The application of an equal standard will therefore result in significant inequalities with respect to the actual distribution of goods and resources, and so the right to be treated equally turns out to be '*in content ... a right to inequality, like all rights*' (MEGA I/25: 14; CGP, 214).[3]

This may look like an attempt on Marx's part to show the need for a principle of equality whose application avoids such outcomes. Yet an unequal distribution of goods is something that Marx himself favours,

---

[3] The problem of how the application of the principle of equality within a society committed to this principle is essentially self-undermining was already identified by Hegel:

> In a society based on a community of goods [*Gütergemeinschaft*], in which provision would be made in a universal and enduring way, either each receives as much as he *needs* – in which case there is a contradiction between this inequality and the essential nature of that consciousness whose principle is the equality of individuals – or, in accordance with that principle, goods will be *equally* distributed, in which case the share bears no relation to the need. (PhG, 283; PS, 258; translation modified).

4.1 Property and Equality

provided it corresponds to differences in the type and the extent of the needs that individuals have. In contrast, treating everyone equally by applying an equal standard is to neglect the differences that distinguish individuals from one another, including their different abilities and their different needs. This implies that 'rights would have to be unequal, instead of equal' (MEGA I/25: 15; CGP, 214). Yet this inequality would violate the essential nature of rights, for rights, unlike privileges, are meant to apply equally and universally. It is significant that the idea of equality is here held to pose a threat to individuality because, as we shall see, Marx's argument for the abolition of private property is motivated by the wish to explain how such threats can be removed. Is it possible, however, to establish a deeper connection between Marx's views on the idea of equality and his argument for the abolition of private property? I shall now begin to demonstrate the existence of such connection with reference to another argument that supports the claim that communist society would not be an egalitarian society.

As we have seen, the first stage of communist society is 'stamped with the birthmarks of the old society'. Marx's most fundamental objection to the idea that equality provides the moral principle that ought to decide the distribution of goods and resources in communist society can then be thought to rest on the following claim: this principle of distribution and the moral idea from which it derives are expressive of a society founded on acts of commodity exchange governed by exchange value, that is to say, capitalist society. This claim is supported by Marx's own claim that in the first phase of communist society, the principle 'is the same as the one that applies in the exchange of commodities' (MEGA I/25: 14; CGP, 213). It also helps to explain the following key claims found in his account of the relevant phase of communist society:

1. The claim that with respect to any division of goods and resources undertaken by applying an equal standard, 'the operative principle is the same as under the exchange of equivalent values: a given amount of labour in one form is exchanged for an equal amount in another form' (MEGA I/25: 14; CGP, 213).
2. The claim that the application of an equal standard with the aim of measuring the contributions and entitlements of each member of society requires viewing individuals 'only in terms of a *specific* aspect, e.g. considered in a given case *only as workers*', so that 'nothing else about them is taken into account, all else being disregarded' (MEGA I/25: 14; CGP, 214).

These two claims are, in fact, bound up with each other, in that both the relevant principle of distribution and the way in which individuals are viewed under only one aspect require the kind of abstraction that is already familiar to us from Hegel's account of abstract right. As we shall see, Marx explains this tendency towards abstraction in terms of how abstract exchange value has come to govern human relations in a society founded on acts of commodity exchange and shape how individuals conceive of themselves and others. In this way, Marx provides the basis for an explanation of the claim that genuine individuality is not possible, or is at least extremely difficult to achieve, in modern capitalist society made by philosophers influenced by him. Theodor W. Adorno, for example, attributes the impossibility of genuine individuality to the effects of an all-encompassing impersonal economic and social system that demands the suppression of any determinate characteristics and attributes that serve to distinguish individuals from one another:

> If the equality of all who have human shape were demanded as an ideal instead of being assumed as a fact, it would not greatly help. Abstract utopia is all too compatible with the most cunning tendencies of society. That all human beings are alike is exactly what suits society. It considers actual or imagined differences as stigmas that attest to the fact that not enough has yet been done; that something has still been left free of its machinery, is not fully determined by the totality.[4]

This passage may appear to refer to any totalitarian form of society that attempts to legitimize itself by claiming that it is founded on the idea of equality, rather than being a description of liberal capitalist society, which views its ability to accommodate individuality, and even to secure the conditions of its free development, as one of its main virtues. Given the Marxist heritage of Adorno's philosophy, however, one may assume that he intends liberal capitalist society as much as, if not more than, any other society which represses individuality in the name of equality.[5] The question then becomes the following one: how are we to explain the connection between the levelling process that Adorno describes and liberal capitalist society in particular, when this type of society is claimed to be one in which individuality becomes truly possible?

---

[4] Adorno, *Minima Moralia*, no. 66. Translation modified.
[5] The connection is even more evident in *Negative Dialectics*, where Adorno explicitly mentions the 'principle of exchange [*Tauschprinzip*], the reduction of human labor to the abstract universal concept of average working time', and claims that 'through exchange ... non-identical single beings [*Einzelwesen*] and services [*Leistungen*] become commensurable and identical' (*Negative Dialektik*, 149 / *Negative Dialectics*, 146; translation modified).

I shall argue that Marx's answer to this question is that if we look below the ideological surface of liberal capitalist society, we shall discover that it is not simply a matter of a society that happens to fail to live up to one of its own central ideals, namely, that of accommodating individuality and facilitating its free development. Rather, this type of society necessarily represses individuality. In other words, liberal capitalist society *cannot* live up to this ideal because another of its ideals, the moral equality of all individuals, is merely the ideological product of social relations and levelling tendencies that make genuine individuality impossible. These social relations and levelling tendencies are explained in terms of the nature of exchange value and how this form of value dominates a society founded on the exchange of commodities. Marx's critique of the idea of equality is therefore not reducible to an attempt to demonstrate how the application of an equal standard produces outcomes that are incompatible with the principle of equality itself. This critique goes beyond such ideological phenomena and thereby finds itself confronted with the question of how the economic and social structures that produce these phenomena can be abolished.

One such structure is private property and the rights that define it because a society founded on the exchange of commodities presupposes this form of property. This is the kind of society in which individuals must come to think of themselves and others as nothing more than rights-bearing persons capable of entering into contractual relations with one another that involve an exchange of items of private property. Thus Marx's critique of private property cannot be understood independently of the historical process in which exchange value's increasing dominance of social relations is accompanied by increasing recognition of the idea of moral equality and the rights associated with it. I shall therefore now turn to Marx's account of how exchange value is the true source of the idea of moral equality and how knowledge of this source becomes possible only at a specific historical moment.

4.2 The Origin of the Idea of Equality

According to Marx, Aristotle recognized that the relation of value that exists between one commodity and another commodity presupposes some way of viewing qualitatively different things as commensurable. If commodity X is to have the same value as commodity Y, then there must be a common measure of their value. This common measure presupposes some way in which commodity X and commodity Y can be viewed as identical despite their differences. Yet Aristotle failed to explain how quantities of different objects or the objects themselves can possess equal value. Marx, in contrast, claims to provide the missing explanation in the form of his labour theory of value. The possibility of treating qualitatively different things as equal in value can be explained in terms of how these things possess the common property of being products of 'abstract' human labour (MEGA II/8: 102; Cap. 1: 166). The measure of the value of each commodity is 'socially necessary labour-time', which is 'the labour-time required to produce any use-value under the conditions of production normal for a given society and with the average degree of skill and intensity of labour prevalent in that society' (MEGA II/8: 71; Cap. 1: 129).

We can already see how applying an equal standard, which is here supplied by the time taken to produce a commodity, involves identifying a property that different things share and consequently requires abstracting from the properties that distinguish them from one another. The idea of equality, understood in moral, legal or political terms, likewise requires the identification of a common property that all human beings possess, and which explains their equal moral, legal or political status, while abstracting from any natural, personal or social properties that distinguish them from one another. By means of this process of abstraction, through which a common essential property is identified, individuals who are otherwise qualitatively different from one another can be viewed as identical. The outcome of this process is captured by a remark of Hegel's concerning the consciousness of oneself and others that finds expression in the legal equality that all persons enjoy in civil society. This equality requires ignoring religious and national differences, thereby allowing everyone to be viewed and treated as equal before the law: 'It is part of education, of *thinking* as consciousness of the individual in the form of universality, that I am apprehended as a *universal* person, in which [respect] *all* are identical. A *human being counts as such because he is a human being*, not because he is a Jew, Catholic, Protestant, German, Italian, etc.' (PR § 209R).

In this way, an analogy between commodities and individuals begins to emerge. Commodities are reciprocally measurable and exchangeable with one another by virtue of the common property of being products of socially necessary labour time. Similarly, individuals are granted the same moral, legal or political status by virtue of their possession of a common property, the identification of which requires ignoring all the particular attributes that serve to distinguish them from one another. I shall now attempt to

4.2 The Origin of the Idea of Equality

strengthen this analogy.[6] I shall begin with the passage from the first volume of *Capital* in which Marx explains why Aristotle was necessarily unable to discover the concept of value that would have provided him with the solution to a puzzle that he himself had identified, namely, how qualitatively different things are reciprocally measurable, and thus exchangeable, with one another. The passage in question is the following one:

> Aristotle himself was unable to extract this fact, that, in the form of commodity-values, all labour is expressed as equal human labour and therefore as labour of equal value [*gleichgeltend*], by inspection from the form of value, because Greek society was founded on the labour of slaves, hence had as its natural basis the inequality of human beings and of their labour-powers. The secret of the expression of value, namely the equality and equivalence [*gleiche Gültigkeit*] of all kinds of labour because and in so far as they are human labour in general, can only be deciphered once the concept of human equality has already acquired the permanence of a fixed popular opinion. This however becomes possible only in a society where the commodity-form is the universal form of the product of labour, hence the dominant social relation is the relation between human beings as possessors of commodities. (MEGA II/8: 90; Cap. 1: 151–52; translation modified)

This passage contains a series of claims that need to be separated from one another.

1. Given his historical situation, it was not possible for Aristotle to achieve full insight into the essential nature of exchange value. A central feature of this historical situation was the institution of slavery, which presupposes and expresses a radical inequality of status. The fundamental difference in status between the master and the slave was explained and justified in terms of natural differences, including by Aristotle himself.[7] The modern moral, legal and political idea of equality, in contrast, presupposes the ability and the willingness to view human beings in abstraction from all the natural and other contingent features and factors that serve to distinguish them from one another, so as to discover an essential attribute by virtue of which all human beings can be considered identical and, on this basis, accorded the same status which demands that they be treated equally.

---

[6] Although the analogy ultimately depends on Marx's labour theory of value, I do not intend to engage with the issue of this theory's validity. All that matters to the argument that I shall construct is the assumption that there is some way of viewing commodities as identical, and thus exchangeable, with one another, and that this identity concerns their exchange value, which abstracts from those properties that distinguish the things themselves from one another.
[7] See Aristotle, *The Politics*, 1254a–1255b.

2. The modern idea of moral, legal and political equality provides the key to the discovery of an adequate theory of the value of commodities, that is, a theory that explains how commodities are reciprocally measurable and thus exchangeable with one another. This is the theory according to which every commodity embodies a certain amount of abstract, socially necessary labour time.
3. It follows from (1) and (2) that Aristotle was necessarily not in the position to gain knowledge of the concept of exchange value, for the key to the discovery of this concept and the theory of value that explains it, namely the idea of legal and political equality, was unavailable to him in the society in which he lived. In modern liberal capitalist society, in contrast, the key to the discovery of the concept of exchange value and the theory of value that explains it is available precisely because in this society the idea of the moral equality of all individuals is generally recognized, and to such an extent that it has assumed 'the permanence of a fixed popular opinion' and various legal and political forms, even if a completely consistent, universal application of this idea has yet to be achieved.
4. The idea of the moral equality of individuals and the corresponding demand for its legal and political realization can, however, achieve general recognition only in a society in which the 'commodity-form' has begun to dominate human beings by becoming that which ultimately determines how individuals view themselves and their relations with others. Thus, although general recognition of the idea of the moral equality of individuals and its legal and political expressions are historical conditions of knowledge of the true concept of exchange value, it is exchange value's dominant role within society that explains general recognition of this idea and its legal and political expressions. Marx himself makes this clear when he states that '[e]quality and freedom are thus not only respected in exchange based on exchange values but, also, the exchange of exchange values is the productive, real basis of all *equality* and *freedom*' (MEGA II/1.1: 168; G, 245).

From (4) we can see that there are two stages and directions of inquiry. The first stage and direction of inquiry consists in inferring the concept of exchange value from the historical fact of recognition of the idea of the moral equality of all human beings in a legal and political form. The second stage and direction of inquiry consists in explaining this general recognition of the idea of the moral equality of all human beings and its legal and political expressions in terms of the concept of exchange value that has been inferred from them, but that is, in fact, the 'real basis'. Thus economic relations between commodity owners governed by exchange value explain the ideological phenomenon of general recognition of the idea of the moral equality of all human beings and the legal and political forms in which this idea finds expression. We must assume, then, the existence of a historical process through which exchange value has increasingly come to dominate society and, in so doing, produced the relevant ideological forms.

I shall now focus on the second stage and direction of inquiry with the aim of explaining the relation between moral, legal and political equality and Marx's account of a society in which social relations are governed by exchange value. By explaining the surface phenomenon of general recognition of the idea of the moral equality of all human beings in terms of social relations governed by exchange value, we can begin to see why Marx would want to advocate the abolition of private property. Essentially, the abolition of private property is the most direct and effective means of abolishing a society that is the source and expression of a false conception of oneself and others, and that is incompatible with genuine individuality and freedom. This is because private property, in the form of the right to dispose freely of a thing of which one is the full legal owner, is a presupposition of this society. Communist society, in contrast, will be the source and expression of a more adequate conception of oneself and social relations that is compatible with 'real' individuality. It will also provide the economic and social conditions of this individuality's free development.

4.3 Exchange Value and the Idea of Equality

According to Marx, the commodity is characterized by its 'double existence'. On the one hand, there is the commodity in its 'natural' existence. This is the 'real' commodity in the sense of a determinate thing that is exchanged because of the distinctive properties that enable it to satisfy a specific human need, thereby giving it a use value. On the other hand, there is the commodity in its 'purely economic' existence as exchange value. The commodity here stands in a purely quantitative relation to other commodities (MEGA II/1.1: 76; G, 141–42). A relation of this kind requires viewing the commodity in abstraction from all properties other than the property by virtue of which it is identical with all other commodities and can be exchanged with them *qua* exchange values. This leads Marx to describe exchange value as 'a generality [*ein Allgemeines*], in which all individuality and peculiarity [*Eigenheit*] are negated and extinguished' (MEGA II/1.1: 90; G, 157). The relation between commodities governed by exchange value must find symbolic expression in a third thing that can be exchanged for any commodity whatsoever, namely money.

The double existence of the commodity mirrors the double life of the individual in the modern state that Marx describes in 'On the Jewish Question'. The state 'abolishes' (*hebt ... auf*) distinctions based on natural, personal or social factors that serve to distinguish individuals from one another by treating all such distinctions as politically irrelevant (MEGA I/2: 148; JQ, 219). Rather, every individual, as a citizen, enjoys the same political status based on his or her identity with others. In this way, the individual comes to live a double life, by existing 'in his *immediate* reality, in civil society ... where he regards himself and is regarded by others as a real individual', on the one hand, and as someone who 'is divested of his real individual life and filled with an unreal universality [*Allgemeinheit*]', on the other (MEGA I/2: 149; JQ, 220). In the first case, the individual is the human being 'in his sensuous, individual and *immediate* existence', whereas in the second case, this same individual is 'abstract, artificial man, man as an *allegorical, moral* person' (MEGA I/2: 162; JQ, 234).

Three analogies here emerge. First, there is the analogy between the individual as a real, perceivable being who is 'particular' in the sense of being qualitatively distinct from other individuals and the commodity in its natural, real form. Second, there is the analogy between the same individual as an abstract political being from which all distinctive attributes have been abstracted to create an artificial entity that is numerically distinct but qualitatively indistinguishable from all other such entities and the commodity in its economic form. Third, the political identity of individuals in the modern state finds expression in a third thing, law, which, by virtue of its formal character, applies to all individuals and unites them in an external way. This corresponds to how each commodity in its economic form is governed by exchange value and the laws of commodity exchange in such a way that it stands in a purely external relation to other commodities. The relation is a purely external one because any actual connections that exist between commodities are established by the act of exchanging them as part of a contract. This act is facilitated by a third thing, money, in which the relative value of the commodities exchanged finds symbolic expression and can do so only if all properties other than their abstract exchange value are ignored.

So far it looks as if Marx has suggested some possible analogies while leaving the following question unanswered: how are general recognition of the moral equality of individuals and the legal and political expressions

4.3 Exchange Value and the Idea of Equality

of this recognition to be explained in terms of the way in which exchange value governs social relations? As it stands, Marx has not shown that the implied connections between the legal and political forms in which recognition of the moral equality of individuals finds expression and exchange value's dominance of society are anything more than accidental ones. It could also be the case that the idea of moral equality explains exchange value's dominance of society rather than the other way round. Part of Marx's answer to this question relates to another claim found in 'On the Jewish Question'. The claim is that 'species-life itself, society, appears as a framework extraneous to the individuals, as a limitation of their original independence' (MEGA I/2: 159; JQ, 230).

A society in which exchange value governs social relations is one in which the exchange value of commodities becomes the immediate object of production. The same would be true in relation to any productive capabilities or other saleable attributes over which an agent enjoys initial effective control. The stage at which objects produced by human labour, productive capabilities and other saleable attributes are viewed primarily, and even exclusively, in terms of their exchange value draws ever closer with an increasing division of labour. This is because each producer's activity becomes more restricted in terms of its scope, making individuals correspondingly more dependent on others to produce or otherwise provide the means of satisfying their needs. These needs have themselves become more extensive and more complex in the course of history. This development itself presupposes an increasing division of labour, whereby 'the needs of each person have become very many-sided and his product has become very one-sided' (MEGA II/1.1: 128–29; G, 199). Given the way in which exchange value governs society, individuals cannot acquire from others the commodities that they need without first converting their own products, powers or activities into money, which is the universal medium of exchange. Once an individual has done this, he or she can exchange the value of his or her commodity for any other commodity of the same value.

Economic agents are in this way constrained to produce objects or to provide services that can be exchanged for money, with the result that the distinctive properties of the things exchanged, which may include natural or personal attributes of these agents themselves, become of secondary importance compared to their exchange value. Even if an individual wants to act or to produce something with a view to the specific properties of the action or the object and how this action or object promises to satisfy the determinate needs of other individuals, he or she will be constrained by his or her own needs and the desire to obtain the means to satisfy them to act and to produce things primarily with a view to the exchange value of the action or the thing. For an individual's ability to satisfy his or her needs has now become dependent on whether he or she can turn a commodity of which he or she is the legal owner into the symbolic expression of its exchange value. In this way, money assumes a 'seemingly transcendental power' (MEGA II/1.1: 81; G, 146). Moreover, the degree of social power that each agent possesses relative to other agents has becomes a function of the amount of exchange value in the form of money that he or she possesses, so that, as Marx puts it, 'The individual carries his social power, as well as his bond with society, in his pocket' (MEGA II/1.1: 90; G, 157).

The developments described above are features of that which Marx calls 'bourgeois society'. This is the same society in which the legal and political equality of individuals is generally, if only imperfectly, recognized. Even if this indicates a historical connection between increasing recognition of the moral equality of individuals and exchange value's increasing dominance of society, it has yet to be shown how the one explains the other. To demonstrate this, Marx needs to establish a causal connection between exchange value's dominance of society and the legal and political expressions of increasing recognition of the moral equality of individuals within the same society in such a way that the former explains the latter. This challenge can be illustrated with reference to Marx's theory of history.

In the canonical account of historical materialism found in the preface to *A Contribution to the Critique of Political Economy*, Marx claims that in 'the social production of their lives' human beings 'enter into relations that are specific, necessary and independent of their will, relations of production which correspond to a specific stage of development of their material productive forces'. The totality of these relations of production forms the economic structure of society. This structure in turn forms the basis of a 'legal and political superstructure' to which 'specific forms of social consciousness' correspond (MEGA II/2: 100; PCPE, 159–60). The idea of the moral equality of individuals and any legal or political expressions of it would belong to this superstructure and the forms of social consciousness. This idea and the legal or political expressions of it must, therefore, ultimately be explained in terms of the development of the material productive forces of society by way of the social relations of production.[8] The social

---

[8] For example, moral notions, including the idea of equality and the subjective rights associated with it, especially once they have achieved legal recognition by the state, might be explained in terms of how they facilitate the development of the productive forces by serving to maintain and promote the corresponding relations of production. See Wood, *Karl Marx*, 130ff.

4.3 Exchange Value and the Idea of Equality

relations of production are structured by property rights. This means that the idea of moral equality and the forms of consciousness corresponding to it must, in the first instance, be explained in terms of the property rights that are specific to capitalist society. Marx himself indicates that this is the right approach to adopt when he claims in *The Eighteenth Brumaire of Louis Bonaparte* that '[o]n the different forms of property, the social conditions of existence, arises an entire superstructure of different and peculiarly formed sentiments, delusions, modes of thought and outlooks on life' (MEGA I/11: 121; EB, 56).

How, though, does Marx seek to explain the relation between the idea of moral equality together with the forms of consciousness corresponding to it and the property rights that are specific to capitalist society with reference to how exchange value has come to dominate society? I shall now seek to address this question in a way that avoids the difficulties introduced by a direct appeal to historical materialism and particular interpretations of it. Marx's account of how material factors ultimately explain ideological ones nevertheless requires identifying a sufficiently strong tendency that explains how the relevant material factors produce the relevant ideological effects. This tendency must account for the increased demands for legal and political equality that are features of liberal capitalist society. I shall argue that the relevant causal connection can be explained in the following way. Exchange value's increasing dominance of society, which is a material factor, produces a strong tendency to conceive of both oneself and others in a correspondingly abstract way, thereby making a purely formal notion of equality that reinforces this abstract conception of oneself and others appear natural. The tendency to conceive of oneself in an abstract way is accompanied by the tendency to view distinctive features of oneself as detachable, and thus commodifiable, parts of oneself. Moreover, the capitalist economic and social system exerts a pressure on individuals to think of themselves and others in precisely this way.

Marx emphasizes how commodity exchange requires abstracting not only from any properties other than the exchange value of the commodities themselves but also from any properties that serve to distinguish the parties to the act of exchange from one another. One example of this is provided by the following description of how the worker and the capitalist confront each other as the owners and exchangers of commodities. This description appears to treat legal equality as an implication of the equality of individuals who are viewed as nothing more than the owners and exchangers of commodities:

> He and the owner of money meet in the market, and enter into relations with each other on a footing of equality as owners of commodities [*als ebenbürtige Waarenbesitzer*], with the sole difference that one is a buyer, the other a seller; both are therefore equal persons in the eyes of the law [*beide also juristisch gleiche Personen sind*]' (MEGA II/8: 183–84; Cap. 1, 271; translation modified.

The worker, who owns one commodity in the form of his or her labour power, and the capitalist, who owns another commodity in the form of the money with which he pays the worker for the use of this labour power, are different only in that one of them is a seller and the other is a buyer. Apart from this difference, any other features that distinguish them from each other as natural persons and individuals with their own characters, needs, ends and interests have been abstracted from. Yet even the difference between buyer and seller is not a fixed one, for the worker can, or rather must, also be a buyer and the capitalist must also be a seller within the capitalist system of production and exchange. In any case, whether as buyer or as seller, each of them is identical with the other by virtue of being a person who engages in acts of commodity exchange regulated by contracts: 'each has the same social relation towards the other that the other has towards him. As subjects of exchange, their relation is … that of *equality*. It is impossible to find any trace of distinction … between them; not even a difference' (MEGA II/1.1: 165; G, 241). Abstracting from any determinate features and relations is also necessary if human beings are to be recognized as legal persons who are equal before the law and possess the equal right to dispose freely of their property by entering into contracts with other legal persons.

The following passages provide examples of how Marx is keen to emphasize that the exchange of commodities requires abstracting from any attributes that would distinguish the parties to the act of exchange from each other, and how this corresponds to the way in which the money form, in which the commodity appears, requires abstracting from the specific properties of any object of exchange:

> Each appears towards the other as an owner of money, and, as regards the process of exchange, as money itself. Thus indifference [*Gleichgültigkeit*] and equal worthiness [*Gleichgeltendheit*] are expressly contained in the form of the thing. The particular natural difference which was contained in the commodity is extinguished and constantly becomes extinguished by circulation. A worker who buys commodities for 3s. appears to the seller in the same function, in the same equality – in the form of 3s. – as the king who does the same. All distinction between them is extinguished. (MEGA II/1.1: 169–70; G, 246)

4.3 Exchange Value and the Idea of Equality

> A worker who buys a loaf of bread and a millionaire who does the same appear in this act only as simple buyers, just as, in respect to them, the grocer appears only as seller. All other aspects are here extinguished. The *content* of these purchases, like their *extent*, here appears as completely irrelevant [*gleichgültig*] compared with the formal aspect. (MEGA II/1.1: 174; G, 251)

The causal connection between exchange value's dominance of society at the economic level and recognition of the idea of moral equality at the legal and political levels can then be understood in the following way.

Once exchange value becomes dominant within a society, and thus comes to govern social relations, not only the particular properties of the commodities exchanged but also the particular attributes of the individuals who engage in acts of commodity exchange must be ignored. Individuals, like the commodities that they exchange either primarily or exclusively with a view to their exchange value, will then confront one another as nothing more than abstract entities. Thus the abstract economic and legal relations that exist between them do not require that they have any interest in one another as the individual that each of them happens to be. Individuals instead subsume themselves and others under the general category of buyer or seller, or the even more general category of a legal person with whom another person can enter into a contract. This relation between persons who exchange commodities in a society governed by exchange value presupposes a form of recognition. This legal recognition is reducible, however, to one according to which 'they are, as equals [*Gleichgeltende*], at the same time also indifferent to one another [*Gleichgültige*]; whatever other individual distinction there may be does not concern them; they are indifferent to all their other individual peculiarities [*Eigenheiten*]' (MEGA II/1.1: 166; G, 242). There is, in short, nothing about acts of commodity exchange that requires the existence of more concrete relations between human beings, and thus a different type of recognition.

By its very nature, therefore, a society dominated by exchange value is liable to develop in individuals the tendency to regard other individuals with whom they lack any immediate personal relations (for example, that of a family member) or determinate social relations (for example, that of a fellow worker engaged in a common struggle against capital) as abstract entities, as opposed to human beings who differ by virtue of their particular natural, personal and social characteristics. This abstract, formal conception of others finds expression in legal and political forms of equality that appear natural only because exchange value has come to govern social relations to such an extent that it itself appears natural. Moreover, it is not only a matter of how one conceives of others but also a matter of how one conceives of oneself because the relevant type of relation to others will tend to shape a person's relation to himself or herself, in that being viewed and treated by others as an abstract economic and legal entity encourages individuals to conceive of themselves in the same abstract terms, even if this abstract self-conception may be partially offset by more concrete forms of identity.[9] Indeed, this type of self-conception is almost bound to develop as a consequence of the additional pressure exerted on individuals by how they must conceive of their own productive capabilities and other saleable attributes primarily in terms of their abstract exchange value: 'In exchange value, the social connection between persons is transformed into a social relation between things [*Sachen*]; personal capacity into objective wealth [*das persönliche Vermögen in ein sachliches*]' (MEGA II/1.1: 90; G, 157).

This pressure can be explained in terms of how one's own productive capabilities or other saleable attributes must assume the form of money, the units of which measure the value of those features of oneself that can be commodified and thereby treated as 'things'. This abstract material expression of exchange value circulates in such a way that it remains independent of, and indifferent to, the particular commodities exchanged and the individuals who exchange them, leading Marx to speak of how equality posits itself objectively (*sachlich*) in the form of money (MEGA II/1.1: 169; G, 246).[10] It is difficult to see how an individual's self-conception could remain uninfluenced by the necessity of viewing one's own productive capabilities and other saleable attributes as detachable features of oneself in this condition of 'universal [*generelle*] prostitution', in which social relations governed by abstract exchange value are reduced to 'the universal

---

[9] Marx has been criticized for neglecting the importance of such sources of identity as religion and nationality. This neglect has been said to reflect a more general failure to consider the importance of the self's relation to itself. See Cohen, *Karl Marx's Theory of History*, 346ff. These criticisms are misplaced because they ignore not only the extent to which Marx explains the self's relation to itself in terms of its relation to others in a society dominated by exchange value but also how exchange value's dominance of society may undermine other sources of identity, especially ones that involve thinking of oneself as someone who belongs to a greater whole. This invites the question as to whether modern forms of religion and modern nationalism represent attempts to counter this tendency towards abstraction and atomization while mistaking the true basis of this tendency.

[10] Years before Marx had described how money possesses the property of being able to buy anything. This entails abstraction because individuals become that which they can buy rather than the possessors of distinctive attributes. In this way, an individual becomes the mere placeholder of extrinsic properties. Conversely, if an individual lacks money, he or she will, in effect, lack specific capabilities and needs that he or she does in fact possess, in that the opportunity to exercise these capabilities and the real possibility of satisfying these needs will not exist. See MEGA I/2: 436–38; EPM, 377–79.

4.3 Exchange Value and the Idea of Equality

relation of utility and use' (MEGA II/1.1: 95; G, 163). This may lead one to treat even those features that one considers most unique to oneself as commodities by conceiving of them as separable from one's own self to such an extent that they are, in effect, no longer intrinsic parts of oneself that serve to distinguish one from others. Adorno identifies a phenomenon of this kind in connection with the commodification of an individual's personality, especially certain idiosyncratic features of it, in the following passage from *Minima Moralia*:

> The individualities imported into America, and divested of individuality in the process, are called colourful personalities. Their eager, uninhibited temperament, their sudden fancies, their 'originality', even if it be only a peculiar odiousness, even their garbled language, utilize [*verwerten*] human qualities as a clown's costume. Since they are subject to the universal mechanism of competition and have no means of adapting to the market and coping with it other than their petrified otherness, they plunge passionately into the privilege of their self and so exaggerate themselves that they completely eradicate what they are taken for.[11]

Thus, even those features of one's own self that distinguish one from others and appear to have nothing to do with property rights, such as distinctive physical or psychological attributes, memories and life-defining experiences, as well as abilities and talents, become commodities. This way of viewing and relating to oneself is captured by the following declaration made by one of Marx and Engels's targets of criticism in *The German Ideology*, Max Stirner: 'Over the portal of our time stands not that "Know thyself" of Apollo, but a "*Get the value out of thyself* [*Verwerte Dich*]*!*"'.[12] How one views such features of oneself depends on how they are interpreted and made use of, that is, whether they are treated as essential parts of oneself that define who one is or as detachable parts of oneself that can be interpreted or employed in ways that increase their exchange value but distort their meaning and value for the individual who is the bearer of them. Consider, for example, the case of a person who writes an autobiography that falsifies or trivializes key experiences in his or her life with the intention of making the book more accessible and thus likely to sell more copies. Property rights here play a key role because the system of production and exchange that explains the tendency to behave in this way presupposes a particular historical form of property that allows features of oneself to become commodities in the relevant sense.

---

[11] Adorno, *Minima Moralia*, no. 88; translation modified.
[12] *The Ego and Its Own*, 278.

I shall now summarize the argument. The way in which exchange value comes to dominate society generates the seemingly natural tendency to conceive of oneself and others in terms of purely formal categories, especially legal and political ones. Exchange value's dominant role in society tends to produce these effects because the detachability of productive capabilities and other saleable attributes of a person's own self and their utilization as sources of exchange value reduce the self to a purely abstract entity. Treating such features of oneself as commodities in fact presupposes the reduction of the self to a merely abstract entity that is independent of any determinate content, that is to say, a self that is nothing more than a repository of exchange value. Although legal equality and political equality likewise require an abstract view of the self and others, exchange value's dominance of society is held to be the source of the relevant self-conception and view of others.[13] The moral idea of equality then serves to reinforce exchange value's dominance of society by making that which is purely abstract appear natural.[14]

We are now in a better position to understand why Marx would advocate the abolition of private property beyond the means of production. The reason is that the complete abolition of private property would undermine the capitalist system of production and exchange that produces and requires a false picture of the self and others, for a defining feature of

---

[13] Thus the surface phenomenon that prompts the inquiry turns out to depend on something more fundamental, which concerns material relations between social agents. This would help to explain how increasing recognition of the moral equality of individuals accompanied by more strident demands for its legal and political realization and exchange value's increasing dominance of a society based on commodity exchange historically emerged at more or less the same time in 'bourgeois society'. The 'abstract', 'artificial' and 'unreal' individual is not, therefore, to be identified with the citizen alone. Rather, this individual is also encountered at the level of civil society, which is dominated by exchange value, and whose social relations are governed by it. This implies that widespread and insistent appeals to the idea of equality are most likely to be heard when, beneath the surface, abstract exchange value comes increasingly to dominate society by governing social relations. A claim of this kind poses a problem for Marx's own account of history, however, for it suggests that the historical period in which appeals to the idea of legal and political equality would be the most strident is the same period in which the dominance of exchange value would be at its height. In 'On the Jewish Question', Marx associates appeals of the relevant kind with the French Revolution and key political documents associated with it. Yet it is implausible to claim that at this historical juncture exchange value not only became more dominant in society than it had ever been before but also more dominant than it would ever subsequently be.

[14] This is not to say that Marx is completely hostile to appeals to legal and political equality. He himself acknowledges that, under certain historical conditions, an appeal to them may in fact be expressive of genuine emancipatory demands, and that the idea of equality may then serve as a powerful instrument in political struggles. For example, he claims in 'On the Jewish Question' that '[p]olitical emancipation is certainly a big step forward. It is admittedly not the final form of human emancipation in general, but it is the final form of human emancipation *within* the world order up to now' (MEGA I/2: 150; JQ, 221; translation modified).

4.3 Exchange Value and the Idea of Equality

private property, the right to dispose freely of a thing to which one possesses a legal right, is a presupposition of this system. The abolition of legal ownership of commodities and, in particular, the right to dispose of them freely would therefore end exchange value's dominance of society, thereby preventing it from having the effects described above, whereas restricting this right to one sphere would allow exchange value not only to remain dominant within this sphere but also to encroach on other spheres, including a human being's self-conception and his or her conception of other human beings.

One may nevertheless ask whether there is not ultimately some way of reconciling an individual's conception of himself or herself as an abstract legal entity, on the one hand, and as a concrete individual, on the other, by showing that although the exchange of commodities governed by exchange value and the accompanying idea of moral equality require abstracting from all determinate features of the self, this does not entail that an individual must conceive of himself or herself only in this way. I have already highlighted, however, that for Marx exchange value's dominance of social relations in capitalist society will exert a pressure on individuals to treat determinate features of themselves as detachable parts of themselves, turning the self into an abstract repository of exchange value. Moreover, there are two other reasons Marx has for rejecting what is, in effect, a division of the self into two distinct aspects that corresponds to the separation of social life from political life. Although these reasons may not be decisive, they serve to strengthen my interpretation of Marx's grounds for advocating the complete abolition of private property. As we shall see in the next section, he also has a separate, if closely related, freedom-based argument for the complete abolition of private property.

To begin with, it is difficult to see how Marx could accept a division of the self that corresponds to two distinct spheres that an individual occupies at the same time, for this suggests the kind of alienated double life described in 'On the Jewish Question'. As we have seen, this double life is explained in terms of how an individual abstracts from all the determinate natural, personal and social features that distinguish him or her from other individuals and, at the same time, is a natural, concrete human being. Thus there is an internal division within the same self. The objection identified above would therefore need to explain how these two aspects of the same individual can be successfully reconciled in such a way that the individual's being and life in capitalist society remain sufficiently unified. This brings me to the second reason Marx has for rejecting a division of the self that requires explaining how the different aspects of the same self can be reconciled.

The reason is that even if it were possible to conceive of an initial condition in which there existed an equilibrium between the two relevant aspects of the self and the unification of them, the abstract self will *become* dominant because of the constant pressure to treat determinate features of oneself as detachable, and thus commodifiable, parts of oneself, thereby reducing the self to an abstract repository of exchange value. Thus, once one adopts a less static model of the self, a model of the self as it exists in society and is shaped by it, a satisfactory account of how the required unity of the two aspects of the self can be maintained is required. Ultimately, the question of the extent to which individuals can resist the pressures exerted on them by a system of commodity exchange governed by exchange value and successfully unify the relevant aspects of themselves is an empirical one.[15] Marx nevertheless provides us with a plausible account of why such pressures must be thought to exist and what their lasting effects may be. Since the capitalist economic and social system arises from countless acts of commodity exchange and these acts presuppose the right to dispose freely of things of which one is the legal owner, the complete abolition of private property promises to eliminate the pressure to conceive of oneself as an abstract repository of exchange value and thus view determinate features of oneself as detachable, commodifiable parts of oneself at the same time as one seeks to retain the view of oneself as a unique individual.

The idea that an economic and social system founded on private property will exert irresistible pressure on a society, and thus on the individuals who belong to it, is a theme that Marx discusses in one of the drafts of a letter that he intended to send to the Russian revolutionary Vera Zasulich outlining his views on the potential role of the Russian rural commune in a transition from a largely pre-capitalist society to a socialist one that did not involve all the phases of capitalist development. Marx writes that

---

[15] Some accounts of contemporary capitalism can be seen to support Marx's views on the effects of a system of commodity exchange governed by exchange value even though they highlight certain fundamental differences between modern capitalism and the form of capitalism with which Marx himself was familiar. For example, it is argued that the deregulation of financial markets has produced a situation in which profit extraction based on wage labour takes a back seat to the valuation of capital by financial institutions and thus to the allocation of capital in the form of credit. In this situation, individuals are forced to make their 'projects' and any relevant aspects of themselves, such as their educational achievements or skills, attractive to investors who are the ultimate judges of their value. See, Feher, *Rated Agency*, 41ff. Among such projects, we may include ones that initially have considerable personal significance and value for the individuals who adopt and develop them, but who must then make sure that they are able to turn these projects and the relevant aspects of themselves into alienable assets ('human capital') that are sufficiently attractive to investors who possess the financial means required to realize these projects. This process may deprive the projects of their original personal significance and value, with the result that they become purely external ones in relation to the individuals concerned.

the dualism of private property and communal property (*la propriété commune*) that is characteristic of this agrarian society endows it with a vigorous life. This is because the communal ownership of land and the social relations that follow from it provide a solid foundation, while the private ownership of a house, a yard, a small plot of land for farming and the products of the cultivation of this plot of land fosters individuality in a way that the structures of more primitive forms of society did not allow. Yet this dualism also contains the seeds of the commune's dissolution.

One reason for this is that the private ownership of land, however limited, will gradually undermine the communal ownership of land. The more fundamental reason, however, concerns the fragmentation of labour that accompanies the cultivation of privately owned plots of land. This is a source of further private appropriation, in that it facilitates the accumulation of movable property such as livestock and, more crucially, money in ways that the commune cannot control. These goods may become the objects of individual exchanges in which cunning and chance play their part. This enables individuals to enrich themselves, leading to the loss of the economic and social equality that characterized the original rural commune (MEGA I/25: 237–38; MZC, 120). We can here detect the idea of a process whereby increasing commodification and the accompanying development of a system of exchange governed by exchange value become ever more dominant, resulting in the demise of earlier social forms and the exclusion of alternatives to the prevailing economic and social system. This theme of the pressures exercised on a society, and thus on individuals, by the capitalist economic and social system brings me to another of Marx's reasons for advocating the complete abolition of private property.

The account of Marx's reasons for advocating the complete abolition of private property that I have so far provided invites the question as to how communist society would foster the right self-conception and the right conception of social relations. It is now evident that this self-conception and this conception of social relations will involve thinking of oneself and others as individuals. Communist society will therefore not be an egalitarian society in the sense that each member of it is viewed as a person with the same formal moral status that requires abstracting from those features that distinguish individuals from one another. The self of communist society is nevertheless understood to be a free self as well as a determinate one. I shall therefore now seek to combine my discussion of how individuals can be determinate selves within this society with an explanation of why Marx considers the abolition of private property to be a condition of genuine freedom.

4.4 Freedom and the Abolition of Private Property

One reason for advocating the abolition of private property in order to make 'real' individuality possible concerns the statement 'from each according to his abilities, to each according to his needs!' (MEGA I/25: 15; CGP, 215). The idea of a society in which individuals contribute according to their abilities at the same time as goods and resources are distributed according to need implies the following ways in which the members of this society will relate to themselves and to one another as genuine individuals as opposed to abstract economic, legal or political entities.

Those individuals who contribute according to their abilities are recognized as individuals who possess capabilities that not all individuals share, while those who do share these capabilities may not possess them, or cannot develop them, to the same extent. Recognition of individual differences also manifests itself in the benefits that individuals enjoy, such as the opportunity to develop distinctive capabilities through the exercise of them and social esteem, and in society's expectations concerning the contribution that individuals who possess specific capabilities ought to make to the satisfaction of the needs of others. Those individuals who receive goods and resources according to their needs – and individuals belonging to the previous group will form a subgroup of this group – are recognized as individuals with determinate needs that every other member of society either does not share or does not have to the same degree. Thus in communist society, specific objects are produced by employing specific capabilities with a view to satisfying specific needs, whereas in the capitalist economic and social system objects are produced primarily with a view to their abstract exchange value and the distribution of them is governed by this value.

The statement 'from each according to his abilities, to each according to his needs' implies that individuals would not be entitled to claim the exclusive right to the use and possession of a thing independently of the norm expressed in this statement. The entitlement to the possession and use of a thing will instead depend on whether an individual genuinely needs it, either as an object of consumption or as something required for a specific activity, including a productive activity that contributes to the satisfaction of the needs of others. Individuals cannot, therefore, be thought to enjoy the right to dispose freely of things that they are nevertheless entitled to possess and to use, beyond being permitted to judge what is the most appropriate and effective use of these things in relation to the specific end for which they have been allocated to them. Individuals would not even be completely free to dispose of their own labour power as they please because they ought to exercise their productive powers in ways that serve to satisfy the needs of others as well as their own needs. It might nevertheless be possible to identify at least some things from which individuals have the right to exclude others accompanied by the right to dispose of them freely in such a way that the rights in question do not appear to violate the norm implicit in the statement 'from each according to his abilities, to each according to his needs'. This is because these things are not ones that must be produced and distributed in order to satisfy the needs of others. Thus Marx's argument for the total abolition of private property cannot be explained purely in terms of this statement. Rather, the argument concerning the effects of exchange value's dominance of society on a person's self-conception and the way in which he or she conceives of social relations is also necessary. Moreover, Marx has a further reason for abolishing private property that concerns the threat that private property poses to the freedom of individuals.

We have seen that Marx identifies the amount of social power that an agent possesses with the amount of exchange value in the form of money over which he or she exercises control. The differences in social power here reflect differences in the type of property owned by social agents, which are the means of production, on the one hand, and a person's own labour power only, on the other. The individual is assumed to possess the legal right to this exchange value, including the right to dispose of it freely by entering into contractual relations with other persons. It can therefore be said that the more private property an individual possesses in the form of money or in the form of items of property that can be converted into money, the more he or she will be able to enter into acts of exchange with others, either with a view to the satisfaction of his or her needs and desires or with a view to increasing his or her capital. Thus considerable differences in social power are likely to exist in a society in which private property ranges from ownership of resources such as land, through ownership of any means required by a productive activity under the relevant historical conditions, to ownership of one's own labour power alone. These differences have their source not only in the nature of that which a social agent can exchange but also in the extent to which he or she is able to exercise control over others by means of the greater amount of exchange value at his or her disposal relative to the amount of it that others have at their disposal. In this way, private property generates asymmetries in economic and social power that are the sources of actual or possible forms of domination.

One possible objection to the demand for the complete abolition of private property is that this demand does not follow from the need to prevent, or at least reduce, such actual or potential domination because of the threat that it poses to an individual's freedom. For the state could undertake redistributive measures funded by general taxation aimed at ensuring that individuals possess enough private property to make them sufficiently independent of the wills of others, or it could restrict the right to private property to things that do not serve to increase one agent's social power relative to the social power of other agents.[16] Yet even if the state is assumed to be both willing and able to undertake the relevant measures in the face of the resistance offered by powerful economic and social agents, such as individuals or corporations rich enough to pay others to discover legal loopholes that enable them to reduce their tax burden, this type of objection misses the point in two important ways. First, it neglects the argument concerning the effects of an economic and social system governed by exchange value on a person's self-conception and his or her conception of social relations. Second, the ameliorative measures proposed above would leave the system of commodity exchange intact, whereas this system is the source not only of differences in social power but also of the pressures that lead people to conceive of themselves and others in a purely abstract way. It is therefore still worth seeking to reconstruct Marx's argument for the claim that private property is incompatible with the genuine freedom of all members of society.

If private property exists within a society, then the opportunity to enter into acts of commodity exchange also exists. The exchange of commodities requires a measure and symbolic expression of the value of commodities. As we have seen, Marx argues that a system of exchange will then necessarily develop in such a way that exchange value and its symbolic expression, money, take on a life of their own. The problem cannot be reduced to how individuals will then fail to relate both to themselves and to others as genuine individuals and act accordingly. Rather, there is also a deficient understanding of freedom that is produced by an economic and social system governed by exchange value. Since private property is a presupposition of this system, the complete abolition of this form of property is a condition

---

[16] This type of solution is suggested by Rousseau's claim that legislation must aim to fulfil the following demand: 'as for wealth, no citizen be so very rich that he can buy another, and none so poor that he is compelled to sell himself' (*Of the Social Contract*, 2.11.2).

of the freedom presupposed by the idea of a society in which individuals relate to themselves and to others as truly *free* as well as *real* individuals. Marx lays the groundwork for this type of argument in 'On the Jewish Question', the same text in which he describes how the idea of equality is the expression of an alienated self-relation and relation to others.

With reference to Article 16 of the French Constitution of 1793, Marx characterizes freedom as the right to act in any way that one desires, provided one does not thereby harm others. He claims that this right finds more determinate expression in the human right to private property understood as 'the right to enjoy and dispose [*disponiren*] of one's resources as one wills [*willkürlich*], without regard for other men and independently of society: the right of self-interest' (MEGA I/2: 158; JQ, 229). In civil society, in which the right to freedom and the right to property are located, equality 'in its non-political sense' is nothing more than 'the equality of ... *liberté*', a form of freedom that amounts to regarding each human being as 'a self-sufficient monad' (MEGA I/2: 158; JQ, 230; translation modified). From some of Marx's claims in 'On the Jewish Question' discussed in the previous section, this self-sufficient monad can be identified as an independent moral and legal entity that is identical with all other such entities by virtue of its formal status and its enjoyment of the corresponding set of rights. Each monad will be different from the other ones only because of the choices that it makes through the exercise of its right to freedom, especially in the form of the right to dispose freely of its property. The other monads will remain indifferent to the content of these choices and what they may tell them about the first monad as an individual, provided this monad's exercise of the right to freedom does not violate their own rights.

This shows how Marx's demand for the abolition of private property concerns the type of freedom enjoyed by individuals in capitalist society and the type of relation between them that this freedom entails. The type of freedom in question finds expression in the right to property, which leads one human being to see in another human being 'not the *realization* but the *limitation* of his own freedom' (MEGA I/2: 158; JQ, 230). In other words, the freedom of others and their property rights mark the boundaries of the legally defined sphere within which a person may exercise the right to dispose freely of his or her property without any regard for the needs and views of others. Community, in so far as it exists at all, then 'appears as a framework extraneous to the individuals, as a limitation of their original independence' (MEGA I/2: 159; JQ, 230). As we have seen, Marx identifies this external framework with a society that is governed by exchange value and structured by laws that secure the property rights presupposed by an economic and social system in which commodities are freely exchanged. The power that this external framework possesses in relation to individuals helps to explain another claim made in 'On the Jewish Question'.

The claim in question is that each human being 'as a *private individual* [*Privatmensch*]' not only regards other human beings as means but also 'debases himself to a means and becomes a plaything of alien forces [*zum Spielball fremder Mächte wird*]' (MEGA I/2: 149; JQ, 220). The idea that individuals become 'a plaything of alien forces' implies that their freedom, as described above, is in fact a source of unfreedom. Marx's account of commodity fetishism in the first volume of *Capital* helps to explain this claim, for it shows that the exercise of the right to dispose freely of one's property, which entails freedom in the sense of the absence of moral or legal constraints on the use of one's property, results in a situation in which exchange value dominates individuals and the relations between them.

In his account of commodity fetishism, Marx describes how the social character of labour assumes the distorted form of a relation between products of labour exchanged by private persons for money. In capitalist society commodities *must* be exchanged in this way by individuals who are reduced to abstract legal entities. The relations between these private persons who otherwise remain indifferent to one another then appear to be established by acts of commodity exchange and the contracts governing them. Although the commodities exchanged may well have a use value, for the persons who exchange them they primarily possess exchange value, given how the immediate aim is to acquire the universal means of exchange, that is, money. Marx speaks of fetishism in connection with this reduction of society to a set of formal, external relations because commodities appear to possess the mysterious and seemingly magical power to establish social relations that did not previously exist. In this way, a system of relations between things comes into being, with the relations between things explaining the existence of social relations. This system appears to be independent of the wills of the individuals caught up in it. These individuals must accommodate themselves to the demands of this system, even though the labour of many of them is the real source of the value of the commodities that are exchanged. Since, however, the social relations that characterize a society governed by exchange value are produced by means of acts of exchange, they cannot be regarded as fully objective ones, in the sense of relations that exist independently of human agency. Rather, through repeated and endlessly repeatable acts of commodity exchange, social agents create and maintain the set of relations that constitutes this system, and thus create and maintain the system of exchange that dominates them. This represents a perversion of that which Hegel calls 'ethical life', in that the moment of objectivity is not accompanied by the moment of subjective identification that would remove the alien objective character that society has come to assume.

The relevance of Marx's account of commodity fetishism to the claim that he is committed to the complete abolition of private property can be illustrated with reference to the worker's position within the system established and maintained by acts of commodity exchange. The only commodity that the worker brings to the marketplace is his or her labour power understood as nothing more than the capacity to produce value, for this labour power is the only private property that he or she can repeatedly exchange for money in the form of wages with the aim of purchasing the means of satisfying his or her material needs. The worker lacks the opportunity to exercise his or her productive powers independently of others because he or she lacks free and direct access to the productive forces required to exercise them. These forces instead belong to the capitalist. One may therefore speak of a capacity that 'becomes a reality only when it has been solicited by capital ... since activity without object is nothing' (MEGA II/1.1: 189; G, 267). Once the worker has entered into a contractual agreement with the capitalist to exchange his or her labour power for another commodity, that is, money in the form of wages, this labour power is employed to produce not only the value of the wages paid to the worker but also a value that exceeds it. The production of this 'surplus' value 'is the determining purpose of capitalist production' (MEGA II/8: 236–37; Cap. 1: 338). A relation is here established between two agents with equal legal status, both of whom possess and exercise the right to dispose freely of their property. Thus the relation between them appears to be established by a voluntary act that presupposes this right. Yet Marx identifies how the worker is already unfree when he or she enters into a contract with the capitalist and how the conditions of his or her unfreedom are in part created by an exchange of commodities.

The voluntary nature of the act of exchanging commodities is to a large extent illusory because the idea of a contract into which the worker freely enters conceals the coercive character of the relation between the worker and the capitalist. As we have seen, the worker is not able to produce independently either the means of satisfying his or her basic material needs or commodities that can be exchanged for the money needed to purchase the means of subsistence because he or she lacks free and direct access to the productive forces that would enable him or her to exercise his or her productive powers. The worker must therefore sell his or her labour power to another person who is the legal owner of these productive forces. In this respect, 'the wage-labourer is bound to his owner [*Eigenthümer*] by invisible threads' (MEGA II/8: 540; Cap. 1: 719). These threads are woven by the worker's own act of entering into a contract with the capitalist, in that this voluntary act establishes a relation between the worker and the capitalist through which the latter achieves effective control over the worker's labour power. The worker then proceeds not only to actualize the productive forces to which he or she lacks free and direct access but also, through the employment of these same forces, to increase the amount of surplus value that is the private property of the capitalist.[17] This is, in effect, to increase the power of capital over labour, given that social power is a function of wealth:

> Capitalist production therefore reproduces in the course of its own process the separation between labour-power and the conditions of labour. It thereby reproduces and perpetuates the conditions under which the worker is exploited. It incessantly forces him to sell his labour-power in order to live, and enables the capitalist to purchase labour-power in order that he may enrich himself. It is no longer a mere accident that capitalist and worker confront each other in the commodity market [*Waarenmarkt*] as buyer and seller. It is the alternating rhythm of the process itself which throws the worker back onto the commodity market again and again as seller of his labour-power and continually transforms his own product into a means by which another man can purchase him. In reality, the worker belongs to capital before he has sold himself to the capitalist. His economic bondage is at once mediated through, and concealed by, the periodic renewal of the act by which he sells himself, his change of masters, and the oscillations in the market-price of his labour. (MEGA II/8: 544; Cap. 1: 723–24; translation modified)

The worker therefore does not, and cannot, enjoy genuine freedom, either in the sense of exercising genuine free choice or in the sense of enjoying

---

[17] Any increase in these forces is therefore necessarily detrimental to the worker's freedom during the capitalist phase of their development:

> Thus all the progress of civilization, or in other words every increase in the *powers of social production* [*gesellschaftliche Produktivkräfte*], if you like, in the *productive powers of labour itself* – such as results from science, inventions, division and combination of labour, improved means of communication, creation of the world market, machinery etc. – enriches not the worker but rather *capital*; hence it only magnifies again the power dominating over labour; increases only the productive power of capital. Since capital is the antithesis of the worker, this merely increases the *objective power* standing over labour. (MEGA II/1.1: 227; G, 308).

4.4 The Abolition of Private Property

effective control over the material conditions of his or her life in a way that enables him or her to develop his or her productive powers freely. Rather, both at an interpersonal level and at a systematic one, he or she is subject to 'alien forces' that dominate him or her. This may appear to leave unanswered the question as to why private property beyond the means of production must be abolished, instead of being redistributed in such a way that individuals do not become subject to the arbitrary wills of others and are able to exercise effective control over their lives by making their own choices. The following answer to this question suggests itself in the absence of any satisfactory explanation of how a redistribution of property rights would prevent exchange value from continuing to dominate human beings, not only at an interpersonal level but also, and more crucially, at the systematic one.

A redistribution of property is compatible with the continued existence of a system of exchange in which relations between private persons are established and maintained through the exchange of commodities. The difference is that there would be regular interventions aimed at changing the outcomes produced by such a system. This system of exchange would nevertheless continue to be dominated by exchange value, given that social relations between private persons are, or so it seems, established through the exchange of commodities and how this requires a measure of value that also serves as a medium and instrument of exchange. It is precisely a system of exchange of this kind that over time inevitably assumes the form of a set of independent relations between commodities governed by exchange value. This set of relations dominates individuals and forces some of them more than others to agree to an exchange of commodities that is ultimately incompatible with their freedom, as well as leading human beings to develop a false conception of both themselves and social relations. This system of exchange presupposes an exclusive legal right to things that include a person's own labour power and the labour power of other persons, and especially the right to dispose of these things freely. Thus, even if the general right to things were more equitably distributed, the right to dispose of them freely in acts of commodity exchange would reproduce the same economic and social system and eventually produce the same actual or potential relations of domination. A redistribution of property rights aimed at removing, or at least minimizing, differences in social power that enable some agents to dominate and, in effect, coerce other ones, must therefore ultimately prove ineffective in the long run.

The problem is not simply that the same economic and social system remains intact. The solution of a redistribution of property rights within an economic and social system governed by abstract exchange value fails to take sufficiently into account the inherently dynamic character of such a system. A system of this kind will, in the long run, take on a life of its own and generate the differences in social power based on wealth that the original redistribution of property was designed to prevent or minimize. Maintaining the right balance between the property rights enjoyed by individuals and the amount of social power that they possess relative to one another will therefore ultimately demand constant oversight and repeated acts of redistribution, and thus considerable constraints on a person's right to dispose freely of his or her property. Yet this outcome would be incompatible with the institution of private property under any reasonable *modern* description of it. We encountered an example of this problem in connection with Fichte's attempt to accommodate 'absolute' property within a closely regulated economic system aimed at securing each person's right to live from his or her labour. The complete abolition of private property, in contrast, would make the relevant type of economic and social system impossible, given how this system presupposes this form of property, thereby providing a definitive solution to the same problem. It should therefore come as no surprise that Marx claims that the abolition (*Aufhebung*) of private property is identical with the overthrow of the existing state of society that is to be achieved by means of a communist revolution (MEGA I/5: 42; GI, 55).

Marx's argument for the complete abolition of private property has now been shown to be equally founded on the claim that eliminating this form of property is necessary to pave the way for a society that is not dominated by exchange value and does not itself, therefore, dominate individuals and produce asymmetries in social power that enable some individuals and social groups to dominate other individuals and social groups. Thus the complete abolition of private property is necessary in so far as a free as well as real individuality is at stake. An adequate response to Marx's critique of private property would therefore need to show that a society in which this form of property exists is one that does not necessarily produce the relevant effects, or that these effects can be justified. It is not my intention here to consider what such a response might be. It is enough to have shown that even if Marx's arguments for the complete abolition of private property are less than compelling, they at least demand a response, and that a theory of redistribution that wants to retain private property and the rights that define it while seeking to prevent or to minimize certain undesirable effects of this form of property may struggle to provide an adequate

4.4 The Abolition of Private Property

response. I shall now instead turn to a question that Marx himself must answer if my reconstruction of his arguments for the complete abolition of private property is correct: how will communist society produce the right kind of relation to oneself and to others once private property has been abolished? After all, the abolition of private property is only a negative condition of a society in which the right kind of relation to oneself and to others becomes possible.

In some of his early writings, Marx makes the concept of property central to his answer to the question of how the members of the same society can be free individuals and relate to one another as such. This is consistent with the claim that property, understood as the appropriation of nature, is a constant feature of human society and the claim that property concerns not only a relation between human beings and nature but also a relation between human beings. Since the relation between human beings and nature and the relations between human beings founded on this relation change, the precise form that property assumes will vary. History shows that the specific form that the concept of property assumes is indeed subject to change. We must therefore assume that there will be property of some kind in communist society and that this property will involve a relation between human beings mediated by things that can ultimately be traced back to a relation between human beings and nature. This relation between human beings mediated by things will not, however, generate the type of self-conception and the type of conception of social relations found in a society governed by exchange value. This expectation is confirmed by Marx himself when he contrasts private property with '*truly human* and *social property*' (MEGA I/2: 374; EPM, 333). Yet what would this alternative form of property be like? And how would it overcome the problems associated with private property identified in this chapter?

Marx describes communist society as 'an association in which the free development of each is the condition for the free development of all' (MEW 4: 482; MCP, 20), and as a higher form of society in which 'the full and free development of every individual forms the ruling principle' (MEGA II/8: 556; Cap. 1: 739). If it is through this 'full and free development' that human beings *become* individuals in the required sense, then an account of the possibility of such free development must be combined with an account of how the existence of property in communist society poses no threat to freedom. Rather, communist property will serve to establish the kind of relation to oneself and to others that befits free and real individuals.

4.5 Communist Property and the Free Development of the Social Individual

We have seen that one way of understanding how individuals relate to one another as genuine individuals in communist society concerns how they contribute according to their abilities and are allocated goods and resources according to their needs. There are two distinct ways in which individuality is recognized: (1) there is recognition of the specific abilities that individuals possess and may develop by means of the exercise of them, and (2) there is recognition of the specific needs of individuals. Moreover, the mutual satisfaction of human needs by means of the exercise of distinctive human capacities does not occur within a set of social relations that remain external to individuals in that they appear to be established and maintained by an exchange of commodities. This differs from Hegel's theory of property because individuals are recognized as beings with specific attributes and needs, instead of abstract legal persons whose specific attributes and needs must be left out of consideration because of how in 'formal' right 'it is not a question of particular interests, of my advantage or welfare' (PR § 37).[18] Does this mean that individuals in communist society will be recognized and treated as individuals simply by virtue of the specific abilities and the specific needs they happen to have, irrespective of the actual character of these abilities and needs?

With respect to needs, Marx could have in mind either fundamental human needs or needs that are somehow unique to individuals. In the first case, the needs would be ones that individuals share. They would not then be needs that distinguish them from one another. Particularity would concern only the extent to which individuals experience these needs or some other variation in the set of essential needs that they share. These needs may include needs other than basic material ones, such as cultural needs, and the needs may vary from individual to individual with respect to the ways in which they can be satisfied. In the second case, the needs might be regarded as the products of merely personal, and even idiosyncratic, beliefs and desires, so that they may be termed preferences rather than needs. The demand to satisfy needs of this kind could then be considered unjustified, given how the failure to satisfy them would not harm a fundamental human interest, whereas the efforts made to satisfy them may require a use of another individual's abilities that might have been more appropriately directed at the satisfaction of needs that concern fundamental human

---

[18] For more on this point, see Chitty, 'Recognition and Property in Hegel and the Early Marx', 691ff.

4.5 Communist Property and Free Development 175

interests. This suggests that there would, in fact, be no requirement for others to exercise their distinctive abilities in ways that contribute to the satisfaction of these needs that might be better described as preferences. The willingness to exercise one's distinctive abilities with the aim of satisfying such needs would remain a matter of personal choice once all essential needs had been satisfied. I shall now explain how Marx must be thought to have in mind a type of individuality that is not reducible to desires of this kind or any other arbitrary features that distinguish individuals from one another.

In communist society, there will be a system of production and distribution based on need. This system is presumably one in which items are exchanged directly or the distribution of them is centrally managed. In either case, the production and distribution of goods and resources will not be mediated by abstract exchange value and its symbolic expression, money. Marx provides a clue as to the nature of this system of production and distribution when he asks us to imagine an alternative society to a society in which human relations seem to be established and maintained by an exchange of commodities governed by abstract exchange value so as to break the spell of this society's appearance of naturalness: 'Let us finally imagine, for a change, an association of free men, working with the means of production held in common [*mit gemeinschaftlichen Produktionsmitteln*], and expending their many different forms of labour-power in full self-awareness as one single social labour force' (MEGA II/8: 106–07; Cap. 1: 171).

In this form of association, human beings are free. But in what sense are they free? It is evident that their freedom has to do with common ownership of the means of production and how the members of this form of association, despite any differences with respect to the use made of their labour power, are conscious of themselves as members of one single, unified productive force. The transparent social nature of this single productive force can be contrasted with how individuals appear to be only contingently united when they exchange commodities of which they are the legal owners. Individuals are now conscious of the essentially social character of their productive activity and the larger social process of which it forms an essential part. The total product of their united productive powers is also essentially social in nature, with one part of it serving as fresh means of production while the other part is consumed by the members of this form of association and must therefore be distributed among them according to need. The distribution of the social product nevertheless mirrors the exchange of commodities in so far as 'the share of each individual producer in the means of subsistence is determined by his labour-time' (MEGA II/8: 107; Cap. 1: 172). In other words, the value of an individual's contribution is determined by the amount of time required, on average, to produce the relevant type of thing. This recalls how the value of a commodity is determined by the amount of labour time required to produce it. An individual is then entitled to receive in return goods of an equivalent value.

This corresponds to the first stage of post-capitalist society identified in the *Critique of the Gotha Programme*, not to the higher phase of communism in which individuals willingly contribute according to their abilities and are allocated goods and resources according to their needs. There is nevertheless a fundamental difference between this first stage of post-capitalist society and the capitalist society that preceded it. This difference concerns the explicitly social nature of the organization of the production process and the distribution of goods, for they are both subject to planning with the aim of ensuring the satisfaction of needs, rather than allowing the relation between the production of goods and the distribution of them to be determined by an exchange of commodities that depends on the choices of their legal owners. In other words, by abolishing the mediating function performed by exchange value and its symbolic expression, money, individuals become conscious of how their labour power and that which they produce by means of it serve to satisfy the specific needs of others, so that the 'social relations of the individual producers, both towards their labour and the products of their labour, are here transparent in their simplicity, in production as well as in distribution' (MEGA II/8: 107; Cap. 1: 172). We may assume that at the higher stage of communist society, the ghost of exchange value is completely banished by dispensing altogether with any kind of common standard that is used to measure the value of labour and goods. I shall shortly show that Marx provides some clues as to what this might mean in practice.

Is the transparency that characterizes the social relations of communist society and its members' consciousness of their dependence on one another with respect to the satisfaction of their needs sufficient to explain how individuals relate to themselves and to one another as free individuals? The members of communist society might accept that cooperation in accordance with a social plan is necessary but not also agree that their productive activity should directly aim to satisfy *all* the needs that individuals happen to have. Rather, there might be some agreement concerning the production and distribution of goods required to satisfy fundamental human needs in the absence of any commitment to provide the means of satisfying other, less vital needs. If it is only a matter of needs that all human beings share, however, it becomes difficult to see how we might speak of them as individuals who are not merely numerically distinct from one another but also differ from one another by virtue of who and what they are, as when individuals are described as 'particular' ones because of their personal characteristics, specific aspirations and particular desires.

The particularity of the individuals who are members of communist society must therefore be explained either in terms of how each set of essential human needs is somehow differently configured or in terms of how these needs, although common to all, are not strictly identical because there are certain qualitative or quantitative differences between them. I shall now argue that there is, in fact, another aspect to Marx's account of individuality which helps to explain how the members of communist society would relate to one another as individuals who are immediately conscious of their social nature and act in accordance with this consciousness. This aspect concerns the way in which individuals *become* distinct from one another through both the specific productive activities in which they engage within communist society and that which they produce or otherwise achieve by means of these activities. The individuality in question is not a purely personal or idiosyncratic one, for there is an important sense in which it is of a general kind.

Marx speaks of '[u]niversally developed individuals, whose social relations, as their own communal relations, are ... subordinated to their own communal control' (MEGA II/1.1: 94; G, 162). The ideas of communal relations and communal control imply that these 'universally developed' individuals are members of a form of association governed by a social plan that regulates the production and distribution of goods. Moreover, this social plan is one that these individuals themselves have collectively devised. The form of association in question is presented as the alternative to a society whose 'point of departure is not the free social individual [*das freie gesellschaftliche Indviduum*]' because social relations appear to be established by acts of commodity exchange, and thus assume the form of 'an *alien* social power' that dominates individuals, whereas the social relations are, in fact, the result of their 'own collisions with one another' (MEGA II/1.1: 126; G, 197). As already indicated, an association of genuinely free individuals would be one in which individuals are essentially social as well as free beings because they are directly conscious of both the social relations that they create and maintain through their productive activity and how this activity and its products serve to meet the needs of others. The locating of 'universally developed individuals' within a social context should come as no surprise. Nevertheless, Marx still needs to explain how communist society facilitates the free development of individuals by means of their transparent social relations in a way that it not possible when society is structured by the seemingly contingent social relations established by voluntary acts of exchange that are a defining feature of a society governed by exchange value. This brings me to Marx's understanding of the essentially relational character of the free individuality that he has in mind.

For Marx, society is essentially a set of relations, as opposed to an aggregation of individuals, each of whom is brought into an external relation with other individuals as a result of the spontaneous workings of a free market governed by exchange value: 'Society does not consist of individuals, but expresses the sum of interrelations, the relations within which these individuals stand' (MEGA II/1.1: 188; G, 265). A free society would be one in which the relations are of the right kind, in that the relata remain free in relation to one another, though not in the purely external way of 'atoms' whose legally defined spheres of personal freedom separate them from one another. As we have seen, this external model of freedom is compatible with interpersonal forms of domination and the domination of individuals by the capitalist economic and social system. The idea that the relata stand in transparent social relations with one another at the same time as they remain free corresponds to how communist society will be a free society in that it is governed by a social plan endorsed by the members of this society, each of whom plays an active part in shaping this plan. This presupposes not only the capacity to be self-determining, both individually and collectively, but also the exercise of this capacity.[19] So far, however, any notion of individual development within a social context would concern only common features of human agency, thereby leaving unanswered the question of how one can speak of genuine individuality.

One possible answer to this question is that when individuals collectively construct the social plan that determines the relations between them in communist society, they assign to themselves and to others different roles in the production process. This enables individuals not only to perform mental as well as physical forms of labour but also to fulfil various tasks suited to their personal talents and abilities. This would correspond to the demand to contribute to meeting the needs of others according to one's abilities. Within the capitalist division of labour, in contrast, individuals are typically restricted to one task or function. Support for this

---

[19] For more on this point and how the workers' organization of the production process in communist society can be thought to facilitate freedom understood as self-determination, see James, *Practical Necessity, Freedom, and History*, Chapter 6.

interpretation is provided by Marx's claim that the revolutionary nature of modern industry demands mobility and flexibility on the part of the worker, who therefore no longer occupies a fixed role in the production process that requires perfecting only one type of productive activity at the expense of others. The development of modern industry, or so Marx claims, thereby paves the way for the replacement of 'the partially developed individual [*das Theilindividuum*], who is merely the bearer of one specialized social function' by 'the totally developed individual, for whom the different social functions are different modes of activity he takes up in turn' (MEGA II/8: 471; Cap. 1: 618). The requirement that individuals contribute according to their abilities would nevertheless impose limits on the extent to which variation of this kind is justifiable.

Even if we assume that society does not block the development of any abilities that an individual possesses, the claim that each individual, irrespective of the nature and the extent of his or her abilities, should be allowed to perform any role that he or she desires to perform would amount to a denial of individuality. For it would fail to recognize how the particularity of each human being in part consists in how individuals are not identical with respect to their abilities even when they are provided with the opportunity to employ and develop them. Thus individuals must be viewed as different from one another not only because they perform different tasks within a society in which human beings are directly conscious of their dependence on one another but also because the assignment of these tasks will reflect differences with respect to their specific abilities and the degree to which they are able to develop them within the social division of labour. There would then be certain attributes that serve to distinguish individuals from one another, namely, the distinctive attributes that qualify them to perform specific roles. Moreover, the absence of a society governed by exchange value would result in the disappearance of the tendency to treat such attributes as detachable, commodifiable features of a self that is reducible to the abstract bearer of them.[20]

---

[20] This is to assume a reliable rule of thumb by means of which abilities can be judged without introducing an abstract measure of the social value of the different abilities possessed by individuals. It looks, moreover, as if the possibility of the social plan that is to govern communist society presupposes a natural alignment between people's abilities and the needs of society that can be easily recognized or the possibility of introducing measures that educate and train people to develop the capabilities required to ensure the satisfaction of the fundamental needs of all members of society. There may still have to be a formal assessment process that involves ascertaining whether an individual possesses knowledge or skills that a person sufficiently expert in the relevant field would be able to recognize. A standard of this kind, however, would be directed at, and derived from, something determinate.

The association of free human beings that Marx envisages is less fixed than earlier forms of society in which individuals also stood in direct social relations with one another because individuals are no longer tied to specific social functions, even if there is a social division of labour and constraints on what individuals would be entitled to do within this division of labour. Nor do individuals possess a fixed social identity. Rather, they may to some extent perform different, shifting roles, and in so far as these roles are constitutive of their social identity, this identity itself will not be a fixed one. In this respect, the social relations that characterize communist society are essentially different from those founded on relations of personal dependence, where one social agent directly dominates another social agent and is entitled to do so by a clearly defined, quasi-natural social status which is associated with specific privileges on the one side and specific obligations on the other. Although human beings confront one another as individuals within a society characterized by relations of personal dependence of this kind, in so far as a particular social status and all that follows from it serve to distinguish them from one another, the destruction of such social relations was a historical condition of the liberation of human beings from the type of domination that these relations made possible.

Despite the lack of fixity with respect to social roles and the relations in which individuals stand with one another in communist society, these roles and relations are no longer determined by an unplanned exchange of commodities. In capitalist society, human beings lack genuine control over the material and social conditions of their lives precisely because the satisfaction of their needs and the relations between them and other human beings are determined by how effectively they can operate at any given time within an economic and social system governed by exchange value that remains independent of their own wills. In communist society, in contrast, they exercise some control over their social identities and social relations by playing a role in shaping the social plan in accordance with which society is to be organized. In this respect, Marx's vision of communist society represents an attempt to describe a mean between the disruptive dynamism of capitalist society and a more static, traditional model of society.

Although the features of communist society identified above enable us to make sense of Marx's use of the predicates 'social' and 'free' in connection with the members of this society, it is still only in a limited sense that they can be thought to relate to one another as genuine individuals. The members of this society are individuals in that they have a determinate and

4.5   Communist Property and Free Development

stable, but not fixed, social identity that derives from the different roles they play in a society structured according to a plan that they collectively shape and cooperatively put into practice. Thus, instead of confronting one another as abstract legal subjects who are the owners of commodities that embody a certain amount of exchange value relative to the exchange value of other commodities, the members of communist society will directly relate to one another as individuals who are distinct from one another by virtue of both the differences that qualify them to perform the social roles that they are allocated and the different nature of the roles themselves. Moreover, these roles will require making available to some individuals resources that are not made available to other individuals in so far as the effective performance of a specific role demands this. Yet this type of determinacy is compatible with a state of affairs in which some, or even many, individuals perform identical social roles or the same set of social roles.

An individual would then be like someone who is different from others by virtue of the position that he or she occupies in a particular team. There may nevertheless be many other individuals who play in the same position in similar, if not identical, teams, and whose suitability equally derives from their possession of the same or similar abilities and skills. Although there is some room for individuality in that an individual may perform the relevant role in a way that manifests specific personal attributes, the individuality in question would still be of an essentially general kind. Indeed, it is difficult to see how it could be otherwise if the individual is to remain a 'social' individual. I shall now identify three ways in which Marx attempts to introduce some further particularization. The first way concerns the sphere of material production, and it provides some clues as to the nature of communist property. The second way concerns what lies beyond the sphere of material production. The third way concerns global developments brought about by the capitalist mode of production.

In the *Excerpts from James Mill's* Elements of Political Economy, Marx indicates one way in which the members of communist society will relate to one another as individuals in a stronger sense through productive activity aimed at satisfying the needs of others. We are here presented with the picture of a society in which private property has been abolished and human beings relate to one another through that which they produce in a distinctively human way, that is, as free, creative social beings. Each producer objectifies the 'specific character' (*Eigenthümlichkeit*) of himself or herself in that which he or she produces, enabling him or her to experience his or her productive activity and the object of this activity as a free and affirmative expression of his or her own 'individual' life (MEGA IV/2:

465–66; EJM, 277–78). Moreover, in the other individual's consumption or use of the object produced, the individual producer experiences a sense of fulfilment that comes from having satisfied a specific human need. This looks like the resolution of the opposition between objectification (*Vergegenständlichung*) and self-affirmation (*Selbstbestätigung*) mentioned in another text from the same period (MEGA I/2: 389; EPM, 348).

There is here a twofold sense in which human beings relate to one another as individuals through their productive activity and the products of this activity. The object produced, and thus the activity of producing it, are expressive of each producer's individuality. At the same time, a specific need of the individual who consumes or uses this object is satisfied. Individuals are both the producers of objects that serve to satisfy needs and the consumers or users of them, and so the relation between them is an essentially mutual or reciprocal (*wechselseitig*) one (MEGA IV/2: 465; EJM, 278). This is compatible with the idea that each member of communist society contributes according to his or her distinctive abilities and receives goods and resources according to his or her distinctive needs. This reciprocity claim implies, however, that individuals should not receive products of human labour according to their needs without, in some way, providing others with such products, thereby making the entitlement to goods and resources dependent on an individual's own contribution as well as his or her needs. In this respect, Marx's earlier vision of communist society differs from the final phase of communist society described in the *Critique of the Gotha Programme*.

This view of how human beings relate to one another as individuals through their productive activity suggests an expressivist notion of property, in that the object produced is expressive of both the individuality of the producer who appropriates nature in some way and the direct social relation that exists between this producer and another individual who consumes or uses the same object. This expressivist notion of property requires explaining how we can conceive of the object as genuinely expressive of the producer as an individual, rather than being expressive of human nature in general, and how this object at the same time satisfies a specific need that distinguishes the individual who consumes or uses it from other individuals, rather than a general human need. Otherwise, we would not have gone beyond a general conception of individuality that is defined in terms of social roles.

With respect to the producer, one might claim that he or she possesses abilities that other individuals lack or do not possess to the same degree, such as the power to think creatively and to execute his or her ideas in original ways. These differences then find expression in the unique character of

4.5 Communist Property and Free Development

the object produced. With respect to the consumer or user of the object, one might appeal to how individuals have distinctive needs or sets of needs that only specific objects can satisfy, or distinctive abilities that can be properly exercised and developed only by means of the use of specific objects. Yet it is difficult to explain how a relation between human beings of the relevant kind would exist in the association of free human beings envisioned by Marx, given how communist society presupposes the development of large-scale industry facilitated by the capitalist mode of production, which is a necessary historical stage in that it generates the material and social conditions of communist society.[21] The following two contrasting examples illustrate the difficulties faced by any attempt to explain the relevant relation between human beings at the relevant historical stage:

1. The production of an object that is essentially different from other objects of the same general type by virtue of its possession of unique expressive properties that can be reliably identified as resulting from the productive activity of the individual who produced the object and of this individual only.
2. The production of objects of the same general type that are either indistinguishable from one another or different from one another only by virtue of properties that are not a direct result of the productive activity of any identifiable individual who played a discernible role in producing them.

Although works of art are the clearest examples of (1), an object that is a product of a craftsperson's imagination and ability to execute his or her ideas in the relevant medium is another possible example. It is relatively easy to conceive of how this type of object would satisfy a general human need in such a way as to satisfy a specific need on the part of the individual to whom it is allocated. For example, the individual concerned might possess a unique sensibility which attracts him or her to objects that have specific aesthetic properties as well as purely functional ones and enables him or her to appreciate these objects in ways that other individuals are unable to do. We shall assume, moreover, that the individual to whom the object is allocated on such grounds receives it directly from the producer or is otherwise sufficiently aware of his or her identity. The producer of the object and the consumer or user of it can then be thought to relate to each other as individuals in the required way.

---

[21] See James, *Practical Necessity, Freedom, and History*, 206ff.

In the case of (2), in contrast, the object is not clearly identifiable as the work of an individual, for each worker may contribute very little to the final product. This object may, in fact, be a mass-produced one that is so widely produced and distributed that it cannot even be identified as the work of any single group of workers (for example, the workers of factory X rather than the workers of factory Y or the workers of factory Z). An object of this kind might express something distinctive about the person who designed it, though even then constraints arising from the object's intended function and the demands of mass production may be sufficient to reduce it to a standardized product that is incompatible with any form of genuine individual expression. Moreover, the object may satisfy a general human need without there being any good reason for preferring it to another object of the same general type that is equally desirable viewed in purely functional terms, either because the object forms only part of a larger product in such a way that the expression of any kind of preference makes no sense at all or because the whole product itself is so similar to others of its kind that there can be no non-arbitrary grounds for preferring it to other products of the same general type. An expressive relation between the object of an individual's labour and the consumer or user's individuality would not then exist. The producer of the object could nevertheless be aware of having contributed to the satisfaction of a general human need.

Since (2) is typical of modern industrial societies, whereas (1) is not, it is difficult to see how human beings in communist society would relate to one another as individuals in ways that go beyond the possession of attributes that distinguish *some* individuals from other individuals, but that do not distinguish one individual from *all* other individuals. There would nevertheless be the major difference that individuals no longer exhibit the tendency to conceive of defining features of themselves as detachable attributes whose abstract exchange value allows them to be exchanged as commodities.

Marx's recognition of the limited extent to which human beings can relate to one another as free individuals in a stronger sense within the sphere of production is suggested by his identification of a sphere that lies beyond it, and by how he refers to this sphere as the 'true realm of freedom'. In this sphere, there is 'the development of human powers as an end in itself [*Selbstzweck*]', whereas in the 'realm of natural necessity' freedom is reduced to the collective rational control that the associated workers exercise over nature in such a way that it no longer dominates them as 'a blind power' (MEGA II/15: 794–95; Cap. 3: 959). This true realm of freedom expands with the shortening of the working day, so that the 'economy of time, along with the planned distribution of labour time among the various branches of production, remains the first economic law on the basis of communal production' (MEGA II/1.1: 104; G, 173).

We may assume that the distribution of necessary labour time, on the one hand, and the distribution of time free from work, on the other, will form the objects of the social plan that is to govern the association of free social individuals. During the period in which they are free from necessary labour, individuals will be able to pursue freely chosen personal projects that serve to distinguish them from one another. They will then require access to items of property that enable them to pursue these projects, though they will be entitled only to the exclusive use of these items of property in so far as pursuing a project requires it. The personal nature of these projects implies a clear division between the social individual and the private individual. There may be some overlap between the social individual and the private individual in so far as the personal projects that individuals pursue involve voluntary cooperation with others. There may be a stronger social element in that associating with other individuals and cooperating with them is itself a source of the project's value for the agents concerned. Yet there is nothing to say that the value of a project pursued during the time free from work must derive from its social character. Moreover, if the social character of the project is too pronounced, it becomes difficult to see how sufficient room will be left for individuality in any meaningful sense.

Another issue is that if this true realm of freedom is one in which individuals are free to pursue projects that reflect only their personal preferences, then it is not clear why the complete abolition of private property is required. For there is now a sphere to which the requirement that social relations be of the right kind, that is, transparent social relations that are accompanied by the desire to produce for others with a view to contributing to the satisfaction of their needs, no longer applies. This sphere might then be regarded as one in which individuals should be allowed to enjoy the right to dispose freely of that which is theirs. Marx could nevertheless argue that the existence of private property within this sphere would pose a threat to communist society because of how it may give rise to a system of commodity exchange governed by exchange value and thus threaten to produce the abstract self-conception and mistaken view of social relations found in capitalist society. We can here see how vital this line of argument is to Marx's claim that the complete abolition of private property is a necessary condition of 'real' and free individuality. Marx assumes, in short, that a sufficiently clear division between the sphere of the private individual and the sphere of the social individual cannot be achieved in such a way as to confine private property safely to the private sphere.

Another way in which Marx attempts to explain the possibility of individuality in a stronger sense concerns the greater complexity and interconnectedness of human relations brought about by the capitalist mode of production and how the expansion of a system of commodity exchange has resulted in the emergence of a world market. During this historical phase, the material conditions of individuality have been developed at the same time as human needs have become more extensive and more varied with the increase in the available means of satisfying them:

> Capital's ceaseless striving towards the general form of wealth drives labour beyond the limits of its natural paltriness, and thus creates the material elements for the development of the rich individuality which is as all-sided in its production as in its consumption, and whose labour also therefore appears no longer as labour, but as the full development of activity itself, in which natural necessity in its direct form has disappeared; because a historically created need has taken the place of the natural one. (MEGA II/1.1: 241; G, 325)

This reflects a feature of capital that makes it distinctive when it is viewed from the standpoint of world history, namely its 'universal' (*universelle*) tendency. This tendency manifests itself in how capital 'strives towards the universal development of the forces of production and thus becomes the presupposition of a new mode of production', in which there is the highest possible development of the productive forces and 'the richest development' of individuals (MEGA II/1.2: 438–39; G, 540–41). This tendency can be explained in the following way.

The overriding aim of the capitalist mode of production is to produce surplus value. This is the value that exceeds the value of the goods required to reproduce the labour power that is its ultimate source. Only part of this surplus value is appropriated by the capitalist for consumption purposes. The capitalist reinvests the other part in the production process by purchasing machinery along with the raw materials and labour power required to utilize it. This is done with the intention of creating even more surplus value. The increase in wealth facilitated by an expansion of the productive forces provides the material basis for a society in which the creation of surplus value is no longer the aim. Moreover, in its attempt to expand indefinitely, capital is compelled not only to develop the productive forces but also to expand its markets in order to accommodate the increase in goods being produced, leading to the creation of a world market. In this way, increasingly varied means of satisfying needs and increasing exposure to these means prove to be inevitable by-products of capital's inherent tendency to expand. Thus this tendency results in

4.5 Communist Property and Free Development

the generation of new needs, including the desire to engage in cultural, intellectual or scientific activities, and the desire to acquire the means of satisfying these needs on a global scale.

At the same time as more people are exposed to more products and more activities in the world market, the increasing dominance of exchange value comes to sever natural and traditional ties between human beings, so that the actual and possible relations into which individuals may enter with one another become increasingly complex and varied. This makes it possible for individuals to develop themselves in different directions and in different ways, leading Marx to speak of 'the universal development of the individual', which is not, however, 'an ideal or imagined universality [*Universalität*] of the individual, but the universality of his real and ideal relations' (MEGA II/1.2: 440: G, 542). In short, the greater complexity and interconnectedness brought about by capital's tendency to expand and its creation of a world market provide individuals with more opportunities to develop themselves by means of the manifold relations into which they may enter with other human beings across the world.[22] These relations will lose the appearance of an alien, independent power that they possess in a world market governed by abstract exchange value with the advent of a communist society in which the possibilities of a richer form of individuality can be realized. The idea of this next stage of history finds expression in the following passage from *The German Ideology*:

> [I]t is clear that the real intellectual wealth of the individual depends entirely on the wealth of his real connections. Only then will the separate individuals be liberated from the various national and local barriers, be brought into practical connection with the material and intellectual production of the whole world and be put in a position to acquire the capacity to enjoy this all-sided production of the whole earth (the creations of man). *All-round* dependence, this natural form of the *world-historical* co-operation of individuals, will be transformed by this communist revolution into the control and conscious mastery of these powers, which, born of the action of men on one another, have till now overawed and governed men as powers completely alien to them. (MEGA I/5: 42–43; GI, 55)

---

[22] For Marx, the situation is very different in the case of the nineteenth-century French smallholders (*Parzellenbauern*) who are bound to a form of property that enables each family to be more or less economically self-sufficient but at the price of material impoverishment and the failure of individuals to develop because their isolated mode of life prevents them from regularly interacting with others and forming enduring social relations with them: 'Their site of production, the smallholding, does not allow any division of labour in its cultivation, no application of science and therefore no diversity in development, no diversification of talents, no wealth of social relationships' (MEGA I/11: 180; EB, 117)

Marx himself, however, emphasizes the levelling effects of capitalist society in connection with the class entrusted with the task of bringing about the new society. He in fact identifies the removal of differences in the type of labour that individuals perform and their conditions of life as a presupposition of the unity required for the workers to form a revolutionary class (MEW 4: 470; MCP, 9). Thus individuals appear to be reduced to abstract receptacles for the rich content that the greater complexity and interconnectedness of human relations makes available to them in a way that mirrors how an individual becomes nothing more than a repository of exchange value in capitalist society. As Marx himself puts it, 'standing over against these productive forces, we have the majority of the individuals from whom these forces have been wrested away, and who, robbed thus of all real life-content, have become abstract individuals, but who are, however, only by this fact put into a position to enter into relation with one another *as individuals*' (MEGA I/5: 111; GI, 92). A key question therefore remains unanswered: how can individuals then realize the possibilities that Marx associates with the creation of a world market and thereby relate to themselves and to one another as individuals in a stronger sense than that of the free social individual of communist society as previously described? The abolition of private property does not address this question because it concerns only a negative condition of communist society.

Concluding Remark

In the final chapter, we saw how Marx argues that life in a society in which the relations between individuals are structured by the rights and obligations that define private property is detrimental to how we conceive of ourselves and others, whereas 'social, collective property' will form the basis of a society in which human beings are conscious of themselves as free social individuals and relate to one another as such individuals. Hegel, in contrast, argues that private property is a necessary condition of conceiving of oneself and others as free. This is because a defining feature of it, the right to dispose freely of property, is a presupposition of a contract in which a person places his or her will in one thing at the same time as he or she withdraws it from another thing, thereby demonstrating his or her freedom in relation to another person. Hegel's concept of ethical life, or so I have argued, nevertheless implies a different form of property. This 'ethical' property performs the type of expressive function that Marx assigns to communist property. Indeed, it is as if Marx wants to construct a model of ethical life in which property plays a central role, but not the role of objectifying the freedom of personality, which is necessarily abstract, both in terms of its subject, the person, and in terms of the rights and legal norms that follow from it. This is one example of how, if one looks closely enough, there is some common ground despite any substantive differences.

Where there are areas of fundamental disagreement between the theories of property discussed in this book, it concerns forms of property rather than the concept of property. In addition to the way in which Hegel's attempt to justify private property at the stage of abstract right contrasts with Marx's arguments for the complete abolition of private property, there is Fichte's argument for a form of property that lacks the same essential feature of private property that is integral to Hegel's justification of it, namely the right to dispose freely of a thing. Fichte limits this specific right by privileging a form of property that is restricted to an exclusive right of possession and use which is conditional on whether an activity or a thing is required to live from one's labour, on the grounds that sufficient economic independence is a condition of the consciousness of oneself as a free embodied agent. This not only differs from Hegel's argument for private property and how it implies that this form of property is the most rational one, the extension of which is, therefore, a sign of historical progress, but also introduces a claim that is absent in Kant's *Rechtslehre*, in which property-based forms of dependence are invoked in order to justify a political distinction that entails an inequality of status and thus differences with respect to the rights that individuals enjoy. Once again, however, we should not lose sight of the common ground, for both Kant and Fichte seek to explain the right to property in terms of the independence that is a condition of genuine free choice.

The common ground is most evident in the case of the concept of property. Fichte makes explicit the way in which the concept of property should be understood as a relation between persons that is mediated by things. Some of Kant's statements concerning the right to property indicate that he thinks of the concept of property in much the same way, despite how he entertains the possibility of pre-political property rights that do not initially depend on the recognition of others. Hegel thinks of property in similar terms, even though the triadic structure of the concept of property becomes explicit only at the stage of contract. Marx presupposes essentially the same concept of property, but he does not want to equate it with private property. Rather, there are different historical forms of property that must be explained in terms of the broader context provided by the dominant mode of production and its corresponding social relations. The way in which the concept of property is understood in terms of a relation between persons that is mediated by things is essentially different from the reduction of it to a relation between a person and a thing from which certain rights follow, but that only indirectly establishes a relation to other persons, that is, a relation which consists in an entitlement to a thing on the one side and an obligation not to interfere with the owner's control of this thing on the other.

This fundamental difference is significant for at least two reasons. First, it makes more explicit, and is more consistent with, the way in which property rights both structure social relations and depend on the social recognition implicit in these relations, whereas the dyadic person–thing model fosters the illusion that a specific form of property and the rights that follow from it can determine the structure of society independently of any social recognition of this form of property and these rights. Second, once the moment of social recognition is introduced, a significant constraint on what may count as an adequate justification of any specific form of property and the rights that follow from it emerges, in that this moment of social recognition must be accommodated in such a way that all the relevant agents can be thought to have rational grounds for recognizing one another's property rights. The importance of this principle of reciprocity is captured by Fichte's civil contract, in which we encounter the universalization of the principle that no one would willingly harm himself or herself demanded by Kant. We can detect the same principle of reciprocity at work in Hegel's argument for private property, where it takes the form of the right of the free and rational agent's will to exist in its property and the demand to be recognized as a person. For Marx, once the conditions of communist society are present, property ought to ensure the realization of the free individuality of each member of society, but without reducing human beings to abstract legal subjects and mere repositories of exchange value.

The disagreements about what forms of property are or are not justified can be traced back to a common concern with freedom. This is evident from the diverging accounts of the constraints that ought or ought not to be imposed on the right to dispose freely of property. It is precisely this right that Fichte and Marx want to limit or to abolish altogether because of the threat that it poses to freedom, whereas for Hegel this right is integral to the freedom of the person and must, therefore, be accommodated within the modern form of ethical life. This does not mean that Fichte and Marx want to exclude freedom of choice altogether. It means only that freedom of choice will need to express itself in ways other than the exercise of the right to dispose freely of property. Thus, unless Hegel's argument for private property is judged to be compelling, the identification of freedom of choice with the right to dispose freely of property may be viewed as a historical accident rather than a matter of rational necessity.

In this book, I have sought to reconstruct and critically assess the arguments for or against specific forms of property developed by Kant, Fichte, Hegel and Marx. I have shown that there are problems with the arguments for the form or forms of property favoured by each of them. The absence of a compelling argument for one specific form of property to the exclusion of other possible forms of property may appear too inconclusive. Yet I would argue that this inconclusiveness reflects the undesirability of a theory of property that is absolutist in the sense that it commits itself to one possible form of property in such a way as to exclude sufficient consideration of alternatives. We have encountered evidence of such absolutist claims.

Sometimes this is explicit, as when Hegel argues for private property in the full modern sense and considers the extension of this form of property and the rights associated with it to be a sign of historical progress, even though he limits these rights to some extent in accordance with the demands of ethical life, and when Marx argues for the complete abolition of private property and its replacement by the type of collective property that will structure communist social relations. Sometimes it has more to do with the implications of measures that are proposed, as when private property turns out to be incompatible with Fichte's attempt to apply the concept of right, despite how 'absolute' property in some key respects appears to correspond to private property.

The claim that this inconclusiveness should not be viewed as problem can be illustrated by viewing the task of a philosophical theory of property as an essentially twofold one: to define and justify a general concept of property and to show how this concept is best instantiated in specific forms of property. Kant, Fichte, Hegel and Marx have been shown to agree about the basic logical structure of the concept of property. Any major disagreement concerns what specific forms of property can be justified in terms of the idea of freedom. This disagreement reflects the difficulties faced by any philosophical theory of property that seeks to show that one form of property should be recognized within society to the exclusion of, or in preference to, other possible forms of it. One might even claim that this disagreement indicates that an absolutist approach to the issue of what form of property ought to be recognized is a fundamentally mistaken one, in that this issue cannot be decided once and for all at the level of philosophical theory. Rather, it will depend on various factors even when freedom remains the ultimate source of justification. These factors may include the specific aspect or type of freedom that the right to property or a form of property that is not accompanied by any legal rights aims to secure or to promote and specific historical conditions. A pluralist theory of property is therefore needed, that is to say, a theory which acknowledges that different forms of property may be required within a single, historically evolving society in which the freedom of its members is to be secured and promoted.

This more open-ended approach admittedly faces certain challenges, such as how to reconcile different forms of property if they turn out to be incompatible but equally justifiable in terms of the idea of freedom. Yet the neatness of a theory that avoids such challenges by arguing for one form of property to the exclusion of others is hardly a sufficient indication of this theory's truth. In this respect, the arguments and theories concerning the form of property that is most compatible with the idea of freedom discussed in this book can be viewed as valuable contributions to what ought to be an ongoing debate. These arguments and theories can be said to reflect the complex nature of the question of the form or forms that the concept of property ought to assume in a society that genuinely values the freedom of all its members, as opposed to the freedom of the members of a privileged social group. I shall end by indicating a further reason that this inconclusiveness regarding what specific form or forms of property can be justified in terms of the idea of freedom does not diminish the value of the theories of property discussed in this book. This reason concerns the way in which this inconclusiveness favours a genuine reorientation in how the question of property rights is posed.

With respect to the relative importance of this question, I noted in the introduction how a theory of distributive justice may presuppose the justifiability of a specific form of property and thereby serve to prevent adequate consideration of alternatives. This suggests at least one way in which the question of property can be thought to be more fundamental than the question of distributive justice, namely, that it concerns the justifiability of that which is to be distributed fairly and may form a legitimate object of redistribution in the first place. Thus the more fundamental question is *what* should (or should not) be distributed according to a principle of justice, rather than the question of *how* it should (or should not) be distributed. I shall now provide an example of what I mean by this. This example concerns the issue of taxation, which is central to the issue of distributive justice in at least two ways. First, government spending funded by general taxation is typically the means of redistributing goods and resources in accordance with a principle of justice in modern societies. Second, the issue of taxation invites the question of what can legitimately be taken from some individuals and distributed to others through the tax system. The question of property rights is here clearly more fundamental because the redistribution of property by means of taxation may or may not be thought to violate property rights that are assumed to exist prior to, and independently of, any redistributive act.

An example of a presumption in favour of private property is provided by the claim that property rights act as a constraint on what may count as a legitimate object of taxation. This type of argument is characteristic of a libertarian position which assumes that the outcomes of a capitalist market economy will be just if they result from voluntary contractual arrangements through which individuals exchange things, whether they be goods or services, to which they already enjoy a moral or a legal right.

Some compulsory taxation may be justifiable in terms of the need to fund the government and state institutions that protect basic rights, including property rights, enforce contracts and thereby ensure the effective functioning of the market economy itself. To this type of claim, however, the following objection can be made: there is no such market without government and there is no government without taxation, so that the correct conclusion to draw is a different one. This conclusion is that the question of the legitimacy of taxes cannot be decided with reference to any pre-tax entitlements because people are entitled only to that which is left to them after taxes have been paid to fund government. The legitimacy of taxes must then be evaluated with reference to the legitimacy of the economic and political system in the absence of which any income that remains after the payment of tax could not be generated.[1] The question of the legitimacy of this economic and political system itself can be decided only by appealing to other considerations, goals and values.[2] From this it follows that there are, in fact, no property rights that are independent of the tax system which funds the preferred economic and political system, and thus no rights that compulsory taxation can violate.

On the one hand, this position looks like a restatement of a claim that is explicitly made in Fichte's theory of right, but is also present in Kant's, and that can be traced back at least as far as Hobbes's political philosophy.[3] This is the claim that there are no pre-political or natural property rights because the existence of the right to property depends on the establishment of legal and political norms and institutions to which all relevant agents can be thought to consent.[4] On the other hand, this position does not exclude treating the income and the wealth that remains after the payment of taxes as private property that individuals or companies may dispose of freely. Nor does it entail that the resources that the state allocates to individuals and that are funded through taxation could not be private property and private property only. Indeed, the way in which the issue is framed implies that it should be private property, in that the burden of proof lies with anyone who wants to justify constraints on

---

[1] See Murphy and Nagel, *The Myth of Ownership*, 32f.
[2] See Murphy and Nagel, *The Myth of Ownership*, 58f.
[3] For Hobbes, property rights depend on the institution of a sovereign and therefore do not exist in the state of nature, where 'there be no Propriety, no Dominion, no *Mine* and *Thine* distinct; but onely that to be every mans, that he can get; and for so long, as he can keep it'. *Leviathan*, Ch. XIII, 63. Cited by original pagination.
[4] See Murphy and Nagel, *The Myth of Ownership*, 74, where it is explicitly stated that the right to property in the shape of a pre-tax income is not a pre-political or natural right.

private property in the form of compulsory taxation aimed at funding public goods and services in the face of the libertarian claim described above.

Yet why not begin with the question of what property rights, if any, ought to structure the economic and political system in relation to which the legitimacy of taxation in general and any specific taxes must, according to the argument presented above, be assessed? For the answer to the question of the legitimacy of this economic and social system will, to a large extent, turn on the legitimacy of the rights and obligations that structure it, including those connected with the right to property. The answers given to the more fundamental question concerning the appropriate form of property will nevertheless have implications in relation to the question of how goods, resources and wealth ought to be distributed within a society. Thus the question of distributive justice will not be independent of, and more fundamental than, the question of what form or forms of property there ought to be. Rather, there is no way of determining how property ought to be distributed without deciding *what* is to be distributed and *why* it should be distributed to all members of society or only to some of them. The claim that discovering the principle in accordance with which goods and resources ought to be distributed will provide a reliable guide as to what ought to be distributed risks identifying this principle with the form of property and the corresponding rights and obligations that already structure a society, thereby making a theory of justice that presupposes a specific form of property appear more 'natural' or 'plausible' than other ones. In modern capitalist societies, this form of property will be private property, which is a presupposition of a capitalist market economy.

Is it natural, though, to think of private property as that which generally ought to be redistributed through taxation and as the form of property that ought to be favoured even with respect to the provision of public goods that are funded through taxation? The answers given to such questions may have major social and political implications, such as the development and implementation of policies that aim to recreate a market economy in relation to public goods, as when governments decide to provide such goods indirectly by entering into contractual agreements with private companies that directly provide them, even though these companies' overriding goal is to maximize the value of their shares and the dividends paid to their shareholders. Moreover, policies of this kind are liable to create a competitive environment that is incompatible with a feeling of effective control over one's own life and a sense of social solidarity, thereby producing a specific self-conception and influencing how individuals relate to one another in society.

Aristotle does not appear to have thought that private property is the natural form of property in the relevant sense: 'We will begin with the natural beginning of the subject. The members of a state must either have all things or nothing in common, or some things in common and some not'.[5] This natural beginning concerns the appropriate starting point for an inquiry into the best political constitution. Property rights and the corresponding obligations will structure the relations between citizens living under this constitution, making it natural to begin with the question of the best form of property. Aristotle, however, does not assume that private property is the best form, even though he himself goes on to argue for the principle that '[p]roperty should be in a certain sense common, but, as a general rule, private'.[6] Rather, Aristotle identifies three possible forms of property: full common property, full private property and a combination of common property and private property. Although the third form concerns essentially the same form of property, we can distinguish between incomplete common property and incomplete private property if the former is taken to privilege the role of common property and the latter is taken to privilege the role of private property in a society. Aristotle's own position appears to favour incomplete private property understood in this way. What Aristotle does not do is privilege from the very beginning one form of property, thereby implying that the burden of proof lies with the advocate of any alternative to it. Today, in contrast, this type of openness is threatened by how private property has become the dominant form of property in a particular type of society during a specific historical period.

There may be various explanations of why Aristotle thought it necessary to consider forms of property other than the one for which he himself argues, such as his knowledge of societies in which different forms of property were dominant and the need to engage with Plato's claim that even wives and children ought to be common property. It is nevertheless significant that for Aristotle the natural starting point demands deciding the question of the best form of property by means of philosophical inquiry and reflection in a way that adequately considers all possible forms of property. One may therefore claim that even though philosophical inquiry may not be enough to decide the issue of the form or forms of

---

[5] *The Politics*, 1260b.
[6] *The Politics*, 1263a.

property that ought to structure a society, it may play a crucial role in the development of a genuinely critical theory of society that does not allow this fundamental issue to be, in effect, decided by the course of history and how it has resulted in the increasing dominance of one specific form of property. I hope to have shown in this book that Kant, Fichte, Hegel and Marx provide us with valuable resources when it comes to developing such a theory. Indeed, their combined achievements are so profound and comprehensive that one may wonder what more philosophy can here hope to achieve.

Bibliography

Adorno, Theodor W., *Negative Dialectics*, trans. E. B. Ashton (London: Continuum, 1973).
Adorno, Theodor W., *Negative Dialektik*, in *Gesammelte Schriften*, ed. Rolf Tiedemann with the assistance of Gretel Adorno, Susan Buck-Morss and Klaus Schultz, Vol. 6 (Frankfurt am Main: Suhrkamp, 2003).
Adorno, Theodor W., *Minima Moralia: Reflexionen aus dem beschädigten Leben*, in *Gesammelte Schriften*, ed. Rolf Tiedemann with the assistance of Gretel Adorno, Susan Buck-Morss and Klaus Schutz, Vol. 4 (Frankfurt am Main: Suhrkamp, 2003).
Adorno, Theodor W., *Minima Moralia: Reflections from Damaged Life*, trans. E. F. N. Jephcott (London: Verso, 2005).
Aristotle, *The Politics*, in *The Politics and the Constitution of Athens*, ed. Stephen Everson (Cambridge: Cambridge University Press, 1996).
Balint, Benjamin, *Kafka's Last Trial: The Case of a Literary Legacy* (London: Picador, 2018).
Buhr, Manfred, 'Die Philosophie Johann Gottlieb Fichtes und die Französische Revolution', in *Fichte – die Französische Revolution und das Ideal vom ewigen Frieden*, eds. Manfred Buhr and Domenico Losurdo (Berlin: Akademie Verlag, 1991).
Chitty, Andrew, 'Recognition and Property in Hegel and the Early Marx', *Ethical Theory and Moral Practice* 16(4) (2013): 685–97.
Cohen, G. A., *Karl Marx's Theory of History: A Defence*, expanded edn (Oxford: Clarendon Press, 2000).
Duncan, Samuel, 'Hegel on Private Property: A Contextual Reading', *The Southern Journal of Philosophy* 55(3) (2017): 263–84.
Feher, Michel, *Rated Agency: Investee Politics in a Speculative Age*, trans. Gregory Elliot (New York: Zone Books, 2018).
Herb, Karlfriedrich and Bernd Ludwig, 'Naturzustand, Eigentum und Staat: Kants Relativierung des "Ideals des hobbes"', *Kant-Studien* 84(3) (1993): 283–316.
Hobbes, Thomas, *Leviathan, Volume 2: The English and Latin Texts (i)*, ed. Noel Malcolm (Oxford: Clarendon Press, 2012).
Hume, David, *An Enquiry Concerning the Principles of Morals*, ed. Tom L. Beauchamp (Oxford: Oxford University Press, 1998).

James, David, *Practical Necessity, Freedom, and History: From Hobbes to Marx* (Oxford: Oxford University Press, 2021).
Kühn, Manfred, *Johann Gottlieb Fichte. Ein deutscher Philosoph* (Munich: C. H. Beck, 2012).
Locke, John, *Two Treatises of Government*, ed. Peter Laslett (Cambridge: Cambridge University Press, 1988).
Maliks, Reidar, *Kant's Politics in Context* (Oxford: Oxford University Press, 2014).
Merle, Jean-Christophe, 'Fichte's Political Economy and His Theory of Property', in *The Cambridge Companion to Fichte*, eds. David James and Günter Zöller (Cambridge: Cambridge University Press, 2016).
Mohseni, Amir, *Abstrakte Freiheit. Zum Begriff des Eigentums bei Hegel* (Hamburg: Felix Meiner, 2015).
Munzer, Stephen R., *A Theory of Property* (Cambridge: Cambridge University Press, 1990).
Murphy, Liam and Thomas Nagel, *The Myth of Ownership: Taxes and Justice* (New York: Oxford University Press, 2002).
Neuhouser, Frederick, 'Marx and Hegel on the Value of "Bourgeois" Ideals', in *Reassessing Marx's Social and Political Philosophy: Freedom, Recognition and Human Flourishing*, ed. Jan Kandiyali (London: Routledge, 2018).
Nozick, Robert, *Anarchy, State, and Utopia* (Malden: Basic Books, 1974).
Nuzzo, Angelica, 'Freedom in the Body: The Body as Subject of Rights and Object of Property in Hegel's "Abstract Right"', in *Beyond Liberalism and Communitarianism: Studies in Hegel's Philosophy of Right*, ed. Robert R. Williams (Albany: State University of New York Press, 2001).
Patten, Alan, *Hegel's Idea of Freedom* (Oxford: Oxford University Press, 1999).
Pettit, Philip, *Republicanism: A Theory of Freedom and Government* (Oxford: Clarendon Press, 1997).
Pierson, Christopher, *Just Property: A History in the Latin West, Volume 1: Wealth, Virtue, and the Law* (Oxford: Oxford University Press, 2013).
Proudhon, Pierre-Joseph, *What Is Property?*, eds. and trans. Donald R. Kelley and Bonnie G. Smith (Cambridge: Cambridge University Press, 1994).
Riedel, Manfred, 'Die Aporie von Herrschaft und Vereinbarung in Kants Idee des Sozialvertrags', in *Kant. Zur Deutung seiner Theorie von Erkennen und Handeln*, ed. Gerold Prauss (Cologne: Kiepenhauer and Witsch, 1973).
Ripstein, Arthur, *Force and Freedom: Kant's Legal and Political Philosophy* (Cambridge: Harvard University Press, 2009).
Robespierre, Maximilien, 'Sur les subsistances', in *Œuvres de Maximilien Robespierre*, Vol. 9, eds. Marc Bouloiseau, Jean Dautry, Georges Lefebvre and Albert Soboul (Paris: Presses Universitaires de France, 1910–1967).
Rousseau, Jean-Jacques, *Of the Social Contract*, in *The Social Contract and Other Later Political Writings*, ed. and trans. Victor Gourevitch (Cambridge: Cambridge University Press, 1997).
Sayers, Sean, *Marx and Alienation: Essays on Hegelian Themes* (Basingstoke: Palgrave Macmillan, 2011).

Schottky, Richard, 'Anmerkungen zum Text', in Johann Gottlieb Fichte, *Beitrag zur Berichtigung der Urteile des Publikums über die französische Revolution*, ed. Richard Schottky (Hamburg: Felix Meiner, 1973).
Skinner, Quentin, *Liberty before Liberalism* (Cambridge: Cambridge University Press, 1998).
Stillman, Peter, 'Property, Freedom, and Individuality in Hegel's and Marx's Political Thought', in *Property (NOMOS XXII)*, eds. J. Roland Pennock and John W. Chapman (New York: New York University Press, 1980).
Stirner, Max, *The Ego and Its Own*, ed. David Leopold (Cambridge: Cambridge University Press, 1995).
Waldron, Jeremy, *The Right to Private Property* (Oxford: Clarendon Press, 1988).
Westphal, Kenneth R., 'A Kantian Justification of Possession', in *Kant's Metaphysics of Morals: Interpretive Essays*, ed. Mark Timmons (Oxford: Oxford University Press, 2002).
Williams, Robert R., *Hegel's Ethics of Recognition* (Berkeley: University of California Press, 1997).
Wood, Allen W., *Karl Marx* (London: Routledge & Kegan Paul, 1981).
Wood, Allen W., *The Free Development of Each: Studies on Freedom, Right, and Ethics in Classical German Philosophy* (Oxford: Oxford University Press, 2014).
Wood, Allen W., *Fichte's Ethical Thought* (Oxford: Oxford University Press, 2016).

Index

accumulation
  primitive, 8
Adorno, Theodor W., 146, 159
Aristotle
  on property, 196
  on value, 149–50
autonomy
  Kant's idea of, 50

body
  as property, 4–5, 101, 115
  concept of, 59
  inviolability of, 59

citizenship
  Kant's distinction between active and passive, 20–23
civil society, 113–15, 167
commodity
  double existence of, 151–52
  exchange, 155–57, 169
  fetishism, 168–69
  one's own self as, 158–62
communism, 141
  and equality, 143–45
  and freedom, 173, 175–80, 184–85
  and individuality, 164, 173–88
  and property, 173, 181–82
contract
  and capitalism, 169–70
  and common will, 107–108
  and recognition, 104–106
  as basis of constitution, 49–50
  civil, 65–67, 72
  labour, 24–25
  property, 67–70, 72, 84
  protection, 68
  Rousseau on the conditions of a legitimate social, 17–18, 26
  subjection, 68
  unification, 68

corporation, 116–20, 122
  property of, 117–18

distributive justice
  and property, 2–4, 193–95
  Nozick on, 3–4

egoism
  universal, 87
enlightenment
  and freedom, 41
  concept of, 40–41
equality
  and capitalism, 140
  and commodity exchange, 155–57
  and communism, 143–45
  and exchange value, 148–60
  and individuality, 146–47
  conditions of, 17–18
  innate right to, 16–17
  legal, 148, 155
  of freedom, 167
estates, 122–24
ethical life, 169
  ancient Greek, 91
  and freedom, 126
  idea of, 126–29
  natural, 122

family
  property of, 112–13
  vs. abstract right, 111–12
freedom
  actualized, 89
  and capitalism, 140
  and communism, 173, 175–80, 184–85
  and enlightenment, 41
  and ethical life, 126
  and leisure, 84–85
  and private property, 119–20, 165–71
  and property, 10–13, 94–95

freedom (cont.)
  as independence, 15–20, 24
  equality of, 167
  external, 24
  natural, 67
  of abstract right, 108–109
  of choice, 14–16, 31–36, 56–57, 84
  of personality, 90, 102, 108–109, 115
  of property, 90
  republican, 17
  subjective, 91
  substantial, 128

Grotius, Hugo, 10 n. 15

history
  and private property, 90–92
  and property, 139
  Marx's theory of, 154–55
  world, 90
Hobbes, Thomas
  on the right of nature, 66
Hume, David
  on the utility of private property, 9–10

individuality
  and communism, 173–88
  and equality, 146–47
  and the state, 152

labour
  and property, 4–5, 53–55, 69–70, 72–77, 116–17
  as source of value, 5
  contract, 24–25
  division of, 153, 178–80
  theory of value, 148–50
law
  moral, 49–50
  of coercion, 64
  of right, 14, 45–46, 64
leisure
  and freedom, 84–85
  as a form of property, 84–85
Locke, John
  on property, 4–5

Nozick, Robert
  on distributive justice, 3–4
  presupposes right to private property, 7–8

person, personality, 56, 91, 93–94
  and private property, 96–108, 114–16
  and property, 94
  concrete, 113

freedom of, 90, 102, 108–109, 115
particular, 113
Plato
  on private property, 91
police, 116
possession
  intelligible, 28–31, 34
  physical, 28, 38
property
  abolition of private, 140–42, 151, 160–61, 164–73
  absolute, 75–79
  alienation of, 99, 103–105
  and communism, 173, 181–82
  and distributive justice, 2–4, 193–95
  and economic dependence, 21–22
  and effective agency, 68–71
  and freedom, 10–13, 94–95
  and history, 139
  and independence, 36–40
  and labour, 4–5, 53–55, 69–70, 72–77, 116–17
  and personality, 94
  and recognition, 8–9, 11, 29–31, 38–39, 63, 94
  and the appropriation of nature, 139
  and the public use of reason, 42–45
  and the Russian rural commune, 162–63
  and the state, 121–24
  Aristotle on, 196
  as a condition of freedom of choice, 31–36
  based on mutual declaration, 62–63
  bourgeois, 141
  common, 112–13, 131, 133–34
  concept vs. forms, 10–12
  contract, 67–70, 72, 84
  dualism of private and communal, 162–63
  ethical, 129–34
  exclusive, 74
  formation of a thing as the source of the right to, 50–52
  free, 112
  free and complete, 101
  freedom of, 90
  history and private, 90–92
  human, 173
  Hume on the utility of, 9–10
  landed, 54, 121–24
  leisure as a form of, 84–85
  modern private, 7–8
  national, 125–26
  of the corporation, 117–18
  of the family, 112–13
  one's own body as, 4–5, 101, 115
  personality and private, 96–108, 114–16
  Plato on private, 91

pluralist theory of, 12–13
private, 113, 119–20, 131, 139–40, 165–71
right to dispose freely of, 7–8, 25–26, 28, 33–35, 54–55, 74–76, 81–84, 102–106, 116–18, 121–24, 164–65, 167
right to inherit, 52–54
social, 173
state and private, 91–92, 130–31
state-owned, 129
Proudhon, Pierre-Joseph, 8
Pufendorf, Samuel, 10 n. 15

rabble, 120
reason
   public use of, 41–43
recognition, 58, 67
   and contract, 104–106
   and property, 8–9, 11, 29–31, 38–39, 63, 94
   legal, 109, 112, 117, 140, 157
   social, 117–18
right
   abstract, 92–94, 108–109, 111–12
   application of the concept of, 46, 59–60, 64, 67, 73, 79, 81, 87
   as the existence of the free will, 92–93
   coercive, 108
   concept of, 56–58, 89–90
   formal, 93
   infinite, 66
   law of, 14, 45–46, 64
   natural, 27–28, 65
   of nature, 66
   of necessity, 110–11, 120
   of self-interest, 167
   original, 59, 65, 67
   principle of, 14–15

   private, 27
   public, 27
   rule of, 58
   science of, 57, 89–90
   system of, 89
   universal relation of, 67
Robespierre, Maximilien, 86–88
Rousseau, Jean-Jacques
   on the conditions of a legitimate social contract, 17–18, 26

self-ownership, 48–49, 55, 59
state
   and individuality, 152
   and private property, 91–92, 130–31
   and property, 121–24
   commercial closure of, 81
   police, 86
   rational, 79–84
Stirner, Max, 159

value
   Aristotle on, 149–50
   exchange, 148–60
   labour theory of, 148–50
   surplus, 169, 186

will
   arbitrary, 109, 113, 117
   common, 37, 107–108
   free, 92–95, 102–103, 105–106, 108–109
   general, 37
world market, 186–87

Zasulich, Vera, 162

For EU product safety concerns, contact us at Calle de José Abascal, 56–1°, 28003 Madrid, Spain or eugpsr@cambridge.org.

www.ingramcontent.com/pod-product-compliance
Lightning Source LLC
LaVergne TN
LVHW020345260326
834688LV00045B/1541